THE ELUSIVE AND IMPORTANT VITAMIN P

This invaluable book will be worth whatever you pay for it if you can glean the vitamin wisdom of Martin Ebon on just a few subjects. For example, most people have probably never heard of Vitamin P. Yet in one study, when patients who were hemorrhaging because of anti-coagulants were given Vitamins P and C, the hemorrhaging areas cleared up quickly. Vitamins P and C have also been shown to speed up recovery from infections such as the common cold and influenza.

WHERE DO YOU FIND IT?
The next time you eat an orange, try not to peel away the white skin of the fruit, because that's where the Vitamin P is. You can also find Vitamin P in lemons, apricots, rose hips, black currants, grapes, grapefruit, cherries, blackberries, cabbage, plums, parsley or prunes.

WHICH VITAMINS DO YOU NEED?
An essential guide and reference book for better health.

WHICH VITAMINS DO YOU NEED?

MARTIN EBON

Introduction by Dr. Henry A. Schroeder

BANTAM BOOKS
TORONTO · NEW YORK · LONDON · SYDNEY

RL 11, IL 9-up

WHICH VITAMINS DO YOU NEED?
A Bantam Book / July 1974

2nd printing .... *April 1975*	5th printing .. *September 1978*	
3rd printing .. *September 1976*	6th printing .... *June 1979*	
4th printing .... *June 1977*	7th printing .... *March 1981*	

ISBN 0–553–20130–1

Published simultaneously in the United States and Canada

*Bantam Books are published by Bantam Books, Inc. Its trade-
mark, consisting of the words "Bantam Books" and the por-
trayal of a bantam, is Registered in U.S. Patent and Trademark
Office and in other countries. Marca Registrada. Bantam
Books, Inc., 666 Fifth Avenue, New York, New York 10103.*

PRINTED IN THE UNITED STATES OF AMERICA

16 15 14 13 12 11 10 9 8

Contents

and other difficult-to-prove therapeutic uses. But there is no doubt that it is essential in maintaining the collagen which maintains the stability and elasticity of such connective tissues as bones, cartilage, muscles and blood vessels.   103

Appendices

Index

Introduction

By Henry A. Schroeder, M.D.

The author of this Introduction, who is emeritus professor of physiology at Dartmouth Medical School in Brattleboro, Vermont, notes that "it is difficult to find foods in a supermarket that have not been processed in such a way as to lose some vitamins, although the minerals are generally preserved." Although this book is designed to answer the crucial question "WHICH VITAMINS DO YOU NEED?" by dealing with each vitamin chapter by chapter, the role of minerals in our diet needs to be kept in mind as well. Dr. Schroeder's comments put the relationship between vitamins and minerals in perspective; the text of his paper "Losses of Vitamins and Trace Minerals Resulting from Processing and Preservation of Foods" may be found in Appendix D of this book. Henry A. Schroeder was associated with the Presbyterian Hospital in New York City, the Rockefeller Institute, and Washington University and Barnes Hospital in St. Louis before joining Dartmouth Medical School in 1958. He served as a naval flight surgeon in World War II, engaged in special studies concerning cardiovascular conditions, and is the author of several books, including HYPERTENSIVE DISEASES: CAUSES AND CONTROL *(1953).*

Vitamins and minerals are nutrients found in foods, which are essential for health, growth, and survival of all living things including man. Certain bulk minerals, such as calcium, magnesium, and phosphorus, are the bases of structure—in bones and teeth. Others, such as sodium, potassium, and chloride, form the salty fluids that bathe each cell in the body and in which essential organic substances inside each cell are dissolved. Some minerals act as catalysts; that is, they take part in chemical reactions or speed them up at the relatively low temperatures of the body without changing themselves. There are eight bulk minerals in the body, in addition to the basic elements of organic matter, carbon, hydrogen, oxygen, and nitrogen.

Other basic nutrients are found in small amounts and are therefore called micronutrients. They are made up of the trace elements and the vitamins. Some of these are effective in very small quantities. Vitamin B_{12}, for example, acts to prevent pernicious anemia at a dose of 1 microgram (one-millionth of a gram) a day, containing 0.04 microgram cobalt. The most active form of vitamin D is also effective at 1 microgram a day. These minute amounts make the difference between sickness and health.

There are twelve trace elements, mostly metals, and seventeen vitamins with known or suspected activity, as this book shows. An adult man's need for most trace metals and vitamins is measured in milligrams. He requires about 15 milligrams each of iron and zinc to be healthy, 20 milligrams of niacin, 60 milligrams of vitamin C, 30 milligrams of vitamin E, and 10 milligrams of pantothenic acid. Only 2 to 5 milligrams of copper, vanadium, fluorine, manganese, and vitamin B_6 appear to be needed, less than 2 milligrams of thiamine and riboflavin, less than a milligram of biotin, molybdenum, chromium, and microgram quantities of iodine and selenium. Without these micronutrients, the human body functions at less than optimal levels, and such specialized functions as growth, reproduction, resistance to infections, longevity, and delay of degenerative diseases may be affected.

One important rule in thinking about micronutrients —all nutrients, in fact—is as follows: *An amount sufficient for growth or survival is not necessarily one adequate for optimal function.* Those who raise animals for profit—for meat or fur—know this rule and feed their animals foods high in vitamins and minerals. Mill-feeds are rich sources, making up the 30 percent of the wheat grain removed during the milling of wheat and containing 60 to 85 percent of the vitamins and minerals originally present in the whole grain (see Appendix D). Molasses contains almost all of the vitamins and minerals of the juice of the sugar cane, which modern civilized man loses but cattle thrive on. There is little profit in undernourished cattle and sheep. Farmers, ranchers, feedlot operators, mink raisers, and racehorse breeders are so aware of micronutrients that their animals may be receiving a better diet than their owners get, in terms of vitamins and minerals.

Another postulate to remember is this: *A raw food contains the micronutrients necessary for its metabolism.* Metabolism means the absorption, buildup, breakdown, utilization, storage, and excretion of a substance in the body. I hesitate to use the word *natural* because of its connotation of "health food" stores, but *natural* would be a better word, meaning uncooked, unprocessed, untouched. This postulate has not been shown by scientific analyses, but has been proven for millions of years by land animals, who otherwise would be chronically diseased from malnutrition were it not true. The corollary to this postulate may be true: Some foods contain more than enough micronutrients for metabolism. Examples are infrequent—such as yeast, liver, organ meats, fish, eggs. Certain bacteria synthesize vitamins themselves in plants and animals.

Whereas all vitamins are synthesized by living things, this is not true for the minerals. It is a basic law of nature that animals feed on plants and plants feed on matter, on elements. Plants take minerals from the soil or sea, and carbon, oxygen, and nitrogen from the air, and convert them into food for animals. Animals that live exclusively on animals obtain their elements from the animals they eat, which have obtained them from plants. The minerals cannot be synthesized by living things—they are the basic matter of the earth's crust and the salt of seawater. Therefore, in a sense they are more important than vitamins, for without them no plant—or animal—can exist.

The twelve bulk elements in the human body—sodium, chlorine, potassium, phosphorus, magnesium, calcium, silicon (probably), sulfur, and the ever-present hydrogen, oxygen, nitrogen, carbon—usually occur in adequate amounts in food. Only under exceptional circumstances or in deficient diets are inadequacies of one or another of some of them found: calcium, potassium, sodium, magnesium, which in those cases may be the result of disease or neglect. Deficiencies of the trace elements from dietary inadequacies occur more regularly and are suspected of causing some widespread chronic diseases in the civilized society in which we live.

Deficiencies of iron are well known, and of zinc are beginning to be recognized. Iron is strongly held by the red blood cells, and anemia is often slow to develop when it is lacking. Zinc is quite loosely bound by some tissues, and deficiency may supervene quite rapidly when zinc is not supplied—after an operation, for example. Delayed wound healing, skin lesions, cheilosis, and more serious disturbances may result. Deficiency of chromium probably causes hardening of the arteries and heart attacks, as well as mild diabetes in older persons. Deficiencies of vanadium, manganese, cobalt (except in B_{12}), molybdenum, and selenium have been described only in laboratory animals or cattle. Iodine deficiency, which causes goiter, is well known. Fluorine deficiency is partly responsible for tooth decay and probably responsible for fragile bones in the aged. Copper deficiency can occur in infants.

Some of these trace elements have specialized functions that are necessary for optimal function but perhaps not for survival. Molybdenum, iodine, chromium, selenium, and fluorine are examples. Although it is not known that their absence in adults would be lethal, at any rate, they are needed for health.

A controversy is raging today as to whether or not the American diet is optimal for health. The dictum so often expressed by officialdom is that there are adequate vitamins and minerals in any "well-balanced" diet. This dictum is loudly proclaimed by a few nutritionists, some in great universities, whose departments receive support from the food industry. It is disbelieved by the millions of people who patronize the so-called "Health Food" industry at a cost of over a billion dollars annually. It is questioned by many scientists, who must search out the facts and make up their own minds.

Of the ten leading causes of death, at least five are either directly dietary in origin or have strong dietary influences—hardening of the arteries with heart attacks and strokes, high blood pressure, diabetes, cirrhosis of the liver, gastrointestinal disorders, and possibly cancer.

Some seventeen dietary surveys have been made in this country to ascertain the adequacy of the diets in terms of seven major components, bulk minerals, iron, and vitamins. Inadequacies of one to seven components have been found in sizable percentages in all economic classes, races, and areas. Although the poorer classes generally have more, deficiencies are not confined to them. Standards used were the official requirements or Recommended Daily Allowances (RDA).

The RDAs have been set by committees of nutritionists for many years and revised upward or downward frequently. Because they are not inflexible (in fact they vary from country to country), they represent a sort of moving standard for the incidence of malnutrition. Better and more accurate surveys come from analyses of blood and urine and clinical signs of vitamin deficiency, which are sometimes quite obvious.

No one can deny the truth of the statement "A well-balanced diet provides adequate vitamins and minerals for health," if the definition of the word *well-balanced* means what it should: each food consumed contains vitamins and minerals in amounts adequate for the metabolism of that food. A diet can also be "balanced" when it contains some "empty" calories—empty or partly empty of minerals or vitamins or both—but other foods containing enough extra nutrients to cover the deficiency. Anything less is not balanced. And, in my opinion, if one has to eat yeast to get enough micro-

nutrients to cover dietary deficiencies, that differs little
from taking them in a pill.

Another way of suspecting dietary deficiencies—but
not necessarily deficiency diseases, so prevalent is pill
taking—is by examining the proportions of empty calories in the American diet. The results are surprising.

The average daily consumption of sugar per person
was 121 grams, which works out to about 480 calories per day. Since the ban on cyclamates, consumption
has been higher by perhaps 20 grams, or about 80 calories per day. Most of this sugar is refined, as sucrose or
glucose. The refining of sugar removes virtually all of
the vitamins and minerals naturally present in sugar
cane or beet juice—in other words, the micronutrients
necessary for the metabolism of sugar. Those that are
stable to heat are usually found in raw molasses. Thus,
480 to 560 calories in the average diet are empty, and
micronutrients necessary for the absorption, utilization,
breakdown, storage, and excretion of sugar must be
provided by other foods richer than normal in these
nutrients. As 2,400 calories are in the average diet of a
sedentary male, about 20 to 23 percent of calories are
empty.

These figures, which are rough, do not mean that
everyone takes in that much sugar. Those who don't
are balanced by those who take more.

A considerable portion of our caloric energy comes
from refined white flour. Some 60 to 80 percent of the
micronutrients in whole wheat are removed in the process of refining. Government or quasi-government bu-
reaus have tacitly recognized that white flour is not an
adequate food, by recommending that four of these
micronutrients be added to flour: thiamine, riboflavin,
niacin, and iron. There are some eighteen or nineteen
others that are partly removed but not restored. Thus a
variable proportion, probably 600 to 800 calories of
the diet, or a quarter to a third, are partly empty in
several micronutrients. With sugar, this makes up about
half our daily caloric intake, or 45 to 57 percent, inadequate in most micronutrients (see Appendix D).

Alcoholic drinks contribute calories to our intake, depending upon individual habit. Two cocktails, whiskeys, or glasses of sherry contribute 300 calories or more. Distilled liquors are devoid of vitamins but contain traces of metals. Wines contain the minerals in the grapes and some vitamins. Vodka and gin have practically nothing but ethyl alcohol.

Therefore, an average diet may contain more than half of its calories deficient in one or more micronutrients, which must be made up by other foods rich in micronutrients. This is probably why nutritionists advise us to eat liver, kidney, other organ meats, eggs, and milk.

It is difficult to find foods in a supermarket that have not been processed in such a way as to lose some vitamins, although the minerals are generally preserved. The stable vitamins—stable to light, heat, and storage —may be unaffected by freezing, preserving, and canning. Purification of fats and oils results in losses; when a food is partitioned, generally into fat and nonfat, minerals and vitamins are not necessarily divided equally between the fractions, but some go with one or the other. The unstable vitamins are E, C, thiamine, part of B_6, and several of the less well-known B group.

As we consider the total nutritional picture today, we are led to conclude that the foods we buy, which are supplied in abundance, are clear, pure, and of excellent quality. But they are lacking in some but not all necessary micronutrients, affected by the processing that makes them so available. Therefore, there is a sort of selective deficiency in our foods, which only public knowledge, such as this book provides, and education can detect. I must admit, however, that to buy foods for a truly well-balanced diet one needs to know the vitamins (about seventeen) and minerals (about fifteen) in each food, the daily requirements of each, and a computer to total the results.

Man and his domestic animals are the only mammals needing a "balanced" diet. All other mammals find their foods naturally balanced. The price of making available plenty of foods of all kinds through refining, processing, superheating, cooking, drying, irradiation, storage, and freezing is an unbalanced diet in respect to several essential micronutrients.

Author's Note

The content of this book should in no way be regarded as the endorsement of any commercial product or products. The author has no commercial or other financial relations with producers or distributors of nutrition products.

The author of this volume is indebted, for helpful informational assistance, to the Vitamin Information Bureau and the Nutrition Foundation, both of New York City, as well as to a large number of individuals who supplied him with data and checked various sections of this book whose subject matter fell within their specific field of expertise. As a work of this nature must be the product of research and writing by more than a single individual, the author gratefully acknowledges the help of William R. Akins, Barbara Benton, and Patricia Davies, as well as of his colleagues at Lombard Associates, Inc., Michael Ballantine and Paul Langdon.

I

But Does Your Doctor Know the Answer?

Your body cannot function without vitamins. They are essential to your physical and mental well-being. Without them, you couldn't last a day. But which vitamins do you need? How much of each? And where do you find them? We will sort out the answers to these questions on the following pages.

Chances are you are confused by the conflicting claims that are being made in the field of nutrition. People have become almost fanatical about vitamins: there are the Vitamin Bores, the Vitamin Haters, the Constant Vitamin Counters, and the Condescending Vitamin Despisers. As in so many other things, it is wise to be moderate in thinking about nutrition and in dealing with vitamins in your diet.

The Food and Drug Administration, which is part of the U.S. Department of Health, Education, and Welfare, published *A Study of Health Practices and Opinions* in 1972. The study found that three-fourths of the public "believe extra vitamins provide more pep and energy" and that 26 percent of the sample, representing about thirty-five million adults, had "used nutritional supplements (vitamins, and/or minerals, in pills or liquid tonics) expecting actual observable benefits, and without physician's advice."

1

The survey showed that people in this category "have a greater-than-average general tendency toward self-medication." Those who use vitamin pills tended "to rely on their own judgments over conflicting opinions from physicians." The FDA survey shows that people who are bewildered by contradictory views decide to be on the safe side, which often means turning to nutritional supplements. Of course, some may overdo it. Still, we can't just sit back and say, "Oh well, fifty years from now they may have examined enough rats and chickens to decide, with impeccable statistics, whether or not I should take vitamin XYZ. Meanwhile, I'll just stick to that TV dinner that has had all the vitamins and other nutrients plucked, cooked, frozen, and stored out of it."

In a book such as this, it is essential that we emphasize that you should not engage in self-medication, that you should consult your doctor. The message is quite simple: "Don't douse yourself with vitamins, any more than you would with anything else, even aspirin. If there is something wrong with you, by all means consult your doctor about it, including your nutritional needs."

The question we must all ask is "Just how much does the average doctor know about nutrition?" We have the word of the American Medical Association's Council on Food and Nutrition that "medical education and medical practice have not kept abreast of the tremendous advance in nutritional knowledge." The AMA's Council reported on March 16, 1963, that medical schools give "inadequate recognition, support and attention" to nutrition. The Council noted that nutritional concepts are "integral to the practice of medicine" and should be used in "diagnosis of disease, treatment of disease, in rehabilitation from chronic illness, in disease prevention, and in health promotion." It found that a patient's "nutritional status" influences the development and cure of diseases and that "many disorders, whether infectious, metabolic, degenerative, or neoplastic, influence the nutritional status of the patient."

The AMA's Council observed that medical students

need to learn a great deal more about nutrition, in order to "better appreciate the practical application of biochemistry to prevention and treatment of disease." Certainly, a good many doctors today are well versed in nutrition. Many of them have supplemented their early training through independent study. Others have had personal experiences, in their practices or even in their immediate family, that have alerted them to the health potential of nutrition.

Specifically, obstetricians are frequently knowledgeable about the need for extra-nourishing foods during pregnancy and after childbirth. They are also well informed about the delicate needs of newborn infants. Many doctors are now worried about the faulty eating habits of children, teen-agers, and older people; others are particularly aware of the crucial role nutrition plays in arresting alcoholism. But no doctor can know everything. That is why there are fewer general practitioners, and more and more specialists, including specialists in nutrition.

Nutrition Is a Young Science

The nutrition controversy is lively, because the whole field, and particularly the study of vitamins, is quite young. It is certainly all to the good that nutrition is being openly discussed, and perhaps even shouted about. We all benefit from the expression of differing opinions, and we must certainly know about them if we are to find our own way through the labyrinth of sometimes contradictory statements.

Take, for example, the authoritative booklet *Your Health: Diet in the Balance,* published by the Nutrition Foundation and written by Marie M. Alexander and Fredrick J. Stare, M.D. The authors say: "Vitamins are nutrients necessary for many body processes. Just the smallest imaginable amounts can do the job, and these may be amply supplied by everyday food. The cheapest and surest source of all vitamins is a balanced diet."

The booklet seems to suggest that there is no need for vitamin supplements because you "may" find all the vitamins you need in "everyday foods." It is essential, of course, that you are eating a "balanced diet." Those are key words. But who can really be sure, in this day and age, that he is eating a diet that contains all required nutritional elements? Who can be certain that this particular carrot, this slice of bread, this piece of meat have not been robbed of their delicate vitamin content on their long way to your dinner table? Despite numerous studies on the way key nutrients disappear during processing and storing, no one really knows the precise degree of deterioriation that takes place.

Then, too, we're not all alike. Our bodies do not follow some general statistical average. And that is why we are simply forced to make up our own minds, at times even in areas where more expertise is available. Certainly, your doctor can guide you in nutrition, but he cannot stand over you like a mother hen. He has just taken your blood pressure, given you an electrocardiogram, x-rayed you, sampled your blood and urine, tapped you from top to toe. And if you need it, he may give you a prescription. While you are facing him across the desk, exhausted and a bit sheepish, you may ask, "I've been taking 400 International Units (IU) of vitamin E daily. Do you think that's all right?" And he, aware of the limits of medical knowledge and of the crowded state of his waiting room, is likely to say, "If you feel that it helps you, certainly."

Against the background of our everyday experience, let us take a second look at the FDA survey of nutritional habits. It noted that many people engage in "rampant empircism," tend to believe that "anything is worth a try," and "approach health problems by trial and error, rather than with a grounding in belief and facts." The survey characterized such people as engaging in "questionable practices."

But where does common sense in making our own choice end, and where do "questionable practices" begin? Nutritional facts are elusive. Trying things out, particularly if they are not harmful, is very much like the experimental method used in science. Scientists call this developing a hypothesis, testing it, developing another and testing it, and repeating this procedure until positive results are achieved. We go through life, from babyhood, gaining knowledge by trial and error.

Our body is subject to such a variety of psychosomatic or somatopsychic influences, and it changes so rapidly, that we could arrive at a complete picture of its functions only if all parts of our body were constantly linked to a computer. As that can't be done, and we are a long way from even knowing how to build such an all-knowing computer, trial and error—or, better still, trial and success—are simply part of living.

Despite the FDA survey's concern about "rampant empiricism," careful personal testing in nutrition, including the use of vitamin supplements, is probably laudable rather than detrimental. Again, we must ask, "Where does healthy and inquisitive independence of judgment end, and where do 'food faddism' and being 'a health nut' begin?" The answer is: "They seem to begin and end with the attitude of whoever makes this judgment." Quite often, the Health Establishment's attitude toward the layman is this: "I am a scientist; he is a charlatan; you are a gullible fool." The charlatan, from this point of view, might be anyone from a vitamin-conscious Nobel Prize winner to your friendly neighborhood nutrition freak who advocates an exclusive diet of betel nut and jasmine tea.

The magazine *Medical World News* observed in its issue for April 27, 1973, that "many physicians are just not very knowledgeable about nutrition." It quoted Dr. Morton B. Glenn of New York City, an internist who is past president of the American Nutrition Association, as saying that nutrition and dieting are even now "hardly taught" in medical schools. He added: "That is why, I am convinced, the medical profession has lost the lead in nutrition to nonmedical people—to nonmedical experts like Jean Mayer, as well as to quacks. I think that academia is at fault." Academia is, of course, the academic world of the universities and medical

schools, the whole area of scholarly instruction on
which human knowledge depends.

Our Cautious Doctors

Our question "But does your doctor know the answer?"
was given an authoritative reply by Dr. Mayer, quoted
in the same periodical, who said: "Nutrition and preventive medicine in general are very poorly taught in
medical school. In surveys of what people know about
nutrition, we found that junior and senior physicians in
a Boston hospital had a very fragmentary knowledge
of nutrition. This knowledge tended to be very highly
theoretical—they had no knowledge of food composition and therefore were unable to translate their theoretical knowledge into practical advice."

Norman Cousins noted in the *Saturday Review* of
May 15, 1971, that the attitude of the medical profession toward vitamins is, to say the least, "cautious and
unenthusiastic." Mr. Cousins, a sophisticated observer
of the world scene for many decades, admits that there
may be a sound basis for such an attitude, because
"vitamins are the ready stuff of quackery," as they lend
themselves easily "to all sorts of unproved notions
about quick cures." He feels that millions of dollars are
being spent on useless vitamins and that some are "toxic
in large doses." But, having said this, Cousins concludes that "much of the medical profession has allowed doubts about vitamins to carry it far past the
point of reasonable criticism." He adds:

"Important research and careful documentation of
vitamin efficacy for some illnesses have often been casu-
ally evaluated or disregarded altogether. Resistance to
vitamin therapy has become institutionalized—indeed,
almost ritualized. Until very recently the entire field of
nutrition, in fact, has been a curriculum stepchild at
many medical schools. There has been a tendency to
take malnutrition seriously only at the extremes—as in
cases of scurvy and kwashiorkor. A related assumption
by some physicians is that the average American supermarket shopping bag contains all that is necessary to

meet required vitamin levels for good health. Similarly, it has not been unusual to hear some doctors say that vitamin deficiencies are rare among the American people. These assumptions have no basis in fact."

They certainly don't. Dr. Mayer, who is professor of nutrition at Harvard University, told the Senate Committee on Nutrition and Human Needs that eating habits in the United States have reached such a low level that government and the food industry should spend $100 million yearly on education in nutrition. At the same hearing, on December 5, 1972, two California nutritionists, Drs. George M. Briggs and Helen D. Ullrich, estimated that the annual cost of hunger and "personal mismanagement of food to the detriment of one's health is approximately $30 billion." They urged the food industry to live up to its "responsibility to produce nutritious foods" and denounced as irresponsible "the development of fabricated foods containing nothing but calories."

Fruits and Vegetables Are Best

Vitamins are at their best when taken as part of fresh fruit and vegetables that have moved quickly from garden to table or have been quick-frozen. Robert Choate, a critic of "empty calorie" products, told the committee that children are now out of touch with fresh food. A generation ago, he recalled, "whether it was shelling peas, scrubbing potatoes, rolling pie crust or cleaning fish," a child "picked up food knowledge by helping in the kitchen." Today, Mr. Choate said, fun foods and convenience foods are "the rallying cry of food merchandising," and "nutrition losses in the ever more sophisticated manufacturing processes" are ignored.

Television is the builder of food images today. The impact is visual. Emphasis is on appearance, including colorful packaging. Quite often, a phrase such as "vitamin C added" is part of the sales pitch. Claims can be confusing. Information is fragmentary.

We must keep in mind, when looking at advertising

claims, that processed foods suffer from loss of vitamins almost inevitably. The manufacturers in some cases try to restore lost vitamins later. Adding vitamin D to milk, for instance, is an excellent thing; in this case, happily, there is total agreement on everyone's part. The late J. I. Rodale, of Emmaus, Pennsylvania, was a pioneer in the struggle for better knowledge in nutrition. His son Robert, now editor of the monthly magazine *Prevention,* also writes a syndicated newspaper column on nutrition. He stated early in January, 1973, that food manufacturers and nutritionists tend to favor "fortified" food—the manufacturers, because it is cheap and makes a good selling point; the nutritionists, because they think it is better than leaving processed foods without additions. Rodale noted, however, that in many cases "additional nutrients were added to items with substantial food values to begin with." The new trend, he wrote, was "to fortify foods that contain few nutrients of their own." According to Rodale, "manufacturers like the idea of adding vitamins to food because the enrichment chemicals are cheap and they add sales appeal as well as nourishment."

Robert Rodale feels that "nutritionists tend to love food fortification because they aren't very hopeful about encouraging most people to stop eating junk foods. Just enrich the junk, they seem to say, and the nutrition problem will be solved." Not so, he maintains. The processing takes away nutrients that can't be put back by chemical means, and "the very cheapness and easiness of fortification could well lead to a continuing downgrading of overall nutritional levels." There is an ongoing argument over the relative virtues of "natural" vitamins and synthetics.

Dr. Linus Pauling, best known for his advocacy of large doses of vitamin C against the common cold, sees no difference between natural and synthetic C. Nor does the Food and Drug Administration. The Rodale people disagree strongly, much as they approve Pauling's concept otherwise. In line with other advocates of natural-versus-synthetic foods and vitamins, they maintain that other, possibly as yet unknown, nutrients may be present in such C-rich plants as rose hips. It is a valid controversy, made difficult by lack of precise knowledge.

The "Well, Maybe Factor"

This paucity of generally accepted judgments makes for a lot of "Well, maybe . . ."-saying on the part of people who should speak with authority. The result is what we might call the WMF (Well, Maybe Factor) in professional attitudes toward the role of vitamins in nutrition. When the medical profession is irritated about vitamins, or in turn irritates others by sweeping statements, it does so by ignoring the WMF. Instead of saying, "Well, maybe . . . ," it often speaks brusquely of "unsupported claims," of "expensive placebos," or of "lack of broadly based experimentation."

By asking, in this chapter, "But does your doctor know the answer?" we do not wish to plant destructive doubts or to drive a wedge between doctor and patient. But when it comes to nutrition and vitamins, we should aim at a grown-up dialogue between mature adults, where neither side puts down the other without valid reason, and in which the physician is a participant and skilled adviser, rather than a bearer of superior wisdom.

In his book *Nutrition Against Disease,* Dr. Roger Williams deals with this delicate problem candidly. Williams is a professor of biochemistry at the University of Texas in Austin, former president of the American Chemical Society, and a member of the President's Advisory Panel on Heart Disease (you will find the text of his Minority Report in Appendix C of this book). Professor Williams believes that "the most basic weapons in the fight against disease are the most ignored by modern medicine: the numerous nutrients that the cells of our bodies need."

Williams is of the opinion that "the very people who should have been able to give expert guidance" on nutrition "have, in fact, virtually abandoned the field." He states, "If more doctors really were experts with respect to nutrition and heredity, they would be able to give their patients sufficiently intelligent advice so that quackery and faddism could have little scope. A depressing aspect of the situation is that laymen's intuitions, uninformed as they may be, are more often justified than the physician's neglect." Dr. Philip L. White, director of the American Medical Association's Department of Foods and Nutrition, has spoken of the prevalence of "food neuroticism and faddism," and he notes, in his book *Let's Talk About Food,* that many consumers regard themselves as "nutritionally impoverished" unless they consume esoteric nutrients and that "the consumer loses faith in conventional foods and becomes a nutrition neurotic."

While we face such psychiatric terminology, let's make sure that we do not get paranoid about the whole vitamin controversy. Neither the medical profession nor the food industry is out to poison us. We are simply dealing with varying degrees of ignorance, and it is all too human to try and look knowledgeable, or to make money from people's laziness and search for higher status even in the things they eat.

We are not victims of a nutritional conspiracy. The consumer, meaning you, does have a choice and a veto. He can ignore useless foods and refuse to buy foods that have been processed into mere shells with little in vitamins or other nutritional content; he can go after fresh fruit and vegetables, use vitamin supplements wisely—and avoid overpriced, gimmicky vitamin compounds—and generally refuse to stampede along with the mass of buyers who want their TV dinners, those it's-all-prepared-for-you snacks, those gorgeous thick steaks without vegetables, or the soft drinks that are largely water and chemical preservatives. The choice is yours. Your doctor may be able to advise you, provided he has kept up with nutritional research, but don't count on it—if only because he is too busy, too expensive, or too specialized.

As you read the following pages, consider the various vitamins first in terms of the natural foods in which they may be found; examine the degree to which you have access to vitamin-rich foods in lean meats and fish, in

WHICH VITAMINS DO YOU NEED

fresh fruits and vegetables; try to build the kind of diet that incorporates your personal vitamin needs; then, and only then, select the vitamins you may require as food supplements. And if you mention all this to your doctor, he may even smile and say, "Well, maybe . . ."

II

Vitamin A: For Vision and Delicate Lubrication

One of America's leading nutritionists, Dr. Jean Mayer, has tried to set vitamin A to music. A high-school group asked him how to feature the vitamin in a musical designed to dramatize and symbolize nutrition. Dr. Mayer, a member of the faculty of Harvard University, suggested in his syndicated newspaper column that a "tuneful charade" should be used, featuring popular songs. As nostalgia is popular and, anyway, Mayer's taste in "jazzing-up nutrition" runs toward an earlier musical period, he admitted that some of his choices might be dated. Writing for the *New York Daily News* and other papers, he said vitamin A, "essential to the maintenance of the outer skin and the inner mucosae," should be set to the music of "I've Got You Under My Skin." And as it is essential to vision, it ought to be dramatized with "Jeepers Creepers, Where'd You Get Those Peepers?"

The mucosae of which he speaks are in the many body areas that must be constantly lubricated, kept moist or mucous. Of the needs for vitamin A, that in vision has probably been most thoroughly researched. And although the vitamin can be found in many foods that are, or should be, part of our daily diet, we must make sure that our intake responds to the needs placed on our bodies by daily stresses and dangers.

A *New York Times* article (October 15, 1972) stated that vitamin A is being used to fortify sugar in Central America. This is a way of getting the nutrient to the general population and particularly to thousands of malnourished children who suffer from blindness caused by vitamin A deficiency. According to Dr. Guillermo Arroyave of the Institute of Nutrition of Central America and Panama, 80 percent of the Central American population suffer from vitamin A deficiency.

Another *Times* article (April 30, 1972) recounted efforts by the United Nations Children's Fund (UNICEF) to distribute vitamin A to blind and otherwise malnourished children in central Java. This is part of a program that emphasizes better health in developing countries. The idea is that better-fed, healthier populations can more readily achieve their goals.

A Common Deficiency

Vitamin A deficiency is one of the two most common nutritional deficiency diseases in the world today. It does not occur only in developing countries with starving populations. Deficiencies may occur in your own home. Most vulnerable are children, elderly people, and vegetarians. People in these three categories are most likely to avoid meat, a primary source of protein, which is necessary for the absorption of vitamin A.

What are the symptoms of deficiency? The most common is night blindness, or the inability to adapt to darkness or bright lights. Advanced symptoms are abnormal dryness of the eyeball, softening of the cornea (called keratomalacia), death and ulceration of eye tissues, and finally blindness. The most common cause of blindness in malnourished children is xerophthalmia, also resulting from lack of vitamin A.

George Wald of Harvard University dramatically demonstrated the relationship of vitamin A to function of the retina. A substance called rhodopsin, or visual purple, in the rods of the retina contains a vitamin A derivative called retinene. When light strikes the retina, this substance breaks down into two constituents which, in the dark, recombine to again form visual purple. Light strikes the retina again (nerve impulses go to the brain to identify what is being seen), the substance breaks down again, re-forms, and the cycle goes on. The rods of the retina assure peripheral vision and vision at low levels of illumination, while the cones influence vision of color and in bright light. The cones contain a pigment called visual violet. Day vision and night vision both depend on vitamin A, but night vision is entirely dependent; so a subtle vitamin A deficiency shows up first in the form of night blindness.

Vitamin A is necessary not only to the eye but to all mucous membranes of the body. Its absence can cause respiratory, gastrointestinal, and genitourinary tracts to become dry, hardened, and unable to resist bacteria. According to Dr. Luigi M. Deluca of the Massachusetts Institute of Technology, moisture in the lungs is a primary defense against invading microorganisms and pollutants from the atmosphere. The lung itself must be lubricated in order to exchange new air for old. Dr. Umberto Saffiotti of the National Cancer Institute found that doses of vitamin A can inhibit the appearance of malignant tumors in the lungs of laboratory hamsters.

Dry, Rough Skin

Vitamin A deficiency can cause dry, rough skin and pimples at the site of hair follicles. One of the vitamin A-related diseases is psoriasis. It is not considered a serious disease, unless, of course, you have it. Victims suffer from itching, scaling, eruptions, and sometimes severe lesions. Progress has been made in fighting psoriasis with vitamin A in its acid form. In the *Journal of the American Medical Association* (March 10, 1969), Drs. Phillip Frost and Gerald Weinstein reported that vitamin A acid helped twenty-four of twenty-six psoriasis patients after one week of treatment. The study was repeated with patients with really ugly skin conditions that had resisted all other treatments. Results were dramatic. The psoriasis patient may have had a particularly high need for vitamin A.

Other signs of deficiency center in the reproductive organs. Not only is the mucous tissue of these organs itself in need of vitamin A, but the secretion of sex hormones that control their function is also affected. Malfunctioning tissue or hormones may be responsible for infertility, congenital malformations in fetuses, abortion, difficult delivery, or failure to lactate. These abnormalities have been produced in laboratory animals deficient in vitamin A.

As vitamin A is essential for the health of all membranelike (epithelial) tissues—not only for eyes, skin and respiratory, gastrointestinal and genitourinary tissues—it is also needed for the growth and maintenance of glands, bones, teeth, nails, and hair. The vitamin is really essential for the upkeep of almost all parts of the body. Lifelong deficiency can lead to premature aging.

Although the effect of vitamin A on bodily health has been researched extensively, little is known about how it works—except for its direct effect on sight. One theory is that, since many animals die without vitamin A, it may play a vital role in metabolism. Another theory is that, as its deficiency so often goes hand in hand with protein deficiency, vitamin A may contribute to the synthesis of protein. Vitamin A absorption is blocked by acute lack of protein. Kwashiorkor (this is an African word) is a childhood protein deficiency disease that hampers the mobilization of vitamin A into the bloodstream from the liver, where 90 percent of it is stored. Other research indicates that vitamin A plays a role in maintaining stability of cell membranes and thereby influences the release of enzymes.

Vitamin A appears to inhibit cancer development in experimental animals. It is the only substance that has been verified by laboratory studies to have this effect, at least indirectly. The *Journal of the National Cancer Institute* (May, 1971) reported a study by Raymond J. Shamberger, a professor in the Department of

Biochemistry, Cleveland Clinic, Ohio. In Shamberger's experiment, vitamin A, when applied locally, inhibited the development of cervical and vaginal tumors in hamsters treated with a powerful chemical carcinogen. It was also found that vitamin A palmitate, administered orally, dramatically inhibited the growth of lung cancer in other chemically treated hamsters. Shamberger claims that the effect of vitamin A is indirect. It increases the ability of lysosomes (tiny bodies in the heart of every cell) to rupture on demand, thus releasing the enzymes that help break down the premalignant cell.

The Carotenoids

Carotenoids, a group of bright yellow substances from which the body synthesizes vitamin A, are present in green and yellow vegetables (particularly parsley, dandelion greens, chard, chicory, turnip greens, spinach, watercress, kale, sweet potatoes, and carrots), tomatoes, egg yolk, fish-liver oils (especially halibut, cod, and turbot), liver, dairy products (milk, cream, butter), and fruit, especially apricots.

However, although carotenoids are initially present in these foods, they may be partially or wholly lost by storage at the market or at home, may be leached out by overcooking, or, once swallowed, may be destroyed by harmful substances in the body.

To avoid vitamin A loss during storage, fresh vegetables should be quickly washed in cold water (never soaked) as soon as they are brought home from the market, wrapped in foil or placed in a container, and kept as much as possible away from light and air. They should be used as soon as possible. According to a study by J. P. Sweeney and A. C. Marsh in the *Journal of the American Dietetic Association* (1971), the longer the cooking time, the greater the loss of carotenoids. Therefore, vegetables, whether fresh or frozen, should be cooked as quickly as possible, in a tightly covered pot, ideally until just crisp. Cooking water should be just enough to prevent sticking and should not be discarded after cooking, but served with the vegetable. According to the same study, canning and pressure cooking caused somewhat more vitamin loss; blanching and freezing caused none.

Cooking and storing are somewhat under our control. However, there are some causes of vitamin depletion less under our control that specifically apply to vitamin A and should be mentioned here. An article in *Prevention* magazine (January, 1971) stated that one of the greatest obstacles to maintaining an adequate supply of vitamin A is pollution, both of the air we breathe and of the water we drink. The respiratory system, so dependent upon vitamin A, is largely made up of mucous membranes that act as a first line of defense against dust and toxic materials in the air. The more foreign matter there is to filter out, the more vitamin A is used up, and the higher our requirements are. Foreign matter, consisting of such pollutants as poison gases, irritating particles, and carcinogenic matter, taxes the mucous linings of nose, throat, and lungs and makes them easier prey for bacteria causing infections. According to a report from the Battelle-Northwest Institute, the pollutants ozone and nitrogen dioxide themselves destroy vitamin A by oxidation.

Drinking water in some sections of the country is contaminated. As far back as 1966, California, Washington, Oklahoma, Arizona, Colorado, New Mexico, Minnesota, and South Carolina showed levels of nitrates in the groundwater rising to a dangerous level. Inorganic nitrogen fertilizers, in the form of nitrates, eventually leach out of the fields and inevitably into some of the water we drink. Nitrates, under certain conditions, are converted by bacteria in the air or in the stomach or intestinal tract into nitrites, poisonous substances that slow down thyroid activity. A healthy, active thyroid gland is essential to convert carotene into vitamin A.

Your Liver Needs Vitamin A

All poisons that break through our bodies' defensive

barriers eventually end up in the liver, our chief cleansing organ. If the liver is healthy and supplied with all the nutrients it needs, it can remove foreign and harmful elements from our system before damage is done. However, the liver depends on vitamin A in its battle against toxicity. As an ever-growing variety of pollutants is dumped into our environment, our livers must work efficiently.

Other antagonists to vitamin A are food preservatives. Nitrates are in canned meat, frankfurters, salami, bologna, and other sausages. Nitrates in food preservatives have the same effect on the thyroid as nitrates in drinking water. Another preservative is benzoate of soda, found in all kinds of prepared and processed foods. Benzoate of soda is especially destructive to vitamin A (Roels in *The Vitamins*, 1967). A common lemon or rose flavoring, known as citral, is an anti-vitamin A substance, but its name rarely appears on the labels of ice creams, sherbets, candy, gelatin desserts, or soft drinks.

Sometimes vitamin A, though ingested, is inadequately absorbed owing to some malfunction in the upper intestinal tract (the jejunum and duodenum), where most absorption takes place and where most of the conversion of carotene occurs. Malfunctions may consist of lack of bile, which prevents vitamin A from being destroyed by oxygen, or presence of some disease such as infectious hepatitis, diabetes, cystic fibrosis, or colitis. Disease and old age can reduce the body's ability to convert carotene into vitamin A.

Low-fat diets are another threat to vitamin A utility, because the nutrient is soluble in fat only. In an article in the February, 1970, issue of the *American Journal of Clinical Nutrition*, Drs. J. G. Chopra and J. Kevany stated, "Very low fat decreases the availability of vitamin A and carotene," and they indicated that adequate protein is also necessary for absorption, or there is "impairment of intestinal absorption, transport and metabolism" of the form of vitamin A utilized for sight. Those who are cutting down on calories must not exclude too much protein and fat. Also, be careful how you handle constipation: mineral oil interferes with vitamin A absorption. The vitamin is absorbed most rapidly by older children and adults; newborn infants and persons over seventy years absorb it more slowly.

The vitamin content of foods varies seasonally, especially in milk. Summer milk may contain twice as much vitamin A as winter milk. The vitamin content of any milk depends on the diet of the mother (human milk usually contains more than cow's milk). Most infant formulas and milk substitutes, such as soybean milk, do not contain vitamin A. When these are used, supplements should be given, especially to babies too young to eat vegetables.

The FDA Restrictions

We have spoken of the foods in which vitamin A may be found, and of the factors that tend to inhibit its use by our bodies; but we have pretty much ignored the use of vitamin A as a food supplement. One reason for this is the controversial nature of this vitamin: the body, in contrast to other vitamins, stores A, and too much of it can have ill effects. For this reason the Food and Drug Administration has placed high-strength vitamin A pills and other products into the category of prescription drugs. Since October 1, 1973, vitamin A above the strength of 10,000 International Units is no longer manufactured for nonprescription use, although existing stocks of supplements can be used up. In other words: vitamin A in potency up to the 10,000 units limit can be purchased freely, like aspirin; above that, a doctor's prescription is necessary.

The U.S. Government Recommended Daily Allowances (U.S. RDA), published in 1973, specify 5,000 to 8,000 IU of vitamin A for women during pregnancy and lactation, 1,250 to 2,500 for children under four years of age, and 2,500 to 5,000 for adults and children of four years or older. Should one take supplements of vitamin A? Dr. Philip L. White, director of the Department of Foods and Nutrition of the American Medical Association, says in his book *Let's Talk About Food* that the recommended daily amount "is easily obtained from a variety of foods" and that "supplemental sources are not necessary unless prescribed by a physician."

Dr. White is a leading authority, and self-medication with vitamin A is particularly ill advised, as it *can* be dangerous to take too much of it. You may require more vitamin A during periods of physical or emotional stress, when your body uses it at an increased rate. But how much is "more" and how much is "too much"? *The Journal of Pediatrics* (1947) reported experiments involving 200,000 IU of vitamin A, taken daily for six months, without any damage being recorded. What do doctors themselves say about the danger of hypervitaminosis, too much vitamin, in the case of A? One widely used guide for physicians is *The Merck Manual,* an annual handbook published by the Merck Sharp & Dohme Research Laboratories. It states that with one exception, an infant aged six and one-half months who received 60,000 to 80,000 units daily for about six months, overdosage of vitamin A is a "rare condition" and has been "described thus far" only in patients receiving more than 100,000 units per day. Symptoms include loss of hair, dry skin, cracked lips, severe headaches, and general weakness. Vitamin K is used in the treatment of excess vitamin A.

It is worth keeping this in mind, because some people think that you can't have too much of a good thing, including a vitamin. Still, there is no single food, other than polar bear liver, that contains enough vitamin A to cause toxicity. Overdose symptoms usually show up from six to fifteen months after the beginning of a large intake and clear up within three to seven days after the dosage is stopped.

With all the concern over too much vitamin A, the greatest problem is still too little of it. Oswald Roels states in *Present Knowledge of Nutrition* that vitamin A is now being produced so efficiently and cheaply that "to provide the entire annual requirement of one human being would cost about five U.S. cents. It is truly amazing, in view of this, that vitamin A deficiency remains one of the most widespread forms of human malnutrition."

III

Vitamin B₁: Thiamine
Against Alcoholism

Since we are adding vitamin D to milk, shouldn't the distillers "enrich" whiskey with vitamin B_1?

At the risk of sounding flippant, let us give a moment's thought to this idea. But first we must put aside the curious habit of regarding intoxication with a knowing smile, of seeing something irresistibly funny in drunkenness.

We should all know by now that alcoholism is the nation's number one addiction, way ahead of heroin and of other hard and so-called soft drugs. One of the ways in which alcohol undermines physical and mental health is its impact on the body's ability to absorb and utilize nutrients. What wrecks the alcoholic's nervous system, and brings about physical debilitation, is the effect drinking has on eating habits and on the digestive tract's capacity to make full use of important nutritional factors, notably vitamin B_1, or thiamine.

According to *The Merck Manual,* a handbook used by many doctors, "in alcoholism, a combination of decreased intake and impaired absorption and utilization occurs. Dextrose requires thiamine for its oxidation, and frequent or long-continued dextrose infusions, coupled with a low thiamine intake, are potent factors in precipitating thiamine deficiency."

The same handbook notes the following "most important conditioning factors in the U.S.A." that create a lack of vitamin B_1: "(1) disorders increasing the vitamin requirement, such as hyperthyroidism, lactation, and fever from any cause; (2) diseases causing impaired absorption, such as long-continued diarrheas; and (3) diseases causing impaired vitamin utilization, such as severe liver disease."

In its discussion of neuritis, an inflammation of nerve fibers, the *Encyclopaedia Britannica* notes that this illness, "accompanying both beriberi and alcoholism, is the result of deficiency of vitamin B_1." As outright beriberi is uncommon in our society, but alcoholism is widespread, we might do well to increase the vitamin B_1 intake of any person who tends to drink heavily, or at least with regularity.

There are many different stages that precede acute alcoholism. The borderline between the "social drinker" and the clinical alcoholic is obscure. But even the moderate drinker should know that alcohol interferes with the body's efficient use of vitamin B_1. Although I do not seriously assume that the distilling industy will ever feature "Enriched with Vitamin B_1" in its glossy advertisements, anyone who drinks regularly should be aware of his special need for vitamin B_1.

When American prisoners of war returned from Vietnam in 1973, several reported that their limited prison diet caused symptoms of beriberi. This illness, still widespread in many parts of Asia, results from the disastrous habit of "polishing" rice, which removes its vitamin-rich outer hull. This discarded silverskin of rice has been used successfully as an antiberiberi medication. Cases have been reported from Malaysia, where the native Malay population suffered from beriberi, while Indian workers who ate "red" or "parboiled" rice remained well. Parboiling forces nutrients of the husk into the inner grain of the rice, which can then be easily dehusked.

Thiamine Deficiency

Like another seemingly "archaic" disease, scurvy, beriberi is widely regarded as absent from the contemporary American scene. Its very name is exotic. According to *Steadman's Medical Dictionary*, it comes from Sinhalese, the language of Ceylon (Sri Lanka), and means "extreme weakness." One prominent American nutrition scholar, Dr. W. H. Sebrell, Jr., of the Institute of Nutrition Science at Columbia University, has stated that "the clinical evaluation of a slight degree of thiamine deficiency is of particular importance in the United States," where "severe thiamine depletion may be seen only as an implication of alcoholism, or of some disease which interferes with the intake, absorption or utilization of thiamine."

Sebrell added: "Unfortunately, the thought still seems to persist that severe thiamine deficiency is a disease of rice-eating people and does not occur in the United States. This leads to a situation where many physicians fail to consider the possibility of beriberi when they are faced with a puzzling diagnostic problem. However, in the past, severe clinical beriberi was widely found in the United States." Among the states in which, according to Sebrell, vitamin B_1 deficiencies have occurred were several in New England, as well as Arkansas, California, and Texas.

A deficiency of vitamin B_1, or thiamine, is difficult to diagnose. Symptoms are fairly generalized and might point to a variety of diseases. Basically, vitamin B_1 is needed to enable the body to make full use of such nutrients as carbohydrates. Long before the body succumbs to beriberi, various complaints accumulate. Such common symptoms as general weakness and loss of weight and appetite may be experienced. In particular, discomfort in legs and feet can be a sign of subclinical beriberi. Such symptoms are difficult enough to pin down by a physician; the average person is likely to ignore them.

The Vitamin Information Bureau notes that "widespread subclinical or mild beriberi is a possibility that cannot be ignored," even right here and now. The Bureau adds: "Long-continued ingestion of a diet poor in thiamine may produce the chronic dry, atrophic type found among elderly adults. Patients are unlikely to be well-nourished generally. They may be heavy drinkers of alcoholic beverages. They may exhibit neuromuscular pathology, ankle or foot drop, toe drop, the thumb drop of tailors, paralysis of the vocal cords."

Because the body is such an intricate biochemical apparatus, lack of other nutrients can create symptoms identical or similar to vitamin B_1 deficiency. On the other hand, B_1 is essential to so many body functions that its lack may be felt in a great variety of ways. The Vitamin Information Bureau says that there exists such "a broad list of indications" for the need of thiamine that "B_1 could be called on to play a therapeutic role in a wide range of disorders." Gerhard Zbinden published a paper on this subject, "Therapeutic use of Vitamin B_1 in Diseases Other Than Beriberi" in the *Annals of the New York Academy of Science* (1962) that surveyed the literature in this area from 1930 to 1960. He found that vitamin B_1 had been used and reported in 230 different conditions. In 1963, replies to his questionnaire showed that physicians had used it in fifty-eight different indications of disease in the United States, including beriberi. The Vitamin Information Bureau states that lack of thiamine "may be quite frequently encountered by the average family physician in the USA, whether the deficiency is recognized or not."

The trouble lies in the difficulty in establishing a B_1 deficiency conclusively. New methods for checking, or assaying, the presence of vitamin B_1 in the various parts of the body are being perfected, notably by Dr. Myron Brin, formerly with the Department of Nutrition of the University of California at Davis and now with the pharmaceutical firm of Hoffmann-LaRoche. Dr. Brin used his method in testing the thiamine level of people undergoing food deprivation. He reported on this work in a paper on "Fasting in Obesity: Thiamine Depletion as Measured by Erythrocyte Transketolase Changes" in the *Archives of Internal Medicine* (February, 1966). Where earlier analytic methods might not have been able to pinpoint a deficiency, Dr. Brin's technique enabled him to demonstrate that "thiamine depletion occurs rapidly in the fasting obese patient." Incidentally, this study did not deal with routine low-caloric diet, but with people who were severely overweight and underwent treatment involving "no caloric intake for periods of a week or more." Conventional methods of measuring the body's thiamine level, such as analysis of urine, apparently have only limited accuracy under specific conditions, and fasting is one of them.

Dangers in Alcohol

The consistent intake of alcohol can create extremely dangerous body conditions. I am emphasizing alcoholism in this chapter, because we now have something like ten million alcoholics in the United States. Chances are you know one or several people who fit into the classifications that range from consistent social drinking to the threshold of serious alcoholism. The difficulties of dealing with alcoholism, despite the admirable record of Alcoholics Anonymous and other groups, are common knowledge. Contributing factors are obviously many, ranging from alcoholic parents and childhood difficulties to business habits. What we don't know precisely are psychological and physiological interactions, the actual metabolic imbalance that is believed to be at work in cases of alcoholism; nor do we know with any degree of accuracy the influence of hereditary, ethnic, and cultural factors.

Let's be quite frank: the early stages of alcoholism are overwhelmingly dealt with outside doctors' offices. A physician is likely to face the problem of dealing with an alcoholic only during some sort of crisis, when alcohol has already taken its toll with severity. *The Merck Manual* speaks of the treatment of Wernicke's syndrome, better known as a form of *delirium tremens,* a severe emotional crisis involving frightening hallucinations. Among the means of treatment under medical conditions are thiamine injections.

The medical handbook advises doctors to look for thiamine deficiency in cases of severe alcoholism, and to use vitamin treatment "until a therapeutic response is obtained or until a strong odor of thiamine in the urine indicates saturation of the tissues." "Although no strictly scientific basis exists" for giving more than 10 to 20 milligrams (mg.) of thiamine per day, the book adds, "experience shows that larger doses may be used safely, since no undesirable side effects have been encountered." The manual states:

"Thiamine either alone or in combination with other water-soluble vitamins in dextrose infusions is good preventive therapy against deficiency disease, since thiamine-containing enzymes are concerned in carbohydrate metabolism. It is recommended in alcoholism and other conditions in which thiamine deficiency is a potential hazard. During refeeding of starved individuals, thiamine should be administered to forestall onset of deficiency."

Having listened in, as it were, on doctors talking to each other about the role of thiamine, or B_1, in an alcoholic crisis, what can we learn from it, and how can we apply it?

This question is of particular importance to anyone who may be married to a heavy drinker, or who may have a relative or acquaintance who has an alcoholism problem in the family. Many things can and must be done to cure or alleviate what we now correctly regard as an illness rather than as a "weakness of character." Among the things to be done is making an intelligent, patient, and sustained effort to strengthen the diet of the alcoholic or prealcoholic.

Although thiamine treatment in alcoholism is well established, nutrition has many other avenues toward the prevention and alleviation of symptoms caused by excessive use of alcohol. As alcohol attacks the cells, nervous system, brain center, and other body centers, the whole spectrum of vitamins and minerals may be required to stem its impact. Dr. Roger J. Williams, in

Nutrition Against Disease, states that "no one who follows good nutritional practices will ever become an alcoholic." But alcoholism and nutritional neglect go hand in hand. Dr. Williams notes that glutamine use has yielded "some highly suggestive results" in the treatment of alcoholics. Extensive experiments have also been made in the use of vitamin B₃ (niacin), the substance that has come into prominence as part of so-called megavitamin therapy against schizophrenia, infant retardation, and related illnesses. (See chap. V.)

People Who Drink Their Lunch

The alcoholic or prealcoholic has a tendency to drink his lunch or dinner, to substitute hard liquor or cocktails for a balanced meal. He or she is skilled at maneuvering around many social hurdles, and just pushing food around on the plate is one of the easiest tricks. Getting the habitual drinker to eat a full meal is often impossible, but he may accept a multivitamin tablet, plus a therapeutic B-complex pill (including a substantial dose of thiamine), if only as a gesture of appeasement.

Naturally, B_1 in the heavy drinker's diet is no substitute for cutting down on alcohol. But it does counteract the destructive impact of alcohol on absorption of nutrients. As we have seen, in serious crisis thiamine is given by injection, so that it goes directly into the bloodstream. One reason for this is the debilitated body's reduced ability to absorb and utilize even vitamins taken in foods or in pill, capsule, or liquid form —injection bypasses the absorption hurdle.

During early stages of heavy drinking, every effort to keep the diet in balance is worth a try. If nothing else, it may alleviate, stave off, or control a more severe condition. It may keep the body better able to fight off the debilitating effects of alcoholism, perhaps even keep the alcoholic in a mental state amenable to self-control or medicopsychiatric treatment. We can't do the doctor's job for him, when it comes to treating alcoholism, but we can make a serious effort to make his job a bit easier by fighting the influence of alcohol on the body's nutritional balance.

If someone you know is a heavy drinker, and you're trying to have him get an adequate thiamine supply in his diet, how much should he take as a supplement? A therapeutic multivitamin capsule may contain something like 10 milligrams of thiamine. On the other hand, in severe cases, over 100 milligrams have been given. Michael C. Latham, writing in *Present Knowledge in Nutrition,* says that "there is a tremendous prevalence of self-medication in vitamins" and that even "physicians tend to overprescribe thiamine, regarding it as a panacea for neurological aches and pains, although the conditions in which thiamine plays a role are fairly limited. He adds that, "fortunately, in the case of thiamine the body is very good at getting rid of the excess."

But, cautious as Dr. Latham is, he, too, concludes that thiamine deficiency in the United States is "by no means a rarity" and is to be found "mainly in the alcoholic population." He writes: "Alcoholism is an increasingly prevalent condition and several clinical features previously believed to be due to alcoholic poisoning are now known to be due to nutritional deficiencies."

Latham specifically refers to the impact excessive drinking has on the eyes, to lack of muscle coordination (ataxia), and to the mental disintegration, which takes many forms—Wernicke's disease, of which we spoke before, and Korsakoff's psychosis, which includes memory loss (amnesia), at times camouflaged by elaborate fantasies. Latham notes that, "if treated early, the signs of the Wernicke-Korsakoff syndrome respond to thiamine alone even if alcohol is continued."

Now we come to the point where help to the alcoholic, even before medical treatment, may be crucial. While Latham speaks in terms of the future, we must keep our eye on the present. He says:

"Of overriding importance in this syndrome is the fact that irreversible brain damage ensues rapidly, and therefore early recognition and treatment are vital. Prevention also calls for considerable public health ingenuity. Possibilities suggested have included fortification of alcoholic beverages with thiamine, frequent immunization of alcoholics with thiamine and development of a suitable depot carrier to reduce the frequency of these injections, and the provision by public health authorities of thiamine-impregnated snacks on bar counters. The cost of any of these measures would almost certainly be less than the present very high cost of caring for those who have suffered from Wernicke-Korsakoff's disease."

These are sophisticated and valuable public health suggestions, which probably won't be put into practice in the foreseeable future. Meanwhile, anyone concerned with the health of a heavy drinker will naturally seek to bolster his intake of thiamine.

Loss in Milling Process

Although alcoholism in vitamin B_1 deficiency is the area of gravest concern in this country at the present time, we must remain aware that thiamine is being removed not only from rice, but also from other grains in the milling process. Throughout the United States, although not uniformly in all states, certain forms of flour and rice are "enriched" with thiamine during their production. Rice is often overwashed in the kitchen, water is discarded, and even steam carries nutrients away when pots are left uncovered.

We shouldn't have to turn to vitamin preparations, and care during cooking is one way to preserve thiamine in rice and other grains. And there are a few other pitfalls to keep in mind. Have you developed a fondness for Japanese *sashimi,* a dish of raw fish? Well, keep in mind that certain uncooked fish contain an enzyme, thiaminase, that can destroy thiamine. And if you eat uncooked clams, keep in mind that they cut thiamine absorption in half. Still, no one is likely to insist that each half shell bear the imprint "This clam has been enriched with B_1 (thiamine) . . ."

IV

Vitamin B₂ (Riboflavin):
Look in the Mirror!

If you are past thirty, next time you stand before a mirror, examine your face carefully, especially the area around the mouth. Are there rows of tiny, radiating pucker lines? Then, if no one is looking, stick out your tongue. Instead of an even, healthy pink, are there red or magenta blotches? If either of these two conditions exists, you may have a mild vitamin B_2 deficiency.

No one knows why we age, what causes aging, or why some people age in different ways and at different rates. Research does indicate more and more conclusively that the balance of nutrients in the body plays an important role. Riboflavin has a specific role in the maintenance of the body. Its absence can cause a number of symptoms, of which pucker lines and a purple tongue are considered mild.

Other symptoms are: sore throat, and inflammation or lesions of other mucous membranes; scaly, oily eruptions on the skin, especially where membranes and outer skin meet; and changes in vision, notably "twilight blindness" which is much like the "night blindness" caused by lack of vitamin A.

There is reason to believe that B_2 deficiency may cause cataracts and corneal disorders. For some time experimenters have been able to produce cataracts in laboratory animals made deficient in riboflavin. Such experiments cannot, of course, be done with humans, but Adelle Davis, nutritionist and author of *Let's Get Well,* gives accounts of persons for whom improvement of diet, sometimes in preparation for surgery, has resulted in recovery from cataracts.

Birth Defects

Very recent research indicates that some birth defects may be due to extreme deficiency in pregnant women. Again in the laboratory, animals made deficient in riboflavin have produced malformed offspring with defects as extensive as those produced by thalidomide. However, researchers are very cautious about these results. They tend to believe more research is needed before any conclusions can be drawn.

This is the case with much of the thinking about riboflavin. Research is still, even at this date, in progress, and there are few conclusive statements to be made, but in addition to sight and to fetal development, there are connections between riboflavin and resistance to cancer (extreme caution here), the health of the thyroid gland, and oxidation (the chemical reaction in which oxygen is carried from one enzyme to another).

Research on riboflavin did not begin until the 1920s. The reason it and many other B vitamins were late in being discovered is that people at that time were so overwhelmed with the discovery of "vitamin B," now know as B_1. It was not suspected at the time that this "vitamin B" was not what it appeared to be, one substance with many operating factors, but was actually a composite of many substances—the whole vitamin B complex. For this reason research was somewhat hindered. It was not until 1926 that a long series of various diets given to laboratory animals proved that the "growth factor" of vitamin B was an entirely separate substance. It was not until ten years after that that B_2 was discovered to consist of four other separate substances.

How does B_2 work? It is part of the structure of two important enzymes that affect many body functions. It was first called the "growth factor" because its absence caused stunted growth in young laboratory animals. We now know that it is vital to metabolism, the mechanism by which food materials are burned in the body. If food cannot be converted to fuel for the maintenance of old cells and production of new cells, there can be no growth.

Family Income Matters

Vitamin B_2 deficiency seems to be a common nutritional problem in many lands, especially in countries with low-protein diets. But the problem occurs here, in the U.S., too. There seems to be a relationship between B_2 intake and family income: the higher your income, the higher your B_2 intake is likely to be because your diet includes more protein and green vegetables. Owing to regional eating habits, you are more likely to be deficient if you live in the South than if you live in the North; in one New York clinic, about one case turns up per month.

You may be deficient if you are guilty of any one of a number of things: lifelong faulty dietary habits, such as skipping meals; food idiosyncrasies, such as refusing to eat liver or green vegetables; alcoholism; prolonged following of a diet selected for treatment of digestive trouble or some chronic disease such as peptic ulcer, colitis, or diabetes. Sometimes persons, especially old people, are unable to absorb the vitamin because of faulty secretion of hydrochloric acid in the stomach or lack of phosphorus in their diets.

Loss of B_2 can occur during cooking, or anytime food is exposed to light. For instance, if you leave a bottle of milk standing on the porch in the sunlight, it can lose 50 to 70 percent of its B_2 content in a matter of a couple of hours. Five to fifteen percent is lost during pasteurization or irradiation with ultraviolet rays.

How can a B_2 deficiency be prevented or corrected? The best way is through a well-balanced dict that emphasizes yeast, milk, liver, lean meat, cheese, eggs, green vegetables, and enriched cereals. As you become more sophisticated in nutrition, you will appreciate the fact that this diet will also take care of a number of other deficiencies as well.

V

Vitamin B₃ (Niacin): Do You Suffer from Subclinical Pellagra?

Now, let us enter a hornet's nest. We must look at a scientific controversy that involves vitamin B_3, known as niacin (or nicotinic acid, or niacinamide). The medical profession is agreed that niacin is needed to steer clear of pellagra. Like scurvy, this is one of the "old" diseases that are supposed to have disappeared from Western civilization. The Vitamin Information Bureau has this to say: "From the beginning, pellagra in the United States was characterized as a disease of disbelief. It was known in Spain and Italy at least 200 years ago, and clearly recognized and even described in the United States in 1864. Yet as late as 1900, American textbooks of medicine failed to mention it or else described it as 'an endemic disease of Italy,' something that happened to other people—foreigners." In 1907 an actual epidemic of pellagra took place in mental hospitals in Alabama. The Bureau adds: "The news was startling. Disbelief was overcome at last, and cases were recognized everywhere—pellagra, unmistakable and identical with the old *pelle agra* (rough skin) of Lombardy. It is recognized frequently even today. Yet, in the absence of an epidemic, the diagnosis is nearly inconceivable, not because it is difficult to make, but because it remains hard to believe."

35

Pellagra frustrates doctors. It combines the symptoms of a half-dozen different diseases and, as the Vitamin Information Bureau puts it, "is as likely to occur in favored debutantes as in chronic alcoholics and with freakish diets as well as in wasting disease." There is a wide variety of symptoms, including blotched skin, inflamed tongue, mental disorientation, digestive difficulties. But you'd have to live entirely on corn, for instance, to really suffer from pellagra. It is a disease that catches people who live too much on polished rice; in fact, rice polishings have been used to cure people of pellagra. The pattern is quite clear in such cases: the patient gets pellagra because his diet habits prompt him to discard the vitamin-containing part of his food; he can be cured by eating the very food elements he has thrown away.

In many Asian countries, there could be pellagra epidemics, because polished rice is a staple food. However, fruits, vegetables, and meats, which are also part of the diet, counteract the bad effect of rice without its polishing cover.

But the really crucial argument about vitamin B_3 is not about the obvious physical ailments its absence brings about. It is about the possibility of using niacin to battle schizophrenia and other mental illnesses, including emotional problems among young children. For these there exist different names, such as perceptually disturbed, minimal brain disordered, hyperkinetic, schizophrenic, or autistic children. We have all read most of these words in news reports.

What are the implications of all this? Well, let's look at a case history, reported by Dr. Glen Green in the journal *Schizophrenia* (1970). On March 31, 1969, Dr. Green was visited by a mother who brought her little girl along, a child whom Green had brought into this world some nine years before. The girl had skidded from a better than average performance in school to a point where she barely managed to get by. She couldn't get along with the other children in the family, and she seemed to be withdrawing into herself. Moreover, the mother told Dr. Green the child suffered from pains in her stomach, vomiting, and pains in her legs.

Vision Problems

The first part of Dr. Green's diagnosis showed nothing that might have accounted for these complaints. However, the physician had brought himself up to date on diagnostic tests that included measurement of such perceptions as sight. He discovered that the girl had severe vision problems. For instance, when she looked in a mirror, her own face seemed to expand. In school, writing on the blackboard seemed to move. She sometimes thought the ground was moving under her, and she heard voices when there was no one present. Her sense of touch was also affected, and she was plagued by vague and undefinable fears.

Green gave the girl what is known as the HOD test, made up of 145 questions the patient has to answer in the traditional true-or-false pattern. The test is named for its originators, Dr. Abram Hoffer and Dr. Humphrey Osmond: it is the *H*offer-*O*smond *D*iagnostic test. The test is a guide toward diagnosing schizophrenia. It helps to discover whether a patient is having trouble with his sight, hearing, smell, taste, and emotional attitude. Dr. Green, in using this method, had adapted it to indicate subclinical pellagra, the kind of pellagra that cannot be readily observed by standard physiological tests.

According to Green's calculations, a patient who scores 40 out of the 145 HOD points may be suffering from subclinical pellagra. The little girl had answered 103 of the 145 questions with "Yes," and Dr. Green decided to treat her with vitamin B_3. On April 1, 1969, he put her on 1 gram (gm.) of the vitamin three times a day. About two weeks later the little girl was still suffering from sensory distortions, but had begun to feel better otherwise. According to Green's paper in the journal, the young patient's disorientations had disappeared by April 30: "She could read without trouble, she could watch television, the ground stopped moving, she heard no voices." Green found her in a happy mood, without the vague fears that had haunted her. She had only two abdominal pains in the month, and they did not bother her. "She looked and acted," said Green, "like a different girl."

Two months later, the young patient scored only 37 points on the HOD test. But, alert to the fact that there might be a family condition underlying the obvious vitamin deficiency, Dr. Green also checked on her two sisters. When their scores were, in one case, 77, and, in the other, 95, he put them on the same diet. Within three months, their scores were down to 10 and 5. These results, and similar cases, prompted the physician to rethink the value of standard diagnostic and therapeutic methods. Although for twenty years he had diagnosed such symptoms as indicating just about everything from neurosis to a sore throat, now Green felt that many of these cases actually might have been subclinical pellagra. Physical symptoms mixed with perceptual difficulties point to the vitamin B_3 deficiency. What might look like symptoms of mental illness could well be treated on a nutritional basis.

That doesn't mean, of course, that typical hallucinations, such as "hearing voices," may not have emotional roots and would not respond to psychotherapy, tranquilizers, or electroshock treatment—but it does mean that a vitamin deficiency could make such a potential condition acute. We just don't know at what point the physical (including the nutritional) cuts over into the emotional (including "vague fears" and perception trouble). Dr. Green's findings, based on the kind of down-to-earth research that goes on in an alert doctor's office, represent one aspect of vitamin use. The doctor said in his article: "In a seven month period since November, 1968, I have diagnosed well over 100 cases of subclinical pellagra; 65 per cent of these cases were under 16 years of age. They all responded to vitamin B_3, which is niacin or its amide, within a few days or weeks. The chief criterion for diagnosis of this disease is the presence or absence of perceptual changes."

It looks pretty much as if there is a direct line leading from very slight symptoms, by way of the perception trouble Green encountered, to more severe emotional difficulties, and so on to schizophrenia—all at least partly due to a deficiency of vitamin B_3, and possibly other nutrients as well. Other physicians, including psychiatrists, doubt this is so. The whole definition of "schizophrenia" is in dispute, and certainly its treatment is. Many psychologists, psychiatrists, and psychoanalysts feel that only one or another form of psychotherapy can get to the bottom of emotional difficulties; the various forms of schizophrenia are among the most difficult to treat.

What Niacin Does

Yet, if only a few patients respond to the vitamin B_3 treatment, important medical victories will have been won. If you look at your multivitamin capsule, you will probably find that it contains 100 milligrams of niacin. Even a physician who does not "believe in" vitamin supplements is likely to tell you that it can do you no harm. People often feel flushed after taking niacin, but the feeling quickly passes, it should not upset you, and it may not recur if you take the vitamin a few times.

Like good nutrition generally, taking such a dose of niacin in addition to whatever you get routinely in your food falls pretty well into the category of preventive medicine. What happens if you don't take it? Probably nothing at all. At least, nothing you can feel, either physically or emotionally. Will you feel better if you do take niacin? Most likely, you won't feel anything you can put your finger on, or that you are consciously aware of. Taking niacin is a sort of insurance against known and possibly even unknown ills that are miles away from either pellagra or schizophrenia.

The evolution of niacin to its present controversial

height runs parallel with our century's knowledge of vitamins generally. The great Polish vitamin pioneer Casimir Funk identified nicotinic acid in rice polishings back in 1913. By 1937, the substance was found to cure the pellagra-type disease of black tongue in dogs, and its role in pellagra generally was confirmed by many other researchers. Doctors have had a tough time pinpointing vitamin B_3 deficiencies in their patients, because its absence can cause a wide variety of common complaints. Among these are a sore mouth, poor appetite, general restlessness. In addition, symptoms may be a reddened tongue, numb and burning sensations throughout the body, forgetfulness, and confusion. But it is hard to test niacin deficiency, which is one reason why the HOD test, originally designed to indicate schizophrenia, has been found useful in tracking down subclinical pellagra.

All of this doesn't mean you and I should go out and consume large doses of vitamin B_3. The U.S. Recommended Daily Allowances for niacin range from 9 milligrams for infants and children under four to an average of 20 for older children and adults, with the top quantity of 40 for pregnant or lactating women. We should get a good deal of the vitamin in bread and other baked goods made from "enriched" flour. But a lot of people are cutting out bread and cakes, because they are sweet and starchy. As I said before, many multivitamin tablets contain 100 milligrams of niacin, and that might well be over your own daily needs.

However, anyone interested in nutrition and its impact on health ought to be fascinated by the kind of discoveries men like Osmond and Hoffer have made, or the kind of uses that doctors like Green have found for niacin. If the treatment of the little girl sounds almost too miraculous and quick, let's not forget that dramatic breakthroughs against such widespread diseases as tuberculosis and polio have only been made fairly recently. The biochemical basis of mental disturbances is only just being explored, and it gains significance against the background of the increasingly dangerous role of chemicals in our lives: in food, in the air, and in the water we drink.

Tests Are Fallible

Niacin may well furnish us with an illustration of provocative possibilities in nutrition. To begin with, it has revealed that deficiency tests don't always show when someone lacks a vitamin. Some people simply require much larger doses of one or several nutritional factors in order to stay on an even keel, physically as well as mentally. Next, there are diseases and cures that can't really be explored by standard statistical means. Dr. Osmond, who is Director of Research in Neurology and Psychiatry for the State of New Jersey, in Princeton, reminds us that the statistical method in research is of fairly recent date. It includes the "double-blind" technique, which demands that experiments with certain nutrients be paralleled by experiments involving placebos, or dummy medication. This certainly creates a wider and more reliable basis for quantitative analysis than do experiments with individuals or experiments that do not include placebos.

However, Dr. Osmond feels the double-blind trial has become "something of a sacred cow," foisted on reluctant clinicians by statisticians and methodologists. He reminds us that James Lind, who published his pioneer research on scurvy—and, thus, on vitamin C —back in 1753, had observed only twelve men. When the two men who had been given citrus fruit got well, Lind decided he had found a way to cure scurvy, and he was right. The editor of the *British Journal of Psychiatry* stated (July, 1970) that double-blind tests have their uses, although "no useful method of treatment was ever yet discovered in a strictly controlled trial."

Dr. Hoffer, who is a psychiatrist in Saskatoon, Canada, believes that twenty years of research suggest "up to ten per cent of any population will need larger doses" than average and "develop dependency conditions." These are people who simply need much more of a nutrient or group of nutrients than do the vast majority of us. They may have suffered deficiency so long they simply can't do without constant and fairly large supplements. Hoffer says: "There is a new kind of vitamin problem or disease called vitamin dependency. In these cases, the person (his body) needs so much of a particular vitamin that it cannot be provided even by the best diet. In these people the problem is not in the diet, it is in the extra need for the vitamins."

In much of science, once you have found a solution for a major problem, chances are you have found out a great deal on the way. Nuclear explosions have led to the use of nuclear energy for peaceful purposes and may help us solve our energy problem. Osmond and Hoffer were dissatisfied with the standard treatment of schizophrenics, of whom they encountered literally thousands in their clinical work. They encountered deficiencies that did not show up by established procedures; they developed the HOD test—and megavitamin therapy emerged.

Special Children's Needs

Hoffer believes that dependency conditions exist in children, adolescents, and adults to varying degrees. Among children, vitamin B_3 dependency shows itself in "overactivity, perceptual changes, difficulty in reading and learning and changes in personality." It can give the impression that a child is a slow learner or "retarded"; some children are diagnosed as schizophrenic, but most are considered hyperactive or hyperkinetic. Among adolescents, such a vitamin dependency shows itself, according to Hoffer, mainly through marked deterioration in school performance, major changes in personality, excessive use of nonmedical drugs, antisocial behavior, unaccountable mood changes. Among adults, the researchers found not only schizophrenia, but that "in a large number, vitamin B_3 dependency expresses itself as great tension or depression which can lead to alcoholism, unusual behavior, etc."

The vitamin B researchers feel there is great difference in individual needs for certain vitamins. They are far from alone in this conclusion. Dr. Roger J. Williams, the "Father of Pantothenic Acid," is also of the opinion that government standards of vitamin requirements have only limited usefulness. Our nutritional needs are as different as fingerprints. One person may get along very nicely with only 10 milligrams of vitamin B_3 daily, whereas someone else gets sick unless he receives 1,000 milligrams of the vitamin. And a need for 1,000 milligrams does not show up in the standard tests, and whoever is in this dependency category certainly won't get his daily requirements in that "balanced diet" we're all supposed to be eating.

The proof of the deficiency is, in other words, in the eating. It is hard to see how this sort of thing can ever be proven with rats, guinea pigs, and other laboratory animals, or how double-blind experiments can be set up that are tight and broad enough to satisfy what Dr. Osmond regards as the tyranny of a purely mathematical approach to scientific certainty. He believes that niacin treatment is "robust enough to survive the scorn and disregard of the orthodox and may even come to thrive on it." Some doctors who used the Hoffer-Osmond method reported failures. Others became enthusiastic supporters of their approach, as they saw patients respond to the treatment, at times with dramatic and heartening effect.

One of these is Dr. Allan Cott, M.D, a psychiatrist in private practice in New York City, who treated over 500 children by using megavitamins and reported that this method "shows greater promise than any other which has been tried." He doesn't believe that vitamin B_3 is any sort of miracle cure by itself. His results have by now been duplicated by several physicians and clinics. Cott reported in *Academic Therapy* (Spring, 1972) that the Institute for Child Behavior Research and the New York Institute for Child Development were similarly successful. Two experiments that brought negative results were due, in his opinion, to the use of niacinamide exclusively, whereas positive results came from using not only vitamin B_3 but also massive doses of ascorbic acid, pyridoxine, and calcium pantothenate (all dealt with in separate chapters in this book). He notes that, until megavitamin treatment began, "most remedial specialists stressed the more peripheral aspects of a handicapped child's performance, ignoring the biochemical basis of his disturbed behavior." Dr. Cott has had some very quick and striking successes, but it usually takes two to six months before one can observe real changes in a child. By then, he writes, "the child begins to understand and obey commands, exhibiting a willingness to cooperate with his parents and teachers." The child no longer avoids people's looks, and hyperactivity (short attention span and restlessness) "subsides slowly." Cott stated:

"The children I see have been exposed to every form of treatment and every known tranquilizer and sedative with little or no success, even in controlling the hyperactivity. The children who are nonverbal begin to make definite vocal efforts. Many parents report that the child begins to babble and becomes 'noisy.' Children who are verbal make greater efforts to communicate through speech and often will begin to use phrases and short sentences to express wants and observations. They show a slow but steady improvement in speech. In their general behavior, they show a greater appreciation in their environment. They become more loving and not only permit cuddling and hugging, but seek it. Initially bizarre food choices change slowly to include a larger variety of foods."

Dr. Cott has found that children treated for the longest time make the most progress. The younger the children, the better their chance for early recovery. Kids from about two and three to seven or eight have a better chance than those who are eleven, twelve, or older. Which is one reason why I am putting all this rather special and clinical information into this book: you may know of such a child, and precious time could be lost if there isn't at least an attempt to see whether the youngster will respond to megavitamin treatment. Incidentally, at the suggestion of Dr. Linus

Pauling, researchers and practitioners in this field have begun to speak of their methods as "orthomolecular treatment." Pauling feels that it provides for optimal molecular composition of the brain. But I'll continue to call it megavitamin therapy, because "orthomolecular" isn't exactly the kind of word that rolls easily off one's tongue.

"No Serious Side Effects"

Anyway, Dr. Cott had some of his young patients under treatment for as long as five years, with improvement in all areas of functioning going on through the years. He uses a combination of vitamins B_3 and B_6, vitamin C, and pantothenic acid. He says, "In my experience, extending over many years, no serious side-effects have resulted from any of the substances used." He may supplement these combinations with other nutrients, including riboflavin, thiamine, vitamin E, and folic acid. That the impact on the child isn't just psychological—"the placebo effect"—becomes evident when treatment is withdrawn, for instance when some other illness interferes: children relapsed into hyperactivity, withdrawal, regression of speech, screeching, self-mutilation. Cott reports that parents encountered "disturbed behavior they had not seen for months." Then, within a few days after the medication was started once more, the children got better.

Over and over again, as you must see throughout this book, the nutritional level of the pregnant mother, the breast-feeding mother, and the baby itself are of the utmost importance. Whatever goes wrong during these periods can have a lasting effect on a child's physical and mental health. There is increasing evidence that malnutrition can have a profound influence on the growth of the infant's brain. During its first year of growth, the child's brain expands to about 70 percent of its eventual adult size. By the second year, it is almost full size. During this crucial period, the brain grows by adding cells and by expanding existing cells. Animal experiments, which certainly can't be duplicated with

human babies, show, according to Myron Winick and
Pedro Roso in *Pediatric Research* (1968, 1969), that
early malnutrition keeps down the number of brain
cells; later nutritional improvement can't make up for
it.

Cott thinks faulty nutrition during pregnancy "probably affects the unborn child by reducing the nutrients
available to it for normal cell growth" and "severe
malnutrition during the first six months of the infant's
life further reduces the number of brain cells the baby
will develop." He also notes that children who are
brain injured or hyperactive, have learning difficulties,
or are psychotic eat food high in cereals, carbohydrates,
sweets, and sugar. School lunches may well fall short
of nutritional needs, and this is an area where parental
and community influence should be exercised. Speaking to his fellow-physicians, Dr. Cott concludes: "It
seems quite clear from the clinical reports of parents,
teachers and others that there is indeed a large number
of disturbed children and children with learning dis-
abilities who can be expected to benefit from orthomolecular treatment. Investigation of this type of
treatment by controlled studies should be given the
highest priority, for we are dealing with a patient population of 20 million children. Moreover, such treatment satisfies the first dictum of good medical practice
—that of doing the patient no harm."

The first thing that strikes people who take niacin
is the fact that they experience skin flushes. It is like
blushing, although it may hit all or parts of the body.
Cheeks, neck, arms, and various parts of the torso may
suddenly feel hot and taut. There is a burning sensa-
tion. Some people like it, because it feels stimulating—
a little like a light sunburn. Others get worried about
it. The flush leaves after a while. It may not recur
after someone has taken niacin a few times, or it may
recur regularly or on and off.

The reason some people like the niacin flush is that
it gives them the feeling that something is really
happening to their bodies. Most medications and vitamins are just popped into the mouth, disappear, and

provide no obvious symptoms to show that they have any real effect. Niacin, because of the overall blush, is more dramatic. It widens (dilates) the blood vessels and thus makes the blood flow more easily. Medicine calls B_8 a "vasodilator," because of this. The Vitamin Information Bureau, in a paper on niacin, notes that "the evident cutaneous flushing about the head and neck and feeling of warmth, early suggested that nicotinic acid in sufficiently large doses might have a pharmacologic benefit in vascular constriction and/or occlusion, for example in coronary artery disease. Such an effect would have nothing to do with coenzyme function, since it is not obtained with nicotinic acid amide, and conversely, there is no particular incidence of coronary disease or peripheral vascular insufficiency accompanying pellagra." In other words, the basic ingredients of B_3 do not cause the flushing, and so they are not responsible for this particular side effect.

Action in the Arteries

The Bureau notes that dilation of the vessels of the skin does not necessarily mean the same thing is happening to other arteries in the body. It probably wouldn't even be a good thing if all the vessels were dilated at the same time; it might upset the overall balance of the blood flow. Nicotinic acid may, however, stimulate blood flow in subtle ways and thus counteract hardening of the arteries (arteriosclerosis). Some physicians suggest that a glass of whiskey can do some good in such cases. Well, nicotinic acid may act as a nonalcoholic factor in similar fashion.

When arteriosclerosis hits the brain, as most of us have observed in elderly people, it causes a number of subtle changes. These run the gamut from forgetfulness to serious disorientation. These symptoms, known together as the "chronic brain syndrome," may well be helped with nicotinic acid acting as a vasodilator. We are dealing here with minute changes in blood flow within the brain. These are difficult or impossible to trace, and doctors have to judge the individual patient's response. The Vitamin Information Bureau states that "this troublesome syndrome is doubtless the commonest single feature of the aging population in chronic hospitals and nursing homes, and, while no known therapeutic regimen is apt to restore these patients to complete clarity, even a slight difference in their functions can be monumental, perhaps making it possible for the patient to be kept at home, or even to remain at home unattended."

Slowing down arteriosclerosis is not a dramatic development. It is, in most cases, imperceptible to the person suffering from brain difficulties. We are not aware that we remember something; we are aware that we don't remember something. But somebody who repeats himself won't know that he is no longer repeating himself, or at least not quite as much. This sort of alleviation can't possibly be trapped into a laboratory experiment, with double-blind precautions, placebos, hundreds of identical experimental subjects, and all the mathematical paraphernalia so dear to the statisticians. No one seriously argues that those 100 milligrams of nicotinic acid you might take daily are going to do any harm; as we have seen, there is an excellent chance that they may do you some good.

VI

Vitamin B₆ (Pyridoxine):
Of Rats and Men

What's good for rats is good for people; what's bad for rats is bad for people. Right? Well, probably.

Much of what we know about the human body and mind has been learned from such laboratory animals as rats, guinea pigs, and other creatures whose body apparatus resembles our own and that can be bred quickly and in abundance. Still, the argument is often heard with regard to vitamin research that what's good for a rat may be all wrong for you and me, or be just meaningless. Morally, experimenting with animals is questionable, anyhow; experiments with human beings, whether they volunteer or are tricked into cooperating, are even more objectionable to most of us.

But just as some inventions and discoveries are the results of accidents, so can some vitamin research benefit from what may otherwise be a pretty dreadful experience. Between 1951 and 1953, what appeared to be an epidemic of epilepsy among babies hit various parts of the United States; one infant was only eighteen weeks old. Doctors reported identical symptoms: convulsions; no other signs of illness; standard sedatives and anticonvulsion drugs provided no definitive cure. Finally, a common denominator was found. All the sick babies were on the same synthetic liquid formula. Analysis showed that it was low in vitamin B_6: it contained only 0.06 milligram per liter, as compared to 0.10 milligram in mother's milk. The same formula, available in powdered form, apparently had not lost B_6 in the production process, as had the liquid formula. As soon as the babies got additional B_6, even when they remained on the same formula, the convulsions stopped. As the deficiency affected hundreds of infants, the epidemic amounted to an unplanned mass test. It showed conclusively that the human brain requires a certain minimum amount of B_6, as convulsions are the direct result of brain malfunction.

Convulsion Epidemic

Unwittingly, the convulsion epidemic had confirmed earlier research with rats and other laboratory animals. These studies, begun by Dr. Paul György and others in the 1930s, indicated that vitamin B_6 was an essential nutrient in the chain of vitamins that interact with each other to maintain the delicate chemical balance of the human body. Its role in brain function may be crucial, but is nevertheless only one of many. We really must look upon vitamins generally, and those in the B family in particular, as links in a long chain. When any one of these links is weakened or breaks, the whole structure is in jeopardy. That is why we shouldn't place too much emphasis on a single vitamin, but should see to it that there is no deficiency in any one of them.

Among the most startling and most convincing discoveries is the finding that every woman who is taking birth control pills should take 50 to 100 milligrams of vitamin B_6 (pyridoxine) daily. This is the conclusion of John M. Ellis, M.D., based on his own observations in daily practice, as well as on the findings of his colleagues. In his book *Vitamin B_6: The Doctor's Report* (1973), Dr. Ellis notes that his observations date back to 1964, when patients taking the pill complained of such metabolic malfunctions as swelling in the abdomen, face, ankles, and feet. One patient, who had taken a high-strength birth control pill, said that she "nearly fainted" after the first dose and said: "The next day I felt a little better, but just felt awful. I had a bad taste in my mouth and felt extremely tired and fatigued. I would feel worse in the mornings and then feel a little better in the afternoons. For the next six months I didn't take any more birth control pills."

When Ellis put this woman on a milder pill, she still had leg cramps "almost every night" for five months. He then began giving her 50 milligrams of B_6 daily. Ten days later there had been only one leg cramp. Two months later the patient reported: "My legs don't cramp and my ankles don't swell like they did before my periods." Dr. Ellis sums up the collective findings of himself and his colleagues by saying that "women taking oral contraceptives excrete an excessive amount of xanturenic acid" and that this "biochemical change is reversed by the administration of pyridoxine."

Pyridoxine, being one of the youngest, most recently analyzed vitamins, does seem to have specific uses in warding off brain imbalances and amnesia. But its absence can be felt in a variety of ways, ranging from tooth decay to kidney function, from skin grafts to protein metabolism. Scholars from many walks of life presented their findings at the First International Symposium on Vitamin B_6 in 1964. The United States Army Medical Research and Nutritional Laboratory at Denver submitted its report on efforts to establish pyridoxine requirements in man. All studies were conducted with healthy young men in the age group from eighteen to twenty-two, who were put on B_6-free diets with high and low protein intake.

In line with the baby epidemic, the Denver tests created abnormal brain function. One young man on a low-protein diet experienced a convulsion during the seventh week of his B_6-free diet. The Army researchers placed an optimum B_6 requirement for people on a high-protein diet at 1.75 to 2 milligrams per day; those on a low-protein diet were assumed to require from 1.25 to 1.5 milligrams. The U.S. Government Daily Recommended Allowances (U.S. RDA), first published by the Food and Drug Administration in 1973, suggested that infants and children under four years of age receive an average of 0.7 milligram, and set a lower limit of 0.35 and an upper limit of 1.05. For adults and children over four years, the U.S. RDA for B_6 was placed at an average of 2.0 milligrams, a lower limit of 1.0, and an upper limit of 3.0. For pregnant and lactating women, the B_6 average was suggested at 2.5 milligrams, with a lower limit of 2.0 and an upper limit of 4.0.

Protein and B_6

The more protein you have in your diet, the more you need B_6 for proper protein management. The Denver study suggested that a high-protein diet, by increasing the body's metabolic demand for B_6, may lead to a deficiency of niacin (B_3). Reducing your protein intake is not the way to avoid a B_6 deficiency. Your body must have protein because it breaks down food protein into amino acids and rebuilds the acids into new body protein. The amino acids in turn form enzymes, complex chemical substances that must be present in order for any body process to take place and for life to be maintained. And fasting can bring about an even worse B_6 deficiency.

An adequate supply of B_6 is important for the utilization of fats, the forming of blood, the harmonious operation of muscles, the health of the skin, and has some effect on the growth, color, and texture of the hair. A deficiency of this vitamin will cause an increase in your body's production of oxalic acid, a component of kidney and gallbladder stones. A poor supply of B_6 has also been found to bring about some forms of liver damage and dental decay. Women on oral contraceptives may, as we have seen, require extra B_6.

Lack of the vitamin can also cause air- and seasickness, dizziness, lessened resistance to middle-ear infection, skin disease, nervousness, insomnia, abdominal pain, irritability, weakness, and difficulty in walking. Peripheral nerve lesions and eventual impairment of motor functions are other "potentials" when you allow a B_6 deficiency.

In the absence of B_6, tryptophan, an amino acid essential to growth, produces xanthurenic acid, a generally useless side product excreted in the urine. In normal metabolism, tryptophan is converted into niacin. But when the body is lacking in B_6, this process is stopped, causing a niacin deficiency. In many cases, the body's inability to convert tryptophan into niacin results in schizophrenia.

According to Dr. Nevin Scrimshaw, head of the Department of Nutrition and Food Science at Massachusetts Institute of Technology, malnutrition in young children can possibly cause lifelong mental retardation: "Early malnutrition which stunts growth has also clearly and repeatedly been shown in experimental animals to reduce subsequent learning ability, memory, and behavior. To the extent that this is true for young children as well, the generations on whom social and economic progress will depend in the remainder of this century are being maimed now in body frame, in nervous system, and in mind."

In 1952 the *Science News Letter* reported the synthesis of the phosphate form of pyridoxine, which is the form in which the body utilizes the vitamin; it added that this finding "is expected to give science a new, useful tool for cancer research," because cancer tissue shows a very low level of B_6 and uses amino acids in a different way than they are used by normal tissues. B_6 has also been useful in treating certain degenerative diseases of the human nervous system and has been used in curing some symptoms of pellagra. And B_6 has been used in ridding pregnant women of "morning sickness." It has been successfully used in certain cases of muscular rigidity, stiffness of the legs, hand tremors, and palsy.

Yeast and Liver

Clearly, our body's need for B_6 is continuous. If
you think you are short on B_6, take natural supplements rich in B vitamins with your meals, preferably
in some natural food substance, such as brewers' yeast
or desiccated liver, which contains all the B vitamins,
known and unknown. Your B vitamins interact with
one another in many ways, and taking only one or two
may throw the function of all the rest out of balance.

Dr. Henry Borsook of California Institute of Technology has suggested fortifying bread and flour with
B_6. He contends that "all the reasons which led to
the original enrichment formula apply, with greater
force, to the inclusion now of B_6." As protein is essential to our diet, and as we seem to need B_6 to
help utilize protein, Dr. Borsook's suggestion seems
well founded. But until such an enrichment program
is undertaken, the average person has to get B_6 elsewhere. We don't seem to be able to manufacture
pyridoxine right in our bodies, as we do, for example,
biotin.

Among foods that supply B_6 are pork, liver, lamb,
veal, milk, egg yolk, legumes, potatoes, oatmeal, bananas, wheat germ, rice bran, and yeast. Actually, we
should be getting enough of the vitamin, even if we
eat only reasonably well. Yet, children who eat a lot
of candy and snacks, and adolescents who live on
pizza and soft drinks, may well teeter on the edge of
deficiency. The Committee on Nutrition of the American Academy of Pediatrics has made this comment:
"Unfortunately, the wide fluctuations in the quantity
and quality of food consumed by the adolescent, the
lack of information concerning the destructive effects
of cooking on the B_6 content of food, and the absence
of adequate measurements of possible biochemical alterations with varying intakes of B_6 during these
periods of growth and development preclude making a
final statement on the matter."

The U.S. RDAs, which we listed earlier in this chapter, are all right as far as they go. When all is said

and done, we don't yet know how much B_6 the body needs during various states of its development and under the impact of such strains as alcohol, smoking, drugs, emotional stress, and pollution. Bacon Chow, the Johns Hopkins nutritionist, feels that our "estimated requirements may be greatly increased," once we "understand the physiological functions of pyridoxine more fully," including its roles in neurology and in the formation of blood cells.

B_6 is a good illustration of the limits of scientific knowledge. The attitude of many vitamin fanciers, which amounts to "When in doubt, take more," is more clearly justified in the case of pyridoxine than in some other nutrients. But "more" should mean taking the vitamin as part of the natural foods that contain it, with supplements a last resort.

VII

Vitamin B₁₂: Against Anemia

Most of us have a friend, usually a woman, who used to complain that she was so tired she didn't want to get up in the morning, that the children were driving her crazy with their quarrels and constant noise, and that she felt dizzy every time she stood up. Finally, this friend went to see her doctor and returned with the news that she was anemic and had been prescribed iron pills or liver injections to get back to a normal state of health and to cope with the demands of everyday life once again. Soon after the treatment began, she became more energetic and got the color back in her cheeks, and the daily household crises no longer threw her into a small panic; even the kids seemed to be less noisy.

This kind of anemia is one of the most frequent bodily disturbances caused by a deficiency in the diet. But what exactly is anemia, and why do women and growing children suffer from it far more frequently than men?

Anemia really means that a person is short of blood, not so much of the actual liquid itself but of its essential red cells. These cells carry oxygen to the many body areas that need it in order to function; if these tissues are deprived, then the body cannot produce energy. Red blood cells are made in the bone marrow, and there should be five million red cells per cubic millimeter of blood. When the amount of cells—or the blood count—falls below four million red cells per cubic millimeter, then the oxygen-deprived victim is said to be anemic.

Red blood cells can be lost by excessive bleeding, either internal or external. Women are prone to anemia during their reproductive years because of the loss of menstrual blood each month. Children and adolescents, while still growing, need larger-than-usual amounts of oxygen in their tissues, particularly for muscle development. Adolescent girls are likely to be anemic as they are losing blood at the same time during their menstrual periods. For this reason, statistics show, young girls suffer more from anemia than any other group.

Most anemias of the simple kind are caused by iron deficiency. The refined foods that are prevalent in our society contribute to this lack. Other anemias are caused by lack of vitamin B_6, or vitamin E, or folic acid (another B vitamin). Sickle cell anemia, a disease that attacks mainly black people, is linked to an acute shortage of folic acid. However, this is a more complicated and serious disease, whereas the deficiency anemias mentioned above, although debilitating and unpleasant, can be remedied by taking whatever mineral or vitamin the body lacks. The anemia that, if untreated, *can* lead to crippling and death is known as pernicious anemia.

Symptoms of Anemia

The first symptoms of pernicious anemia are similar to those of plain anemia: depression, extreme exhaustion, shortness of breath. But, if left untreated, the patient will begin to have difficulty in walking, have a sore mouth and tongue, start stammering, and show signs of a confused mental state. If the problem is still left untreated or undiagnosed, the victim will begin to jerk his limbs, his spinal cord will degenerate, and he may become paralyzed. At the same time his mental state may become psychotic. This deterioration may be caused by lack of vitamin B_{12}.

We might think that it is easy to adjust the diet of these people, to include this vitamin, which is abundant in meats, fish, and eggs, but there is usually an added complication present. Victims of pernicious anemia lack an essential enzyme, which their stomach glands do not produce. Without it they cannot absorb B_{12}, and by the time they have developed the pernicious anemia they are not producing the necessary hydrochloric acid needed by the stomach either. Their treatment can be accomplished only by injections, which bypass the stomach and go directly into the bloodstream.

A group that risks pernicious anemia is vegetarians who avoid all meat and fish. Those who also spurn such animal products as eggs, milk, and cheese are even more likely to be casualities. According to *Nutrition Reviews* (1962), several insecticides, by damaging the bone marrow, cause anemia that can be fatal. That is, unless vitamin B_{12} is given in time.

It is only comparatively recently that this vitamin, with its strong healing properties, has been discovered. It all began back in 1921 when Dr. George Minot, studying the problem of anemic persons' not being able to manufacture red blood cells, found that *all* these people also suffered from wasting of the stomach. At this point in his research, Minot was himself laid low by diabetes but he managed to stabilize his own condition with insulin. By 1924 he had, along with Drs. Whipple and Murphy, made a decisive discovery. According to *Vitamins,* by P. E. Norris, they fed victims of pernicious anemia half a pound of raw liver and quarter of a pound of raw meat each day; in two years, forty-five of them had recovered. Norris writes: "They decided that pernicious anemia was caused by the immobilization or lack of some enzyme created in the stomach which prevents the digestive organs from converting iron into red blood corpuscles, and that extracts from the stomachs of healthy animals (or liver extracts) enabled this element, which they termed the 'intrinsic factor', to function." For this breakthrough in medical treatment the three doctors were awarded a Nobel Prize. Now there was some hope for anemic patients, even if they had to endure a somewhat difficult diet to regain their health.

Discovery of B_{12}

In 1948 the discovery of vitamin B_{12} took a giant step forward through the work of several researchers who were studying the problem independently of each other. All the doctors knew that there was some mysterious substance in the liver that cured anemia but no one knew what it was. J. I. Rodale, in *The Complete Book of Vitamins,* says: "A group of workers at the Merck Laboratories began an intensive search during which they isolated one substance after another from liver trying to find the antipernicious anemia factor, as this element was called. Finally, out of many tons of liver, a few tiny grains of a red crystalline substance were obtained." Then Dr. Randolph West, of Presbyterian Hospital in New York City, who had been working with the Merck Laboratories, injected a tiny amount of the substance into the muscle of a patient who was "bedfast, tormented with upset stomach, pallor, sore mouth, shortness of breath and the indescribable fatigue of pernicious anemia." Although her blood count had been only one and a half million red blood cells per cubic millimeter, in six weeks it had risen to five million and she was healthy again. From then on, pernicious anemia became a disease that was easy to treat.

Also in 1948, according to Norris, "Mrs. Mary S. Shorb of the Maryland Agricultural Experimental Station and her colleague Dr. Folkers, and a team of scientists led by Dr. Lester Smith in Greenford, England, claimed simultaneously to have found this missing factor, a vitamin containing cobalt, which they named B_{12}." It was also discovered that liver need not be used as there is a mold called *Streptomyces griseus* that is rich in B_{12}. Norris goes on to say that, also in 1948, the constituents of the complete structure of B_{12} "were discovered simultaneously by an American

group at the Merck Laboratories in New Jersey, Mrs.
D. M. Hodgkin at Oxford, Sir Alexander Dodd at
Cambridge, scientists at the Glaxo Laboratories, Greenford and workers at the University of California." 1948
was indeed the year of the vitamin B_{12}!

From that time on, of course, doctors all over the
world began using B_{12} as a treatment for cases of
red blood cell impairment, and discoveries continued
to be made. Dr. Castle wrote in *Annals of Internal
Medicine* in May, 1951, "Presumably because of the
lack of the so-called gastric (intrinsic) factor, in most
patients with pernicious anemia the daily oral administration of as much as 50 micrograms of vitamin
B_{12} is relatively ineffectual." As a result, experiments
were made including stomach concentrate from animals
along with the B_{12}, on the basis that this "intrinsic
factor" was something from the stomach although nobody knew just what. This helped, but then it was
found that gastric juice helped even more, and it had
to be gastric juice from the stomach of a human being.

Then, in 1958, Drs. J. G. Heathcote and F. E.
Mooney of St. Helena's Hospital, London, made another
breakthrough. They found that vitamin B_{12} is changed
in the stomach into a substance called "peptide," which
can then be absorbed. They made peptide from mold
and bacteria sources and combined it with vitamin
B_{12}. When they treated anemia patients with this
substance, they had very encouraging results, and they
declared, "We believe, therefore, that intrinsic factor as currently understood, has no real existence per
se, and that the fundamental process preceding absorption of vitamin B_{12} is simply one of normal deg-
radation or digestion of animal protein" *(Drug Trade
News,* June 2, 1958). However, their theory is not
universally accepted, as yet.

Another doctor who has made significant discoveries
concerning vitamin B_{12} is Dr. H. Grabner of Germany.
According to the *Münchner Medizinische Wochenschrift* (October 31, 1958), he used the vitamin for
diseases of the heart and blood vessels in older patients, some of whom had become mentally confused

as their circulation and heart wore out. One of his cases was a retired civil servant of seventy-six, who could not walk without pain and was so mentally confused he did not realize his wife had died five months earlier. When Dr. Grabner began to treat him, he was looked after by a housekeeper because of his mental deterioration and attacks of pneumonia and sciatica.

Dr. Grabner gave him injections of 400 micrograms of B_{12} daily. After only four shots, his patient met him at the door, shaved, dressed, and wearing a tie. Dr. Grabner writes: "This was an unprecedented turn of events when one recalls how helpless and utterly dependent his life had been in the last two years. But not only that—there was no trace of confusion." For two weeks, Grabner gave his patient 400-microgram injections. Then he started cutting them down to 200 micrograms of B_{12} twice weekly. The doctor then reported, "He is in the best of health and completely normal mentally. He is fully able to leave the house daily, attends to his own purchases personally and even occasionally visits taverns."

"Improvement in Every Respect . . ."

Another dramatic case treated by Dr. Grabner was that of a sixty-eight-year-old man too weak to stand up. He had difficulty breathing, mental confusion, and acute vascular disorders of the legs. So hopeless was his case that the hospital had sent him home to die in peace. Grabner gave him injections of 200 micrograms of vitamin B_{12} every other day. By the end of four weeks the patient was able to leave his home for the first time. Four months later, Dr. Grabner reports, "The improvement in every respect has continued to a point where the patient and his wife were able to take a vacation. He is completely and entirely the person he formerly was, able to fulfill all his social commitments and to visit regularly with his cronies at their regular table for his evening half-pint of beer."

Dr. Grabner also alleged marked results with patients suffering from displaced spinal disk, acute skin disease, and shingles after they were treated with vitamin B_{12}. Another condition that has proved responsive to B_{12} is asthma. Dr. M. Caruselli writes in *La Riforma Medica* (1952) of his work with twelve asthma patients who were given 30 micrograms of B_{12} daily. In twenty days, ten of the patients had no more symptoms. After three and eight months, respectively, two patients suffered asthmatic attacks again but they also responded to renewed treatment.

There are also indications that some cancers seem to respond to vitamin B_{12} treatment. According to the *British Medical Journal* (September 4, 1954), ten children with tumors of the nervous system were given vitamin B_{12}. Four of the children showed "striking regressions," and three others had survived when the report was made for thirty, thirteen, and fourteen months, respectively, although the normal survival rate is under one year.

Another advantage of vitamin B_{12} is that large quantities are not dangerous or toxic. Researchers from the Merck Institute for Therapeutic Research (*Nutrition Reviews*, February, 1951) gave laboratory animals doses of up to 1,600 milligrams (not micrograms, or one-thousandths of milligrams, as are normally given), and these injections were absolutely harmless.

So we see that it is very important to ensure that we get enough vitamin B_{12} in our diets and even more vital that growing boys and girls are well supplied. The best sources of all are organ meats: kidney, heart, liver, brain, and tongue. Brewers' yeast, soybeans, and wheat germ are recommended for vegetarians. Dr. Norman Jolliffe of the New York City Health Department reported in 1955 that a selected group of children given vitamin B_{12} showed greater-than-average growth, and B_{12} even restored growth in cases in which the children had stopped developing.

If you are one of those who can't seem to give up smoking, remember that B_{12} is a vital ingredient for prevention of eye damage. Tobacco smoke can injure the myelin surrounding the optic nerve. B_{12} has been found to resist this, as was reported in the *Canadian Medical Association Journal* (February 28, 1971).

It seems plain that there is no harm in taking vitamin B_{12} and that it can clear up a lot of problem conditions. The question of how much is needed by a healthy person each day is still not resolved, however. Although long and tedious studies have been made, they were done before it was possible to obtain reliable counts of vitamin B_{12} in the blood and urine and are, therefore, inconclusive. So one is bound to say that it is best to play safe and make sure that vitamin B_{12} is present in the diet.

When you or a friend feels tired and headachy for days on end, however, it is wiser to consult a doctor rather than dose oneself with any vitamin, including B_{12}. The cause could well be an iron deficiency anemia but it may be one of the other types, and for any anemia it is necessary to have your doctor make tests and read your blood count accurately.

VIII

Pantothenic Acid: Resistance to Stress

He was a twenty-five-year-old Ph.D. dropout. After completing a year of his studies toward a degree in mathematics, he was drafted into the Army. Upon returning to civilian life, he did not return to college. Instead, he found himself a changed person, without any interest in the things that had fascinated him before. Mathematics was forgotten. So were art, music, literature, and, so it seemed, all ambitions.

This young man appears in Dr. George Watson's book *Nutrition and Your Mind* as "Bob Walsh," which is not his real name. Dr. Watson met him at a party and quickly decided that Walsh's energy level, which supported his earlier intellectual activities, had somehow been lowered, and that this accounted for the startling personality change. In fact, Bob Walsh spoke of himself as being a totally changed person.

Watson, engaged in nutritional research on mental health for the Lancaster Foundation, offered to test Bob Walsh as part of his "study of the effects of certain vitamins on behavior, particularly those vitamins that were known to play a part in the release of energy from food." Dr. Watson states in his book that "one of the most important" of these vitamins is pantothenic acid, a member of the vitamin B complex.

He notes that "an average diet of 2,500 calories will provide about 10 milligrams of pantothenic acid, but our research suggests that this may not be sufficient to support the highest energy-producing capacity of the cells."

At first, Bob was given pills labeled "Calcium Pantothenate, 100 milligrams," but these were dummy pills, or placebos. He was asked to take one pill daily for two weeks. When that period was up, Walsh felt no improvement and said, "I'm pretty sure I don't need pantothenic acid or any other vitamins, as I first said." Watson persuaded him to continue the experiment, but now he put him on honest-to-goodness pantothenic acid.

After ten days, Walsh brightened visibly. He bought himself a camera and became interested in photography as well as other activities. He stepped up his intake to 300 milligrams. Watson feels that such a higher dose usually does no harm but also is no more beneficial than 100 milligrams daily. To make the story short: Bob Walsh requested admission to his university five months after he first took pantothenic acid, and he received his Ph.D. in mathematics two years later.

More Than One Factor

Does this sound too good to be true? Does it present pantothenic acid as a sort of miraculous potion? Sure it does. But Dr. Watson admits that this is one of the more dramatic cases he has experienced; he writes: "It doesn't often happen in trial-by-error clinical testing that one succeeds on the first trial. The number of ways one can be wrong is so great that one soon comes to expect frequent failure. One of the reasons, in addition to the large number of other possibilities, is that most nutritional problems involve more than just one factor. If one's diet has been inadequate over a long period of time, simply administering big doses of a single vitamin isn't likely to have much effect."

Still, the case of Bob Walsh illustrates that pantothenic acid, one of the younger and least known vitamins, plays a crucial role in man's well-being. Dr. Robert J. Williams recognized the vitamin as a nutritive requirement of yeast in 1933. He gave it its name: *pantothen,* in Greek, means "from everywhere," indicating that the vitamin can be found in all living cells.

It isn't easy to trace pantothenic acid, and Williams and his associates began to investigate its influence on yeast growth as far back as 1919. It is present in relatively large amounts in liver, kidney, brains, yeast, egg yolk, oats, alfalfa, whole milk, and royal jelly. The Vitamin Information Bureau reports that "a spontaneous deficiency disease of pantothenic acid alone is not likely to occur in humans." Usually, it happens when there are other vitamin deficiencies as well.

Pantothenic acid is not the only vitamin that is spread throughout our bodies. Dr. Williams notes in his book *Nutrition in a Nutshell* that this particular vitamin was the first "for which such universal occurrence was demonstrated." Since then, researchers have discovered that "other vitamins for which human deficiencies are well recognized—vitamins B_1, B_2, B_{12} and niacinamide—are widely distributed in the same way that pantothenic acid is."

Aside from such colorful cases as that of Bob Walsh, why do we need pantothenic acid? As usual, we have to depend mainly on our fellow-animals for research data. Microorganisms have been found to require pantothenic acid, and so have rats, mice, cats, chicks, swine, and dogs. Laboratory animals can easily be put on a diet deficient in pantothenic acid, their deficiency symptoms can be observed, and then they can be cured by giving them appropriate quantities of the vitamin. Dr. Williams, who combines a dry sense of humor with a good deal of disdain for the Nutrition Establishment, has little use for the Food and Drug Administration, which pretty well ignores the animal experiments, and asks that vitamin labels state, in the case of pantothenic acid, "Need in human nutrition not established."

Williams notes that biochemical experts familiar with the functioning of pantothenic acid "in the whole biological kingdom and in all oxygen-using organisms in particular" do not need a specific demonstration of man's need for the vitamin. Williams says: "I would not want any part in an experiment feeding human beings a pantothenate-free diet. It might turn out like the [earlier] experiment with dogs in which they appeared reasonably well until a day or two before they suddenly died."

Let us take a look at some of these animal experiments. In some cases, withdrawal of pantothenic acid resulted in observable changes in the nervous system, the adrenal cortex, and the skin. One startling discovery was that, without the vitamin, the hair of black rats turned gray. (Unfortunately, efforts to discover whether pantothenic acid would prevent graying hair in human beings were, on the whole, not successful.)

Experiments with pigs showed that a withdrawal of the vitamin caused locomotor disturbances; the pigs could not walk straight or lost their equilibrium. Also, their spinal cord was damaged, as were some peripheral nerves. Damage to the spinal cord was also found in chicks. Two researchers observed that the offspring of rats deprived of the vitamin had trouble walking properly and had motor spasms and poor head coordination. The two researchers, B. H. Ershoff and L. Kruger, reported in *Experimental Medical Surgery* (No. 20, 1962) that these symptoms in the baby rats "persisted without apparent abatement into adulthood."

Occasionally, there are frustrations of animal experiments. William B. Bean, M.D., writing in *Present Knowledge in Nutrition,* reviewed detailed studies on the food requirements of the Chinook salmon. He noted that pantothenic acid was found to be "essential for their proper growth, development and well-being." Without it, or with an insufficient supply, they were reported to suffer from "clubbed gills, exudate on the gills, prostration, loss of appetite, and general sluggishness." Dr. Bean wondered, dryly, just "how one diagnoses prostration in a small growing salmon," but was willing to concede that "no doubt, they seemed tired."

Pregnant Guinea Pigs

Dr. Bean felt that not much research on pantothenic acid took place in the 1960s. He did note rather clear indications of a special, even "critical" need of pantothenic acid in pregnant guinea pigs, just before they give birth. Lacking the vitamin, the test animals lived only half as long as nonpregnant or male guinea pigs on the same deficient diet. Rats can go without pantothenic acid more easily than guinea pigs, but there are also differences among different strains of rats. All of which makes it difficult to draw clear-cut conclusions concerning the vitamin's role in the human body.

Dr. Williams's reluctance to do research with people notwithstanding, there have been experiments with volunteers. But, over a period of fifteen years it was impossible to separate pantothenic acid in experimental diets without, as Bean says, "other deficiencies of essential food factors, as well as combined deficiencies." Bean referred to reports in the *American Journal of Clinical Nutrition* (1962) that dealt with experiments on six volunteer subjects. The object was to find out whether lack of pantothenic acid changed their resistance to illness. For thirteen weeks, the control subjects —those who were receiving a diet *including* the vitamin—remained well, while those who did not get a full ration of pantothenic acid experienced weakness and vomiting in the third and fourth weeks. One of them continued to have abdominal distress and burning cramps. Later, the test subjects experienced tenderness in the heels, fatigue, and insomnia.

Two of the men were not only on a deficient diet, but also receiving medication that holds down pantothenic acid. Their symptoms began earlier: pain and soreness in the abdomen, frequent nausea, occasional regurgitation of the formula, personality changes (perhaps related to insomnia), weakness, and cramps in the hands and feet.

The men's reactions to tests of their immunity to illness showed a variety of effects. There were tests to see how the body accepted skin grafts; others dealt with diseases ranging from tetanus to typhoid. They responded well to polio, but badly to others. Finally, Dr. Bean states, "after restoration of the vitamins to their diet, responses in antibody formation were normal." Obviously, then, pantothenic acid does play a role in keeping body chemistry in order, enabling it to fight attacks of illness by helping to mobilize the antibodies to provide immunity.

What does all this mean to you and me?

Quite obviously, pantothenic acid is, indeed, universal in its impact on our bodies. Together with other vitamins, it forms an essential chain of protection, and so we must see to it that we have a sufficient amount of it in our diets. Dr. Mead reminds us that pantothenic acid is "unstable to heat, and in heat-dried and in canned and in cooked meats there may be losses ranging from 15 to 30 per cent." In other words, eat steak tartare, rather than well-done hamburger!

IX

Inosital: Does It Reduce Blood Cholesterol?

Inositol, one of the B vitamins, is one of those many nutrients that vitamin manufacturers must give an asterisk and state: "Need in human nutrition has not been established." That means science recognizes the existence of the nutrient, but doesn't know how it functions or how much of it is needed. However, there can be no doubt that inositol exists for a purpose, and we do have a few clues as to what that purpose is.

When laboratory animals are deprived of inositol, some species lose their hair, others develop severe digestive troubles. These symptoms clear up when inositol is reintroduced into the diet. Inositol has also been given to clear up a paralysis that occurs when animals are given an excessive amount of caffeine.

What about us humans? Adelle Davis, in her *Let's Eat Right to Keep Fit,* voices a strong opinion that a lack of inositol causes baldness in men, who probably have a greater need for it than women. She infers this from experiments in which inositol-deficient animals lost their hair. She cites examples of previously gray and balding men who, after supplementing their diets with inositol and other B vitamins, grew thick, dark thatches of hair. She also admits that others grew not one encouraging wisp. Possibly the latter were bald from some reason other than inositol deficiency.

Hair Loss in Rats

The most authoritative and up-to-date scientific evaluation of inositol is contained in the symposium *The Vitamins* (Vol. III), edited by Drs. W. H. Sebrell, Jr., and Robert S. Harris. This volume, which contains scholarly papers on the chemistry, physiology, pathology, and methods of dealing with vitamins, includes fourteen papers on inositol, covering such aspects as industrial preparation, biogenesis, and biochemical systems. Hair loss in rats is analyzed in detail in T. J. Cunha's paper on "Deficiency Effects in Animals." He also reports on tests with other animals, such as guinea pigs and hamsters, but does not arrive at specific conclusions, because a variety of factors outside the presence or absence of inositol might have influenced experimental results.

In the same symposium, a paper on "Deficiency Effects on Human Beings," by A. Y. Milhorat of the Institute of Muscle Disease, New York City, states that "evidence of a specific need for inositol by human beings has not been presented, nor have symptoms of its deficiency been described. However, wide distribution in the body and the data accumulated in investigations in animals make it reasonable to postulate an important role in the human organism." Milhorat takes note of animal experiments that suggest inositol might be useful in "management of fatty infiltration and cirrhosis of the liver in patients"; still, he adds, the character of such abnormality may vary and "rarely, if ever, may be attributable to inositol." There is, he says, lack of evidence of the vitamin's "therapeutic usefulness in liver disease."

Milhorat deals with the hope that inositol may be useful in counteracting hardening of the arteries (atherosclerosis), not necessarily because it directly reduces blood cholesterol levels, "but in some manner

not yet defined," such as regulating the ratio of cholesterol to other fats in the blood. Milhorat feels that
theoretically inositol "would appear to be of therapeutic
promise," although its practical usefulness "remains
to be established." Scattered experimental evidence
shows inositol effective in reducing blood cholesterol
levels of heart patients, diabetics, psoriasis sufferers,
and people with atherosclerosis, all with previously
very high levels of cholesterol. It may be that these
people either become more deficient in or have a greater
need for inositol than most of us.

When given with vitamin E, inositol has been shown
to be effective in dealing with nerve damage resulting
from certain forms of muscular dystrophy. When given
with choline, it has a greater power to break up fat,
and with biotin it has a beneficial effect on fat in the
liver and on bacterial flora in the intestine. Since there
are large concentrations of inositol in the heart, eye,
and brain, it is extremely likely to be important for
the normal functioning of these organs.

Roger J. Williams, in his *Nutrition Against Disease*,
states that a preparation is available in Canada that
contains niacin and inositol. "This is used to treat mental illness and is tolerated by individuals who cannot
take niacin or niacinamide in large amounts."

All of the above have to do with the outward signs
of inositol—we know what the results of its presence
or absence are and we know that it is a "symbiotic
cell nutrient." That is, it is not needed by the whole
body, but is produced by some cells and needed by
others. Other than these few facts we know little about
its function.

Much more research must be done, and for the time
being we must live with the phrase "Need in human
nutrition has not been established." However, we cannot assume that this nutrient is of minor importance.
Every time we have done this in the past, we have
in the end been proven wrong. Until science is sure
just what inositol does and how much we need, keep
your diet rich in meat, fish, poultry, organ meats, leafy
green vegetables, seeds and whole-grain cereals, nuts,

wheat germ, brewers' yeast, and fruits. All of them are known to contain inositol. You can also get it in natural food supplements where it occurs with other members of the B complex.

X

Choline: Little Known, but Essential

Not much more is known about choline than is known about inositol. Like inositol, choline is a B vitamin for which science and the government have not established a need in human nutrition.

There is some experimental evidence for how it works, but most of these tests were done with animals. The National Academy of Sciences summarizes all of this work very well: "Dietary choline protects against poor growth, fatty liver development, and renal [kidney] damage in many experimental animals, and against perosis, or slipped tendon in the fowl. . . . Also it has been reported to protect against abnormalities in pregnancy and lactation in the rat and mouse, anemia in the guinea pig, rat and dog, cardiovascular disease in the rat, and muscular weakness in the guinea pig and rabbit."

Well, what about us people? So far, scientific investigations have proven that choline has an effect on our nerves, blood pressure, kidneys, fat metabolism, and livers.

You may remember that the brain sends "messages" via the nerves to the muscles to make them move. But there is a small gap, or "synapse," that separates a nerve cell from a muscle, and this gap must be bridged in order for the muscle to get the message. The gap is filled with a liquid (acetylcholine) that serves as a relay, but this liquid is dependent upon choline for its existence. According to *Prevention* (November, 1971), "If there is a shortage [of choline], the muscles cannot be properly stimulated, and will become damaged. If that happens, the whole body as a result becomes weak and listless. A severe deficiency can result in paralysis, cardiac arrest and death." Serious consequences for the absence of a nutrient we know so little about.

Choline also has an indirect effect on the nerve fibers themselves, which are insulated by a thin covering of a substance called "myelin," which is secreted by the liver. Myelin is also dependent upon choline, an absence of which causes a loss of control of certain nerve functions. Infants have not yet developed this myelin coating, and that is why they cannot control their bladder and rectal muscles. They must have choline in order to develop this control.

Influence on Blood Pressure

It is not understood exactly how choline helps control blood pressure, but the fact is it does. Back in the fifties a study was done in which 158 patients suffering from hypertension (high blood pressure) were given choline. Headaches, dizziness, palpitations, and constipation were relieved within ten days. Blood pressure in all patients had dropped by the third week of treatment and that of one-third of the patients had returned to normal. If choline was discontinued, however, blood pressure rose again and other symptoms returned. But hypertension is a complex condition, and one experiment is not enough to prove anything convincingly.

Although there has been no research with humans that we know of, experiments with rats and other young animals have shown that a choline deffciency can produce nephritis, or inflammation of the kidneys. Don't be surprised if sometime in the near future medical researchers find that choline is essential to normal functioning of the human kidney.

Possibly the most important function of choline is its relation, along with inositol, to the metabolism of fat. When there is enough of both choline and inositol, the body manufactures a substance called "lecithin," which controls the level of cholesterol (fat particles) in the bloodstream. Apparently, lecithin keeps cholesterol in such an emulsified state that it cannot settle on artery walls or collect as gallbladder stones. So it seems that choline may well be an important weapon in our fight against heart problems and hardening of the arteries.

Fat has its effect on the liver as well. The complete absence of choline from just one meal causes an immediate accumulation of fat in the liver. The liver must, of course, stay free of fat in order to carry out its work: detoxifying substances that enter the bloodstream, metabolizing proteins and carbohydrates, and regulating the electrolyte balance in the body's tissues. *Prevention* (November, 1971) states that, without choline, "in time the whole body may eventually become diseased by poisons that the liver has been unable to eliminate."

It is very difficult to diagnose a choline deficiency before it gets serious. There are no telltale rashes or wrinkles. Usually it comes up in connection with gallbladder trouble, cirrhosis of the liver, hardening of the arteries, and other serious disorders. But you can prevent a choline deficiency by getting the right foods. These are the same foods that give you other B vitamins: meat, fish, poultry, eggs, whole grains, green leafy vegetables, and seeds of all kinds.

XI

Folic Acid: The Green in Your Blood

"The existence of massive numbers of vitamin-deficient women in our affluent society suggests three things. First, special priority should be given to this problem among pregnant women, who are probably the most neglected group and the most vulnerable. Second, we must make available the wherewithal for a decent diet, preferably through jobs with decent pay, or alternatively through food stamps or other kind of aid, to people who traditionally are undernourished. Third, we still have a massive job of nutrition education to do, especially among people who are transplanted from other cultures."

These are the words of Dr. Jean Mayer, the noted Harvard nutritionist. They were prompted by reports on a special type of anemia, apparently caused by lack of folic acid in the diet, which counts among its victims mostly women, as many as one out of two Puerto Rican women in New York City. That is what Dr. Mayer means when he speaks of people who have been "transplanted" to the United States from other cultures. There is, indeed, a "culture shock" that extends into such everyday activities as the selection, preparation, and serving of foods.

We noted in an earlier chapter that B_{12} can prevent a certain type of anemia, pernicious anemia. Lack of folic acid can create yet another form of blood weakness: megaloblastic anemia. (It gets its meaning from the Greek words *megalos,* which stands for large, and *blastos,* which means center; it is a disease that causes blood cells to become abnormally large.) Dr. Mayer said in his newspaper column syndicated by the *New York Daily News* (September 14, 1972) that women during the last three months of pregnancy are in particular danger of this blood deficiency, as are infants.

We have noted in various parts of this book that people who drink a lot of alcohol are very likely to destroy the vitamins they consume. A good deal of the physical and emotional deterioration of alcoholics may be due to deficiencies. Although knowledge of alcoholism and its treatment remains frustratingly limited, it is safe to say that anyone who drinks liquor regularly—whether he calls himself a "social drinker" or anything else—ought to make sure of replenishing his body's vitamin supply with a balanced diet, if possible, or with vitamin supplements.

Spinach in Your Salad

Alcoholics must have extra folic acid, because their absorption of nutrients may be imperfect. In fact, malabsorption—the body's impaired ability to make maximum use of the food we consume—is probably a factor in folic acid deficiency. Scientists have had a difficult time trying to track down the existence and causes of this particular deficiency. Actually, we ought to get a good deal of folic acid in our food. Its very name comes from "foliage," because it can be found in such green and leafy vegetables as spinach. You might do well to mix a few leaves of fresh spinach into your salad. You will find that it supplements the standard lettuce salad marvelously; it adds color and, among other things, folic acid in good quantities.

Other sources of folic acid are organ meats, such as liver and kidney, lean beef, veal, oranges, lemons, and grapefruit. You also get it in yeast, soybeans, kidney and navy beans, in nuts and whole-grain cereals. As with other vitamins, folic acid tends to get lost in processing, storage, and cooking. High cooking temperature destroys it, and the green leafy vegetables lose folic acid if they are kept at room temperature; you should keep them under refrigeration.

One way of getting around the problem of malabsorption of folic acid, which occurs with anyone who drinks a good deal of alcohol, appears to be with fruit juice. Dr. Richard R. Streiff, of the University of Florida College of Medicine, said at a luncheon organized by the Florida Citrus Commission in Chicago (October 3, 1971) that orange juice is a particularly good source of folic acid, because it has from five to fifty times more of it than tomato, prune, apple, and cranberry juice. He said that grapefruit juice has "approximately one-third of the folate found in orange juice." Although one would naturally expect someone lecturing under the sponsorship of the citrus commission to speak fondly of citrus fruit, Dr. Streiff's findings would appear to mesh with those of other researchers. His research showed that vitamin C is necessary to keep folic acid from disintegrating. This is what he found: "The high concentration of vitamin C in orange juice is very important in protecting the folate from oxidation and breakdown, therefore insuring that the folate content in the orange juice remains relatively stable. In assaying [evaluating] serum blood or food for folic acid, it is necessary to add large amounts of vitamin C to protect the folate from destruction in the assay procedure. Older assay methods did not use vitamin C as a protective agent in the assay and the levels of folate found were at least ten times less than the levels actually present."

Folic acid in most juices is easily absorbed by the body, as it does not have to pass through the absorption process necessary for vegetables, meat, and other foods. Not only alcohol, but some commonly used drugs, may hamper absorption of folic acid.

Streiff echoed the views of virtually all nutritionists

by saying that "people who overcook their food can easily destroy parts or almost all of the folate in that food." He added: "For example, meat cooked ten minutes in an open frying pan can lose between 60 to 90 per cent of its folate content. Boiling vegetables in water can destroy at least 50 per cent of the folate, with most of the remaining folate staying behind in the water if the water is drained from the food." Does this sound familiar to you? The same point has been made with regard to other vitamins earlier in this book. But I feel that if you bring away nothing else from this book but the knowledge that vegetables and fruit should be eaten fresh and preferably raw, you will have learned a highly valuable lesson.

One more point made by Dr. Streiff is worth passing on. It concerns the subclinical role of folic acid deficiency. Actual megaloblastic anemia may not be a problem that affects you personally or members of your family. But, as Streiff puts it, "many people on borderline diets or others with mild to moderate malabsorption problems do not reach the stage where they develop anemia but they continue for long periods of time with low serum folate levels [a low level of folic acid in their blood], blood abnormalities other than anemia and some biochemical abnormalities." He agrees that pregnant women need more folic acid than other people and are often deficient just before giving birth: "The incidence of folate deficiency in pregnant women has been found to be up to 20 to 30 percent by some investigators. Most of these patients were not found to be severely anemic but they had definite objective findings of deficiency."

Again: Alcohol and Diet

With a vitamin as elusive to researchers as is folic acid, there is still some hesitation to apply results of studies with animals to human consumption. Even lack of it in the blood may not prove conclusively that folic acid is deficient in your body or mine. This point was made by Dr. Joseph J. Vitale, writing in *Present Knowledge in Nutrition,* who said that "serum folate level may not be predictive of folate deficiency." He added that "there is still some question as to whether man, like the rat, may not derive enough folate from bacterial synthesis (intestinal flora) to meet daily requirements." Dr. Vitale also provides insight into the complexity of folic deficiency in alcoholics. He notes that "megaloblastic anemia seen in alcoholism has usually been attributed to poor dietary habits and low folate intake." He then cites experimental findings with three alcoholic patients with low folic acid in their blood who were suffering from anemia. They were treated with folic acid and its level in their blood was restored to normal. But when they were given whiskey, their bone marrow became megaloblastic once more, although the blood did not show a deficiency.

Still, this diagnostic problem does not alter the basic lesson we can learn from the experiment. Vitale reports that "the effect of alcohol could be reversed by giving large amounts of folate." In addition to alcohol such drugs as those used to fight convulsions have brought about megaloblastosis, and there is a good chance that they destroy folic acid. There is interaction between vitamin B_{12} and folic acid, whose absences create different forms of anemia; their relationship to each other is so complex that scientists are not sure just how it works. Both are obviously required, and both are particularly needed in pregnancy.

Dr. Robert Angier of Pearl River, New York, synthesized folic acid in 1946. Dr. Tom Spies, one of the nation's leading nutritionists, was of the opinion that the folic acid "molecule must be prefabricated outside the body" and is therefore "an essential nutrient." This assumes that we cannot produce folic acid in our own bodies. The views of Spies, who was chairman of the Department of Nutrition and Metabolism at Northwestern Medical School, have not been accepted by all his colleagues. That was the point made by Dr. Vitale. Since folic acid was found in normal intestines, it remained possible that healthy people could synthesize the vitamin right in their own bodies, independent of direct folic acid intake from food.

As we know, experiments with people are risky. But one courageous researcher, Dr. Victor Herbert, then at the Thorndike Laboratory at Boston City Hospital, made a guinea pig of himself and offered convincing proof that Spies was right. Herbert put himself on a diet that contained only 5 micrograms of folic acid per day; that is very little, being a 5,000th of a milligram. He committed all the nutritional sins we should avoid. His food was boiled three times. He took all essential vitamins in capsule form, so that he had all other nutrients in his body, with the exclusion of folic acid.

As a result, Dr. Herbert came down with all the classical symptoms of folic acid deficiency. After three weeks, the folic acid level of his blood had gone down. After seven weeks, there were observable symptoms of blood abnormality. After sixteen weeks, the experimenter suffered from insomnia, had lapses of memory, became increasingly irritable, and lost a good deal of weight. By the nineteenth week, his bone marrow showed evidence of megalobastic changes. The next step would have been outright anemia.

The Herbert experiment stopped at this point; or, rather, it went into reverse. Dr. Herbert put himself on folic acid therapy. Within 48 hours, his bone marrow was back to normal, as was his mental equilibrium. In his book *The Megaloblastic Anemia,* he expands on his conclusions from this and related experiments. Herbert convinced himself that Spies had been correct, right along: the body does not produce its own folic acid, although it accumulates reserves that can last for about one month.

Dr. Herbert decided that the absolute daily minimum of the vitamin is 50 micrograms (0.5 milligram), just to keep ahead of deficiency and anemia. The U.S. Recommended Daily Allowances, published in 1973, provide for an average for children under four years of age of 0.2 milligram; for children above four and for adults, 0.4 milligram; and for pregnant or lactating women, 0.8 milligram.

One last point on folic acid: its absorption may be blocked by oral contraceptives. The *Journal of the American Medical Association* published an analysis of this problem (October 5, 1970), "Folate Deficiency and Oral Contraceptives," by Richard R. Streiff, M.D., whose lecture we have quoted earlier in this chapter.

The study began with the observation of seven women, between the ages of twenty-one and thirty-nine, who were treated at the University of Florida for folate deficiency and anemia. They had taken no medication except oral contraceptives for about one and a half years. Streiff thought the contraceptives might have had "an adverse effect on the absorption of dietary folate." A resulting study led him to conclude that "several types of orally administered contraceptives have been found to cause folate deficiency." He thinks that oral contraceptives need not be discontinued to arrest their effect on vitamin absorption, but that "folic acid therapy is definitely indicated." Dr. Streiff cautions his medical colleagues that "this cause of folic acid deficiency will undoubtedly continue to be rare when compared to the usual causes, such as malnutrition, malabsorption and pregnancy." Still, any woman who is on the Pill does well to watch for unusual physical or emotional symptoms, as the impact of oral contraception on the body's biochemical mechanisms is still not fully known.

XII

Vitamin C: Can It Stop the Common Cold?

There once was a retired banker, still quite well-to-do, who practically withdrew from active life after his wife died. Lonely and depressed, he did most of his own cooking. At first glance, his meals look limited but average. He usually had a glass of milk for breakfast, a hamburger for lunch, and, in the evening, two martinis and a steak. Not much. But then, he didn't really feel like eating anything else. His physical health began to deteriorate. Among the symptoms he noted were pains in arms and legs, extreme overall weakness, skin rashes, and bleeding.

What was wrong with him? The case became well known after a doctor presented an account of the patient's personality, background, and symptoms at a medical meeting. Various diagnoses were suggested by the participants, but no one hit on the man's actual illness: he had developed scurvy. There was some angry murmuring among the conference participants. After all, they had been told that the patient was a wealthy man. "Bankers," as one of the doctors put it, "shouldn't have scurvy."

The case has been cited by three nutrition researchers from Vanderbilt University: Harold H. Sandstead, M.D.; James P. Carter, M.D.; and William J. Darby,

Ph.D. In their article, "How to Diagnose Nutritional Disorders in Daily Practice," that appeared in *Nutrition Today,* Volume 4, No. 2, the three researchers noted that the banker had fallen victim to scurvy, an illness supposedly eliminated from modern society, because he just did not include fresh fruit and vegetables in his diet. In his own way, he ate like the British sailors of earlier centuries who died from scurvy by the hundreds. Traditionally, their diet consisted of items that could be stored for months without spoiling: hardtack, salted fish, smoked meat, and similar staples.

One eighteenth-century pioneer, Dr. James Lind, published *A Treatise on Scurvy* (1753) in which he concluded that sailors needed citrus fruit to keep them free of scurvy, and he suggested that their diet include lemon or lime juice. But decades passed before this principle was adopted. The use of lime was responsible for the half-affectionate, half-derogatory label "limey" that attached itself to British sailors and other inhabitants of the British Isles.

The widowed banker of our day and the British soldiers who suffered and died because of scurvy lacked vitamin C (ascorbic acid).

You may say, and you'd be right, that the case of the widowed banker is unusual, in this day and age of nutrition. But look around you. We are eating more hamburgers on rolls, pizzas, hot dogs, and other dishes that have no relation to vegetables or fruit. Whatever vegetables do find their way onto our plates, in our homes or in restaurants, are likely to have vitamin C driven out of them. Even the British sailors who discovered that lemon juice was good for them first made the mistake of boiling the daylights out of the lemons.

The fruit and vegetables that reach us are certainly much lower in vitamin C than in the days of our grandparents, when they either came directly from farm or vegetable garden onto the table or arrived truly garden-fresh at the grocery. I won't talk about what happens to your average brussels sprout that is soaked and boiled before landing on your dinner plate—we'll get around to cooking procedures toward the end of the book. One thing is clear, however: the amount of essential vitamin C in our diets has been shrinking rapidly.

You and I, being human, are odd creatures when it comes to vitamin C. Most of our fellow-animals, including the dogs and cats under our roofs, are quite capable of producing vitamin C right in their own bodies. They don't have to get it, day in and day out, from fruit or vegetables. We have very limited company, in the animal kingdom, when it comes to this need. Only the other primates, the big monkeys with whom we probably share our ancestry, guinea pigs, and such exotic creatures as two Indian inhabitants, the red-vented bulbul (a type of nightingale) and the fruit-eating bat, share our curious biochemical condition.

Black-and-Blue Spots

Fido can produce his own vitamin C, but we must get it daily in our food. Since we also excrete it rather quickly and can't store it in our bodies, lack of it can be disastrous. The symptoms of scurvy are spongy gums, swollen or discolored tongue, extreme fatigue, and bleeding in the body tissues. People who get black-and-blue spots on the skin from just a slight bump may have what is called "subclinical" scurvy; this does occur with older people, often because they can't get or don't bother to get fresh fruit or vegetables.

A list of symptoms caused by vitamin C deficiency leaves no doubts. As presented by C. G. King, Ph.D., in *Present Knowledge in Nutrition,* it reads as follows "Decreased urinary excretion, decreased plasma concentration, decreased tissue and leucocyte concentration, weakness, lassitude, suppressed appetite and growth, anemia, heightened risk of infection, tenderness to touch, swollen and inflamed gums, loosened teeth, swollen wrist and ankle joints, shortness of breath, fevers, petechial hemorrhages from venules, beading or fracture of ribs at costochondral junctions, x-ray 'scurvy lines' of tibia or femur, fracture of epiphysis, massive subcutaneous, joint, muscle and intestinal hemorrhages."

Scary as this list sounds—the symptoms are listed "approximately in order of evidence"—it is reassuring to know that vitamin C can make them disappear rather rapidly, and with little or no permanent damage. Just why we, and such species as the red-vented bulbul and the fruit-eating bat, should be so dependent on outside supplies of vitamin C is a subject of speculation. It may have something to do with our relatively recent, as these things are counted in earth history, migration to northern regions. In places such as the Caribbean, or wherever fruit and vegetables grow all year round, there was no problem about adequate vitamin C in the diet—our human ancestors, or our cousins the big apes, just took that orange off the tree and ate it. The North American Indians had various leaves and roots that they either ate raw or made into a broth. When the potato was brought to Europe from Latin America, another source of vitamin C was tapped. Now, the potato is either being downgraded as vulgar or fattening, or it is robbed of vitamin C by peeling, overcooking, or being made into "french fries," so that vitamin C just disappears.

Our Tropical Bodies

Living in cold or temperate zones is, in a larger sense, "unnatural" for man. We need clothes, insulated housing, and various forms of artificial heating just to survive. With air conditioners in the summer, dehumidifiers during the humid months, coal, oil, gas, or electric heat in the winter, plus humidifiers in our dry and heated homes, we manage to live. But the human body underneath all these protective layers and devices is still the old tropical one, daily in need of replenished vitamin C, unable to store it, and unable to do without it.

One of the most annoying and perennial diseases of our civilization is the so-called common cold. It isn't really just one disease. As far as we know, its symptoms may be caused by as many as 100 different viruses. Recently, Dr. Linus C. Pauling, who twice won the Nobel Prize, created wide attention with his position that large doses of vitamin C can be effective in fighting the common cold. Since the cold, in Dr. Pauling's words, "occurs more often than all other diseases combined," it is important to every one of us whether Pauling is right or wrong. Let us ask three questions: What is the common cold? Who, exactly, is Dr. Pauling? And what, viewed in terms of the common cold, is vitamin C?

You may already have read Dr. Pauling's book *Vitamin C and the Common Cold* (Bantam Books, 1971); if not, by all means do so. We catch the cold from others. The cold virus is likely to be in the air we breathe, and it takes about three days to develop. The symptoms, as we all know, include a sore throat, runny nose, sneezing, a stuffed feeling toward our forehead, overall fatigue, headache, and a variety of other discomforts. We may develop a queasy stomach, redness and inflammation around the nose and lips, and there is always the danger that the cold may affect other areas. Secondary infections may hit the ears, the sinuses, the bronchial area, and even the lungs. There is danger of mastoiditis and meningitis.

We have somehow developed a black-humor type of attitude toward the common cold. There are such sayings as, "With treatment it lasts seven days, and without about a week." Generally, we know we should stay in bed, drink fluids, take some sort of soothing medication, and be patient about the whole degrading and irritating onslaught. Pauling notes that medical literature usually says that "no clearly effective treatment" exists and that the drugs used in treating a cold "may have some value in making the patient comfortable, by giving him relief from some of the most distressing symptoms," but do not affect the length of the illness. Pauling writes, "I believe, on the other hand, that most colds can be prevented or largely be ameliorated by control of the diet, without the use of any drugs. The dietary substance that is involved is vitamin C, which is known to be the substance ascorbic acid."

Pauling's Bombshell

Thus, calmly, Pauling placed a bombshell in certain medical quarters. Look at his words again; he makes it very clear that he is not advocating some kind of medication. Vitamin C is a "dietary substance," and its use means "control of the diet" to prevent a cold from happening or make it briefer or less severe. He states very clearly, "Ascorbic acid is a food. It is, in fact, an essential food for all human beings." He goes into further detail:

"A person who eats no vitamin C, even though his diet is adequate in other respects, will become sick, and then die, in a few months. A small intake of vitamin C, which for many people may lie somewhere within the limits 5 milligrams to 15 milligrams per day, is enough to prevent a human being from dying of a vitamin C deficiency, which is called scurvy. The amount that keeps him from dying of scurvy may not, however, be the amount that puts him in the best of health. The amount that puts him in the best of health, which may be called the optimum amount, is not reliably known; but there is some evidence that for different people it lies in the range between 250 milligrams and 10,000 milligrams per day; that is, between ¼ gram and 10 grams per day."

Now that is quite a stretch: from 250 milligrams to 10,000 milligrams per day. Think of it in dollars, maybe as a weekly salary, and it becomes very, very clear. Even the lower total is way over the standard figures. The British Medical Association's Committee on Nutrition only recently raised its recommended daily intake from 30 to 40 milligrams. In the United States, the Food and Nutrition Board of the National Research Council puts the recommended daily allowance for adults at 60, for adolescents at 80, for pregnant women and nursing mothers at 100 milligrams. If you assume that 10 milligrams are just about enough to keep away from scurvy, then these allowances look quite safe. In fact, the National Research Council thinks its recommended allowance provides a good margin for "added protection against scurvy, promotes wound healing, preserves enzyme activity, favors cellular proliferation, and increases the resistance to common stresses such as those induced by bacterial toxins, low temperature and fatigue."

Perhaps the National Research Council included the viruses that cause the common cold among the "bacterial toxins." Anyway, the NRC believes that 60 milligrams of vitamin C per day are enough to fight such toxins. Of course, the figure 60, which is identical with the dose recommended by the U.S. RDA for adults, is some sort of average; it obviously does not cover a wispy little old lady or a 450-pound wrestler. Although segments of the medical profession may tolerate the idea that vitamin C can fight the common cold, Pauling's ideas of high doses came as a shock to them.

But they should not have been all that surprised. For all his Nobel Prize winner dignity, Linus Pauling has for much of his life been something of a stormy petrel.

A number of subjects on which Dr. Pauling has spoken up in the past have been way out of his field of prime expertise. His Nobel Prizes have been a symbol of appreciation for his work in linking chemistry and quantum physics, research into the chemical bonds that hold atoms together, his resonance theory of substances, a breakdown of crystalline and protein structure, as well as links between hereditary diseases and molecular abnormality. With this kind of achievement and prestige in chemistry and physics behind him, Pauling antagonized a good number of people in the 1950s by his advocacy of such controversial causes as U.S. nuclear disarmament and abandonment of the antiballistic missile program.

All this, in the view of some, put him on the side of forces and nations antagonistic to the worldwide interests of the United States. Sometimes out of sheer ingrained attitude, and sometimes for good and sound reasons, people tend to distrust the political judgment of baby doctors and folksingers—or that of chemists, whether or not they win Nobel Prizes. On top of Pauling's bluntness in backing unpopular or even questionable causes, he won the Soviet Union's Lenin Peace Prize in 1970 in appreciation of his "activity in defense of peace."

Eminence in his own field, as well as rough-hewn directness, at times give the impression that Dr. Pauling enjoys notoriety and provokes it with his personal mixture of apparent guilelessness and seeming arrogance. He appears to be lacking guile by speaking out in a way that makes him vulnerable to outrage; he seems arrogant by his casual disregard of critics. Jerry Tallmer, writing in the *New York Post* (December 18, 1970), quoted a friend as describing Pauling as "a dear puckish man," who "has pointed ears and he kind of twinkles." I don't doubt for a minute that Pauling enjoys the anger he provokes among the Political and Medical Establishments, whether they are represented by the Senate Internal Security Subcommittee or by the American Medical Association. His appearance, whether spontaneous or cultivated, is that of a folksy sage, sparse, white-haired, blue-eyed. On television interview shows, he comes across like everybody's foxy grandpa—all wisdom, charm, candor, and self-assurance.

Linus Carl Pauling, now in his mid-seventies (he is as old as the century, having been born in 1900), was born in Portland, Oregon, with English ancestors on his mother's side, German on his father's. Herman Henry William Pauling had married Lucy Isabelle Darling. Linus Pauling's father was a pharmacist. The youngster was a high-school dropout, but graduated with a B.A. in chemistry and physics from Oregon State College in 1922. He received his Ph.D. *summa cum laude* at the California Institute of Technology in 1925. He stuck with Cal Tech until 1963, when he joined that super-think tank at Santa Barbara, the Center for the Study of Democratic Institutions. At the time of the vitamin C controversy, Dr. Pauling taught chemistry at Stanford University, while living in nearby Portola Valley. He married Ava Helen Miller in 1923. They have three grown sons and one daughter.

The Sage of Stanford

If one were to imagine the Battle of Vitamin C as a prizefight, it would look like an uneven match. On the one hand, a crowd pleaser from Oregon and California, the White-Haired Sage and slayer of the dragon known as the common cold; on the other hand, the opponent, the seemingly dour chairman of Harvard University's Nutrition Department, Dr. Fredrick Stare. With an air of mixed tolerance and contempt, Dr. Stare has referred to Pauling as "a man of peace and chemistry, not of nutrition." Seeking to rebut Pauling's suggestions, Stare said: "I think it is absolutely ridiculous to recommend huge doses of vitamin C since most of it will be eliminated in the urine in two to three hours." An easy answer to this would be: "Well, we're not going to stop inhaling oxygen through our nostrils and pushing it through our lungs, just because we exhale this same air within seconds and minutes." And we won't give up drinking liquids, or we'll shrivel up and die, just because we pass them through our body as perspiration or urine within a very short time." I will admit this is not a very scholarly way of putting it, but it is on about the same level as the Stare argument.

As far as I can find out, Pauling had the better of the fight when he discovered that Stare had erred quite seriously in summarizing a key experiment. Quoted in *Mademoiselle* (November, 1969), Dr. Stare cited a test made in 1942 by Drs. H. S. Diehl, D. W. Cowan, and A. B. Baker at the University of Minnesota, and said: "Vitamin C and colds—that was disproved twenty years ago. I'll tell you about just one very careful study. Of five thousand students at the University of Minnesota, half were given large doses of C, half a placebo [a neutral pill]. Their medical histories were followed for two years—and no difference was found in the frequency, severity, or duration of their colds."

Dr. Stare may have been speaking from memory to the magazine's interviewer, but his memory would seem to have been selective in an anti-vitamin C direction. Reading Stare's statement, Pauling went back to the full text of the Minnesota study as it appeared in the *Journal of the American Medical Association*. And this is what he found: the study had involved 400 students, not 5,000; it had lasted for six months, not two years; and it had involved daily doses of only 200 milligrams, which Dr. Pauling regards as "not a very large dose." The investigators reported that the students who received the vitamin had suffered 15 percent fewer colds than those who had been given the innocuous placebo.

Now, even we as laymen can tell that a difference of 15 percent is pretty big: imagine receiving 15 percent interest on your savings bank deposit, instead of the usual 5 to 6 percent! But not only did Dr. Stare disregard this percentage; the experimenters themselves played it down. An exchange of letters between Drs. Pauling and Diehl appeared in the *New York Times* (December 15 and 16, 1970, and January 26, 1971). Answering a letter from Pauling, Diehl said his study had yielded "no indication" that large doses of vitamin C or other vitamins had "any important effect on the number or severity of infections of the upper respiratory tract when administered to young adults who presumably are already on a reasonably adequate diet."

Odds of 100 to 3

In his reply, Pauling noted that the experimenters had, in the summary of their paper, ignored the fact that 15 percent of students had not caught a cold during the experimental period. He stated that, statistically, such a difference "would arise only three or four times in a hundred through chance alone." He added:

"One may therefore consider this as probably a significant difference, and vitamin C supplements to the diet may therefore be judged to give a slight advantage in reducing the number of colds experienced." Odds of 100 to 3 or 4, as any gambler will tell, are pretty good, and nothing to quibble about. What is puzzling, and Pauling says so, is the lack of enthusiasm the Minnesota experimenters felt over their results. If 200 milligrams give you a 15 percent effectiveness, would several times that amount do even better? Why weren't these experiments repeated, anyway?

Dr. Pauling, in his book, speculates on this curious reluctance to follow up the Minnesota results. First, he feels, medical researchers tend to look for medication that is 100 percent effective. Second, the experimenters seemed to feel that it was best to keep the dose of vitamin C as small as possible. "This attitude," writes Pauling, "is, of course, proper for *drugs*— substances not normally present in the human body and almost always rather highly toxic—but it does not apply to ascorbic acid. Another factor has probably been the lack of interest of the drug companies in a natural substance that is available at a low price and cannot be patented."

Certainly, no one can assert about Dr. Pauling that he does not know methods of scientific experimentation, the use of statistical significance in evaluating experiments, or the manner in which a new experiment builds on the concept, procedures, and results of tests that have preceded it. In addition to being an experienced scientist, Pauling is also a human being who resents the havoc colds have played with him. We all share this attitude. As Jane E. Brody wrote in the *New York Times* (December 6, 1970), the interest in vitamin therapy "reflects the failure of medical science to come up with anything reliable to prevent or cure the common cold. The average person is reminded of this failure about three times a year when he is struck down by the earmarks of a cold: runny nose, sore throat, cough and fatigue. Scientists have been working on anti-cold vaccines for more than 25 years;

but the more they learn, the farther away they seem
to be from developing an effective vaccine. At the
outset, it was thought that no more than a handful
of different viruses might be responsible for cold mis-
eries. Modern laboratory techniques have unveiled in
excess of 100 of them that may be the culprits. The
hope of producing one or even several vaccines
against so many viruses is just that—a hope."

The *Times* article noted that researchers are busy
looking for drugs that "may be able to halt an
incipient cold." However, "none of the many cold
remedies now on the market—including antihistamines,
which only affect symptoms—can shorten a bout with a
cold. Nonetheless, Americans spend about $500 million
a year on them 'just in case.' " As we all know, our
body is inhabited and surrounded by a multiplicity
of viruses and bacteria, all just waiting to pounce on us
when we are weakened or lacking in biochemical
resistance to them. In a sense, our body is constantly
under siege, engaged in a day-and-night struggle to
fight off disease. If something like vitamin C helps the
body's resistance, provides ammunition to fight off or
hold down the virus enemy, we should certainly give
it a good try.

Dr. Pauling goes further. He is looking forward to
wiping out the common cold completely. He thinks the
cold could be "controlled in the United States and some
other countries within a few years, through improvement of the nutrition of the people by an adequate
intake of ascorbic acid." He says in his book, "I look
forward to witnessing this step toward a better world."

Dr. Pauling wants you to catch the cold before it
catches you. To start with, he advises you to take
between 1,000 and 2,000 milligrams of vitamin C
per day. If it sounds like too much in milligrams,
think of it as between 1 and 2 grams per day. As
vitamin C often comes in pills averaging 250 milligrams, it may be easier and certainly cheaper to take
it in powdered form. Of course, we are all different,
and Pauling agrees that many people may remain
in good health and even pretty immune from colds on

just 250 milligrams. If so, fine! Others may need even less, still others a great deal more.

Insurance Against Colds

Taking your own optimum amount of vitamin C daily is, then, according to Dr. Pauling, a sort of insurance against the cold. But if you do feel a cold coming on, try to knock it out with vitamin C immediately, or at least keep it from hitting you with full force. Pauling says in his book that "it is wise to carry some 500 milligram tablets" with you at all times. If you get a sore throat, the sniffles, or the kind of muscle pain that indicates cold, take one or two of 500-milligram tablets, and then go on to one or two tablets every hour "for several hours." Dr. Pauling adds: "If the symptoms disappear quickly after the first or second dose of ascorbic acid, you may feel safe in returning to your usual regimen. If, however, the symptoms are present on the second day, the regimen should be continued with the ingestion of 4 grams to 10 grams of ascorbic acid per day."

It is cheapest and easiest to take vitamin C in powder, or crystal, form. It is marketed this way commercially in rather large quantities, because it can be used to keep fruit from oxidizing—if you put it on a freshly cut apple slice, you'll find that it doesn't turn brown. The crystal-type vitamin C dissolves quickly in orange juice, where it sort of feels at home, but you can put it into just about any liquid. A level teaspoon of C is equal to about 4,000 milligrams.

Dr. Stare is not the only one to disagree with Dr. Pauling. But neither is Dr. Pauling the only scientist to advocate large doses of vitamin C or, for that matter, of other vitamins. In recent years, the concept of megavitamin therapy has found an increasing number of followers inside and outside the medical profession. Writing as a layman, I am happily outside the conflict areas of the medical profession. I was frankly troubled by some of Pauling's political notions but equally intrigued by his medical concepts. Therefore, in all fairness, I shall now give you a bird's-eye view of the opinions that differ from Pauling's.

To begin with, there are people who feel that taking a great deal of anything is dangerous. I'm sure that's true; you can drink too much water, and you can certainly poison yourself with huge numbers of aspirin tablets. The *Medical Letter* (December 25, 1970), in a review critical of the Pauling position, mentioned that large doses of vitamin C can have "adverse effects, despite Professor Pauling's assertion that it is harmless even in large amounts, except for a laxative action when taken without food." The publication stated that "when four to 12 grams of vitamin C are taken daily for acidification of the urine, however, as in the management of some chronic urinary tract infections, precipitation of urate and cystine stones in the urinary tract can occur." It added that people who tend toward gout and uric acid formation should avoid high doses of vitamin C, as it might contribute to the formation of uric acid stones in the kidney. Pauling feels that there is no clinical evidence for this assertion; that it is a mere assumption; that no medical literature exists to indicate that vitamin C in large doses encourages uric acid kidney stones, nor have individual cases been reported. I have spoken to urologists who remain worried about vitamin C, however.

Another argument against the Pauling position is based on a study undertaken among twenty-one prisoner volunteers at the University of Maryland during 1971, directed by Dr. Andrew R. Schwartz. In the Maryland study, the volunteers were kept in isolation for one month. Eleven of them were given vitamin C pills, the other ten were given a placebo, a sugar pill that looked like a vitamin pill. Neither the volunteers nor the researchers knew who was taking the pills until the time for tabulation came.

After two weeks of taking the vitamins, each of the prisoners was given an intranasal dose of a cold virus known as rhinovirus 44. Before the test, the men's blood was examined and showed that they were not immune to the virus. Within twelve to twenty-four hours after being exposed to the virus, all twenty-one men developed cold symptoms, including stuffy noses and sore throats. They continued to receive 3,000 milligrams, or 3 grams of vitamin C daily or the sugar pills, for another week after exposure to the virus. According to Dr. Schwartz, the study "showed no preventive or therapeutic effectiveness of vitamin C against the common cold on the subjects studied with the dosage level used. Whether larger doses might be therapeutic we couldn't say. But we saw no evidence of a preventive effect at three grams a day, which is the level Dr. Pauling recommended." Actually, Pauling suggested that doses might vary widely with each individual, but he himself has taken the 3-gram dose as a cold preventive.

Norman Cousins, editor of the *Saturday Review,* has published an article entitled "Linus Pauling and the Vitamin Controversy" (May 15, 1971) that reviewed the disagreement between Dr. Pauling and the segment of the medical profession represented by Dr. Stare. Cousins noted that three questions need to be examined objectively: "How much ascorbic acid can the human body metabolize in a given period? What are the circumstances of varying needs? Do the demands of the body for vitamin C increase sharply with infection or inflammation?"

Cousins' analysis noted that Stare seems to make no distinction between the body's needs under conditions of health and under conditions of illness, whereas Pauling bases his theory on the fact that the human body neither manufactures nor stores vitamin C, yet cannot live without it. This means that large amounts of the vitamin ought to be available at all times, so the body can utilize them when needed. Does the need for vitamin C increase with the severity of the illness? If there is a low fixed metabolic need, then it makes no difference how much vitamin C we take, or how ill we are. Cousins concluded that this controversy has its uses, particularly if it leads to serious new research that seeks to answer all these questions; he wrote:

"Here, then is a clearly defined question for medical researchers. Indeed, it is difficult to conceive of a medical project which might be productive of more valuable answers. For the fact is that, despite the supposedly advanced state of knowledge about how ascorbic acid functions there are crucial gaps in our knowledge. It is thought to play a role in the formation of collagen, the mysterious glue that holds cells together. Dr. Pauling believes ascorbic acid helps to prevent or cure colds by acting as a factor in the synthesis of interferon, a substance believed by some medical scientists to prevent the entrance of the cold virus into the cells.

"Perhaps the most significant single fact about vitamin C is that it helps to activate the adrenal glands, which produce powerful anti-inflammatory substances —epinephrine and steroids such as hydrocortisone. The quantity of epinephrine produced by the adrenal glands in response to the body's needs is so minute that it can barely be measured, though its effects on bodily function are remarkable."

Disdainful Sniping

Cousins probably speaks for the majority of interested laymen, and for professionals in nonmedical fields as well, when he states that "it would be salutary indeed if medical researchers could look into the central question at the heart of the debate between Professor Pauling and Professor Stare—that is, what the body's needs are with respect to ascorbic acid, under ordinary and extraordinary circumstances." Mr. Cousins, I think quite rightly, objects to disdainful sniping at Dr. Pauling. Cousins feels that such a discussion should proceed "on the highest ground" and that "professional prerogatives or even traditions should not be allowed to outweigh the possibility that his work could lead to a genuine improvement in the human condition."

What is there, actually, about the common cold that seems to encourage flippancy and mediocre jokes? It is all very well to say, as a British medical officer did, "If I get a cold, I treat it with the contempt it deserves."

Sure, laugh it off; laughter is the best medicine, and all that. But colds may lead to dangerous complications, and they really are more than just a passing nuisance. When one reads the esoteric titles of research projects underwritten by the National Institute of Health, one wonders why government-sponsored or foundation-financed research has never put the Pauling thesis to a thorough, broadly based test. This would not be something with twenty-one prisoner volunteers, as in the Maryland experiment, but a carefully controlled series of linked experiments, at various research centers, using a wide enough cross section of age and other groups to make the test easily quantifiable, as airtight as these things can be made, and statistically sound. In other cases, such as the use of vitamin E in heart ailments, it is simply not possible to turn human beings into guinea pigs; with vitamin C and the common cold, only minor martyrdom would be involved.

Until this sort of thing happens, one has to rely on more limited studies. Two such experiments were published in 1972. The first appeared in the British medical journal *The Lancet* (June 24), based on work carried out in Glasgow by Drs. Charleston and Clegg. They undertook a double-blind study, using placebos as a check, which showed that large quantities of vitamin C do tend to reduce the impact of the common cold. The second test was published in the *Canadian Medical Association Journal* (September 23), reported by Drs. Anderson, Reid, and Beaton. One of the participating researchers, Dr. Reid, had published a highly critical review of the Pauling book, but he and his colleagues did the fair and proper thing: they decided to test their judgment in the laboratory. Pauling had told Reid that his studies with a mere 200 milligrams of vitamin C were almost useless, and they decided to meet Pauling's challenge.

The results achieved by the Beaton group were startling. They not only found that, after their subjects took vitamin C in large doses, their "disability was substantially less" than in those who had not taken it.

They also were candid enough to admit that these findings were "entirely unexpected"—sure, they had made the tests in the expectation of proving Pauling wrong. They added that the results, which confirmed the usefulness of large vitamin C doses, "may have important theoretical and practical implications."

The continuing research dilemma was illustrated in the summer of 1973, when the relationship between vitamin C and the common cold was the subject of a symposium at Stanford University, which had been organized by Dr. Pauling. The reports on quantitative experiments gave hints that the vitamin erects a barrier against the common cold, but there were problems in the satisfactory execution of the experiments. One experiment, held among Navaho school children at Fort Defiance Hospital, near an Arizona boarding school, used 641 subjects for tests over a period of fourteen weeks. They had been divided into different age and sex groups. The health service director, Dr. John L. Coulehan, reported that "in most vitamin-C-treated groups, significantly more children remained well throughout the surveillance." He recorded a "very highly significant" statistical contrast between 32 percent of children on vitamin C who were not sick during the test period and the 16 percent in the control group, who were given a neutral pill, or placebo. The results were not crystal clear, however, as some of the older boys had been swapping pills with each other.

Another problem arose with 311 employes of the National Institute of Health. Those who took vitamin C had colds that lasted only 5.92 days on the average, while those who took placebos had colds that averaged 7.14 days. But some of the test subjects said they had been able to tell the C tablets from the placebos, and this forced the researchers to recalculate their results, restricting them to those who had not noticed a difference in taste; among this group, the average length of colds was found to be "fairly identical." A third study, undertaken at Stockton State College in Pomona, New Jersey, showed that those who took C lost only half as much time with colds as did others; but only 107 persons were involved in these tests, and that was regarded as too narrow a base for proper statistical evaluation.

But when, you may ask, will they know for sure? Not for a while, that's certain. Until then, you may engage in some relatively harmless self-medication (a word redolent with sin in the medical profession). Still, to be on the safe side, check with your doctor if you suffer from gout or if your blood has a high uric acid content. If there are even the slightest side effects, go to your physician immediately. And if you have a heart condition, make sure your vitamin C is made with ascorbic acid, not with sodium ascorbate, which might give you too much sodium. I will add further details on this caution in the following chapter, which deals with uses of vitamin C in areas other than the common cold—of which there are plenty.

XIII

More on C, the Versatile Vitamin

"Our son, who is 19, has never developed a tooth cavity. Since he was ten he has received at least 10 grams of ascorbic acid [10,000 milligrams of vitamin C], daily, by mouth. Before age ten, the amount given was on a sliding scale."

This statement was made by Fred R. Klenner, M.D., of Reidsville, North Carolina, who says that "the relationship between vitamin C and the health of the gums and teeth has long been recognized." Lack of ascorbic acid may affect dentin of the teeth, and this can weaken tooth enamel to the point where entry is permitted to cavity-causing bacteria. Dr. Klenner reported on his son's immunity to tooth decay in his introduction to *Vitamin C,* by Ruth Adams and Frank Murray.

It is difficult to find a wide experimental basis for the utilization of vitamin C against tooth decay. However, experiments with guinea pigs have been reported in the *Journal of Dentistry for Children* (No. 3, 1943) that showed that lack of the vitamin retarded formation of dentin. The process was reversed when the intake of vitamin C was restored. Teeth are not just solid matter; their structure and function closely resemble those of the rest of the body, bones, nerves, cells, and their delicate interrelation. It is no surprise, therefore, that vitamin C is of crucial importance to our bones. Above all, it is essential to the production of collagen, which functions as a sort of glue or binder in many parts of the body.

The role of collagen was explained by W. J. McCormick, M.D., in the *Archives of Pediatrics* (January, 1954). He said that vitamin C helps in forming "collagen for the maintenance of stability and elasticity of connective tissues generally, and this would include the bones, cartilage, muscles and vascular tissues." According to McCormick, lack of the vitamin may cause "the breakdown of 'intercellular cement substance' [collagen], resulting in easy rupture of any and all of these connective tissues, which would include the intervertebral-discs." Cartilage is the semi-soft tissue, neither flesh nor bone, that can be found in parts of the body that must bend and combine strength with lubricated movement: the knee joint is perhaps best known for its cartilage (we always hear about it in football injuries). When Dr. McCormick wrote of "intervertebral-discs," he referred to the soft disks in our backbone, separating the vertebrae from each other and giving the backbone its flexibility.

Backache: C Deficiency?

When you have a backache, it may well be due to a wearing-away of the disk, with vertebrae pressing against each other or, what may be even worse, pressing on nerves that are linked with other parts of the body—such as the sciatic nerve, which runs down the back of the leg. A breakdown of collagen can be accompanied by a variety of symptoms due to vitamin C deficiency. According to an analysis by Dr. Charles Glen King in *Nutrition Reviews* (February, 1968), these may include decreased effectiveness of the white blood cells, fatigue, lack of appetite, anemia, gum inflammation, a generally increased susceptibility to infection, as well as dangers of bone fractures, hemorrhages under the skin—the black-and-blue marks indicate these—and relative disintegration of cartilage areas.

We examined the role of vitamin C in preventing the common cold in the preceding chapter. But it is wise to consider this function as part of the overall importance of C. No one man has had a more crucial role in the history of vitamin C than Dr. Albert Szent-Györgyi. Now close to eighty years old, but still a strong figure in nutritional research in the United States, Szent-Györgyi is a Nobel Prize winner who isolated ascorbic acid (vitamin C) in crystalline form in 1930. In his recent book *The Living State,* this elder statesman of international nutrition, who was born and worked originally in Hungary, speaks of his personal experiences and conclusions.

As we noted in the preceding chapter, vitamin C prevents scurvy, and as little as 10 to 15 milligrams per day may be enough to guard the human body against this disease. Szent-Györgyi writes that there is a flaw in the persistent notion that "if we lack ascorbic acid we develop scurvy; if we do not have scurvy, we have enough ascorbic acid." But, he counters, "scurvy is not the first symptom of deficiency," but "a sign of the final collapse of the organism, a premortal syndrome, and there is a very wide gap between scurvy and a completely healthy condition."

Dr. Szent-Györgyi is too old and too distinguished to have to mince words or talk in impenetrable academic language to show the extent of his learning. With youthful candor, he admits that "nobody knows" how far the average person is from a state of simple "good health," the state in which "we feel best, work best, and have greatest resistance to disease." There simply aren't any statistical studies to define good health. Szent-Györgyi points out that there are many pitfalls in making such studies: "If, owing to inadequate food, you contract a cold and die of pneumonia, your diagnosis will be pneumonia, not malnutrition, and chances are that your doctor will have treated you only for pneumonia." He adds:

"Is our body such a poor mechanism that it has to break down every so often with a cold or other ailment? Or do we abuse our body, and feed it so poorly that its breakdown is comparable to the breakdown of an unlubricated engine? I am often shocked at the eating habits of people. What I find difficult to understand as a biologist is not why people become ill, but how they manage to stay alive at all. Our body must be a very wonderful instrument to withstand all our insults."

The "Cure-all" Dilemma

Vitamin C is distributed all over our body. Its functions are so numerous that it is easy to see it as a "cure-all" and perhaps dismiss its usefulness for just that reason. We are conditioned to think of vitamins as drugs, which they are not, and so we expect them to have only one specific function. Long before there is likely to be any indication of scurvy, or even of symptoms ranging from swollen gums to black-and-blue spots on our skins, there may exist what are called "subclinical" developments of malnutrition in our bodies. Since we are concerned wth preventing illness, our job is to avoid these from surfacing into clear-cut evidence that something is seriously wrong with us. Just how varied is the usefulness of vitamin C?

The Vitamin Information Bureau has noted that research reports reveal "an impressively wide range of the metabolic repertoire possessed by this versatile chemical." The Bureau states that "the use of supplemental vitamin C has been advocated for many conditions: in wound healing and fracture mending; in exposure to cold, in resistance against infection, in shock, in gastric hemorrhage, in common cold, in arthritis; in pernicious anemia, duodenal ulcer, in iron deficiency anemia." The Bureau says that, although "conclusive evidence of benefits due to vitamin C therapy has not been obtained in any of these conditions," nor has its total effectiveness been fully proven, "researchers have amassed a large store of data on the biochemical and physiological properties of vitamin C."

The details of such research are, of course, primarily of interest to physicians, who have extended their knowledge into the body's biochemistry, with emphasis on nutrition. But we, as laymen, can benefit from getting some insight into this scientific search for knowledge. Dr. Robert J. Williams, of the University of Texas, observed in a paper on "Individuality in Vitamin Needs," published in the *Proceedings of the National Academy of Sciences* (June, 1967), that "medical scientists are still almost completely in the dark" as to the functions of vitamin C, although they know "it has to do in some obscure way with the building and maintenance of collagenous supportive tissue."

The reason for this tantalizing search lies in the leads scientists have found in animal nutrition that cannot be easily checked out with people. But nonstatistical work provides strong indications of human needs. Dr. James Greenwood, Jr., of Baylor University College of Medicine, told the editors of *Prevention* (November, 1972), "We insist on more vitamin C for patients with back problems. We have seen large doses of vitamin C help patients with back, neck or leg pains due to spinal disc injuries. Some patients have been able to avoid the necessity for surgery and others have been able to avoid returns of the syndrome when their vitamin C intake was greatly increased."

Dr. McCormick, whom we have already quoted at the beginning of this chapter, advocated that "therapeutic use of the vitamin should be made a part of the nonsurgical care" in all cases of lesions of the spinal disks, as well as damage to knee cartilages and in the sacroiliac. Writing in the *Journal of Applied Nutrition* (Nos. 1 and 2, 1962), he said that "our knowledge of the pathology of the intervertebral discs has been developed mostly within the last three decades." Recent research has shown that cartilage damage lessens the elasticity of the spinal disks and this may hasten calcium deposits. Dr. McCormick was "convinced that deficiency of vitamin C plays an important role" in creating such damage. He said that use of the vitamin might "result in fixation of a slipping disc or cartilage" and prevent its break or displacement.

One does not get the feeling from these and other research results that the advocates of vitamin C therapy assume disk troubles are exclusively due to vitamin deficiency; rather, lack of adequate vitamin supply may be one of several factors contributing to back pains linked to "slipped disks." Physical and even emotional tensions have been cited as triggering severe back pains. But even in these areas vitamin C use may well be beneficial. In fact, the use of ascorbic acid in counteracting physical and mental stress has been examined with promising results. Muscle strain may be either physical in origin, as from sleeping uncomfortably, or emotional, by bringing about bodily tension.

In either case, vitamin C may be able to act as a muscle relaxer. That, at least, may be deduced from a report by Dr. I. H. Syed in the *British Medical Journal* (July 30, 1966), who has given patients 500 milligrams of C before exercise and 400 milligrams afterward, together with plenty of fluids to drink. He found that this treatment prevented muscle stiffness. "But if it does develop," he wrote, "it is usually very slight and is easily cleared up by taking 400 additional milligrams of vitamin C and extra fluids, and if required, 1 or 2 hourly doses of 200 mgs." Why does the vitamin have this effect? Dr. Syed's clinical explanation is this: "As vitamin C looks after the endothelial lining of capillaries, it may prevent damage or rupture of these in muscles during exercise; it may also help detoxification of metabolites and by its diuretic effects help with excretion."

Against Stress

In other words, the same function that vitamin C has in preventing internal bleeding, which makes for black-and-blue skin blobs, strengthens the walls of the blood-conducting capillaries and thus protects the body at times of unusual physical stress. Jill Klein, writing on "Vitamin C for That Aching Back" in *Prevention* (November, 1972), observes that "many patients with a pain in the back or neck play the martyr and try to ignore it." They drive themselves beyond their endurance. The resulting fatigue, instead of inducing sleep, causes tension. "This nervous tension drives the patient on to greater endeavor, results in more fatigue, and this vicious cycle continues with more pain as the result," say Drs. William K. Ishmael and Howard B. Shorpe of Oklahoma City in their booklet *Care of the Back,* published by Lippincott. Klein quotes the two physicians as saying that "life situations provoking grief, resentment, guilt, anger or other emotional reactions may initiate or aggravate these nervous and muscular tension states." They also note that "lack of calcium, protein, vitamins and other essential nutrients may produce fatigue rendering the back susceptible to strain."

Jill Klein writes that "an emotional strain is a stress situation" and adds: "While vitamin C helps the body to meet its stresses, it is used up in the process so that the stress situation can therefore cause a depletion of this vital substance, making you a candidate for many physical ailments including the excruciating stab in the back. Vitamin C is only one of the nutrients involved in this aching back syndrome." But if nutrition has failed to protect you from such a condition, I should like to add that personal experience prompts me to suggest the services of a chiropractor or osteopath, who may well have knowledge of the underlying nutritional problems that help to create these symptoms.

Experiments with people and animals have given a certain amount of support to the thesis that vitamin

C permits us to withstand physical stress. Naturally, these tests varied greatly in risk. Two Japanese researchers, Kazuo Asahina and Katsumi Asano, of the Toho University School of Medicine, Tokyo, placed test animals in a decompression chamber from which they removed successive units of oxygen. Eventually, the animals were breathing air so low in oxygen that it was equal to the height of 33,000 feet—roughly the level at which a jet plane crosses the Atlantic. They put forty-two rats through this test, the first time around, and all of them died within about thirteen minutes.

The second batch of rats received a dose of vitamin C equivalent to giving a human being 7,000 milligrams. As a result, the rats lived for an average of 23.7 minutes; three remained alive. The researchers doubled the vitamin C dose. As a result, twenty-one out of forty-forty test animals stayed alive. Those that died hung on to life for almost an hour.

These and other research results suggest one basic quality of vitamin C: it acts to give the body strength to resist and overcome the assaults of bacteria, viruses, and other external and internal elements.

This can be seen from diets that are, by their very nature, low in ascorbic acid. Walter H. Eddy and Gilbert Dahldorf report in their book *The Avitaminoses* that a group of ulcer patients were put on the common bland ulcer diet, grossly lacking in vitamin C. Within sixteen days, one-third of the patients developed highly fragile capillaries. But once vitamin C was reintroduced into their diet, 70 percent of those who had experienced damage managed to recover. That is just about as far as experimentation with human subjects can go in vitamin C research, at least as far as the number of subjects in an experiment is concerned. It certainly shows that a diet clearly deficient in vitamin C, as is that of an ulcer patient, requires ascorbic acid as a supplement. J. I. Rodale and staff, who published *The Complete Book of Vitamins,* report that another researcher found that of eighteen ulcer patients, fifteen lacked vitamin C in their blood. The authors ask: "Is it because the diets they are eating are

grossly deficient in vitamin C, or is it that they cannot
utilize vitamin C properly?" They assume that it is
probably a combination of several factors, but "certainly the most important fact is that the usual ulcer
diet is practically void of vitamin C. On the other hand,
if a lack of vitamin C has had something to do with the
formation of the ulcer in the first place—and we
believe it does—then how foolish it seems to prescribe
a diet of milk, crackers, and soft bland foods in which
there is little or no vitamin C!"

Wound Healing

An ulcer is an internal wound. All wound healing
calls upon the body's reserve resources, mobilizing
them to restore damaged tissues and to do battle
against bacteria. A striking instance concerning an
external ulcer was reported in the British medical
periodical *The Lancet* by E. K. Ledermann of the
staff of the Royal London Homeopathic Hospital.
The report, in the form of a letter to the magazine,
stated that "a woman of 78, not showing any other signs
of illness except for glaucoma, developed an ulcer on
her left cheek in 1958." The letter continued:

"She attended another hospital where a biopsy was
carried out, the report being: 'The section of skin
includes a simple inflammatory ulcer lined at the edge
by attenuated squamous epithelium with abundant
inflammatory granulation tissue at its base. The small
ulcer crater is plugged with serocellular keratinous
debris.' The treatment at the Royal London Homeopathic Hospital consisted of homeopathic medicines,
given internally, and external applications of antibiotics. These were matched with results from swabs,
which showed Staphylococcus aureus and Friedlander
bacillus. In addition, eusol dressings and Vioform
ointment were employed. Although the ulcer showed
signs of healing at times, it broke down consistently
and, in fact, became larger."

Thus far, then, the diagnosis had shown an ulcer
that was inflamed at its center, scaly around the

edges, and resistant to external antiseptic medication. By studying the woman's urine, the hospital discovered that she was short on vitamin C. The letter continued:

"The patient was given vitamin C—one gram three times daily and the ulcer started healing. On June 14 [1962] the vitamin C value had risen to 22 milligrams [from 1 milligram] per 100 milliliters. The healing of the ulcer was complete by the middle of July and the condition has remained satisfactory ever since. Throughout the whole period of observation, no signs of scurvy were observed and the patient's diet was not apparently deficient in vitamin C."

Adams and Murray, in their book *Vitamin C*, make these comments on this case:

"This elderly woman had had her facial ulcer for four years. One can assume that she and her family physician had used everything they could think of in an attempt to cure it. It is not likely that something like this would be allowed to continue unattended. It must have bothered her; it must have been painful and uncomfortable, not to mention unsightly.

"A study of the infection present showed staphylococcus germs. These bacteria are at present the nightmare of hospital staffs everywhere. The more antibiotics that are used in a hospital, the more staph infections there are. Epidemics of staph infections occur with increasing regularity among surgical patients and newborn infants in hospital nurseries. Discharged patients going home from infected hospitals take their staph germs along with them and infect their families and neighbors. Years of boils, abscesses, ear infections, urinary infections may plague a family which has been infected at a hospital. No antibiotic "wonder drug" has been found that will kill staph germs. The only answer experts have to staph infections is better hospital housekeeping and sanitation."

The obvious conclusion is that patients must have resistance to staph infections, as to all others, and that in this case the ulcer may have been the indirect result of just such an infection. Perhaps, as a routine precaution, patients in hospitals should be given relatively high doses of vitamin C, simply to heighten their resistance to the stress of hospital confinement itself, the drain that their own illness represents, as well as the danger of infections picked up at the hospital itself.

Internal or external ulcerations, being wounds, are subject to the healing processes that affect all our wounds, whether they are little nicks from a kitchen knife, the results of automobile accidents, or injuries sustained in war. Just as wounds do not heal easily with scurvy victims, it is a virtual certainty that lack of vitamin C retards all wound healing. After all, as we have seen before, C is necessary for the formation of collagen—and collagen is a factor in the skin covering of wounds, the early hardening that seals it against bacteria.

The healing functions of vitamin C were illustrated at the Metropolitan Hospital of New York Medical College. There, Dr. Stephen N. Rous, chief of the service in the Department of Urology, successfully used vitamin C in treating urethra infection in twelve men. The inflammations had caused pain during and after urination. After four days, with 3,000 milligrams of C for each of the men, there was, in Dr. Rous's words, "complete relief of symptoms." Reporting on these cases in the *New York State Journal of Medicine* (December 15, 1971) Rous noted that phosphatic crystals had apparently formed in the patients' urine, and C provided enough acidity to liquefy the crystals.

Lung Protection

Vitamin C's function in strengthening the capillaries, the blood vessels that form a huge network all through our bodies, gives it its universal importance. Speculation and research have gone into such areas as protection of the lungs and even into assuring resistance to that ever-present menace of modern society, air pollution. And, of course, tobacco smoke.

It is always risky to use the word cancer in connection with still controversial work in biochemistry, nutrition, or basic medical research. But a direct line does lead, at least in theory, from vitamin C's role in capillary strength, the delicate lung areas, the onslaught of smoke on the lungs, to the impact of tobacco smoke on lung cancer. In 1954, Dr. E. Schneider, a German researcher, wrote in the *Deutsche Medizinische Wochenschrift* that he used vitamins in treating 100 cases of early and advanced cancer. Together with vitamin A, he gave his patients from 1,000 to 2,000 milligrams of vitamin C. Although he did not cure the cancers, Dr. Schneider reported that the vitamins appeared to cause general improvement; this included a reduction in the size of the cancerous tumors, as well as reduced bleeding, ulceration, and a lower rate of blood sedimentation.

Any kind of stress seems to place an increased demand on the body's vitamin C consumption. And as it cannot be stored, we have no reserves on which to draw: we must get more vitamin C from direct intake. But stress need not only be of a negative sort, it may be the stress that is created by a joyful occasion, a wedding, a reunion of family members after separation, a sudden surprise such as winning a lottery. Illness, crisis situations of all sorts, and finally old age are among the periods that make the highest demands on vitamin C.

The *Journal of the American Geriatric Society* (January, 1972) drew its readers' attention to "potentialities of therapeutic nutrition" among the aged, "with special reference to the role of vitamin C in accelerating the natural processes of recovery from diseases and injuries occurring during the later period of life." The author of this paper, Dr. M. L. Riccitelli of the Yale School of Medicine, observed that aging patients might require added vitamin C when sick or emotionally upset. But as vitamin C is not stored, he emphasized "the extremely low plasma levels of vitamin C observed in severe stress situations."

Dr. Riccitelli pointed out that doses of ascorbic acid must be repeated, since "the body does not metabolize vitamin C any more rapidly in the deficiency state than it does normally." And, unless C is given frequently throughout the day, "large doses are inadequate, since once the body is saturated, a high percentage of the dose is rapidly excreted in the urine." He told his readers to be alert to a C deficiency among their older patients, as its symptoms are so "insidious" that they "may not even arouse suspicion." That, of course, is evidence of the body's fragmented use of vitamin C.

As so many parts of our bodies use the vitamin, the symptoms of deficiency may simply be interpreted as some everyday form of fatigue or lowered resistance. And because the vitamin has an important role in diverse body functions, symptoms of a deficiency are likely to be equally diffuse. Riccitelli asked doctors to be alert to such varied symptoms as general fatigue and listlessness, reduced appetite, withdrawal from activity, emotional disturbance, and even rough skin.

Such symptoms might be due to a great variety of causes. But no matter what the cause, the body's resistance is obviously strengthened by the availability of vitamin C. In the case of older people, vitamin C levels have in some studies been found to be lower than in other age groups. The reasons for this may lie in a number of different facts. Some of these are quite obvious. Older people may simply not want to chew fresh fruit, because of dentures or weaker jaw muscles. They may find shopping difficult and therefore depend heavily on canned and other convenience foods.

"Enriched" Bread

Then, too, the older we get, the more set we are in our ways. Many of us were brought up with emphasis on bread as "the staff of life." This, of course, was before we became aware of the lack of nutrients to be found in processed bread, particularly the ubiquitous white breads that are sold as "enriched," because some of the destroyed nutrients have been put back in again. An older person who lives alone, and this is increasingly the case these days, may live on starches such as bread, drink an occasional cup of coffee, open a can of spaghetti and meatballs, and have a sweet piece of pie for a treat. There's hardly any vitamin C in all this. If an elderly patient is suffering from a heart ailment that calls for less consumption of sodium, it is important that he or she select a vitamin C supplement that is really ascorbic acid, and not sodium ascorbate. Some multiple vitamin tablets also contain sodium ascorbate as C, but this is clear from the label—although you may need a magnifying glass to read the small type.

That older people have a lower level of vitamin C than do younger people was noted by Dr. Constance Spittle, writing in *The Lancet* (December 11, 1971). Her report was particularly interesting as it seemed to indicate that vitamin C may affect the level of cholesterol in blood. Dr. Spittle, who is associated with the Pinderfield Hospital in Wakefield, Yorkshire, England, came across the correlation between C and cholesterol more or less accidentally. To test her discovery, she used fifty-eight healthy persons and twenty-five patients, testing their blood cholesterol over a period of six weeks on a routine basis. She then gave them 1,000 milligrams of vitamin C daily, while checking their cholesterol count during another six weeks.

Among subjects under twenty-five years of age, the cholesterol level dropped by 8 percent while vitamin C was given. Among the older healthy subjects there were no signficant results. But among the patients suffering from atherosclerosis, the cholesterol level rose by 8 percent. Dr. Spittle assumed that this meant a diversion of cholesterol from the blood to the adrenals and the liver. She speculated that the displacement was due to "mobilization of the arterial cholesterol" and concluded: "I suggest that atherosclerosis is a long-term deficiency of vitamin C, which permits cholesterol to build up in the arterial system, and results in changes in other fractions of the fats."

One research swallow does not make a therapeutic

summer, and Dr. Spittle's research would have to be duplicated by quite a few other researchers and with larger numbers of subjects before these results can be considered conclusive. But it is encouraging that individual researchers are looking for new frontiers of knowledge in vitamin C. All of us will eventually benefit from their search.

XIV

Vitamin D: Sunlight and Cod-Liver Oil

How do we get much of our vitamin D? Eating, by mouth? No. By skin. From sunlight.

The function of vitamin D is full of puzzles. We know that it helps our bones and teeth to remain strong, and we've learned a good deal about its sources and needed quantities. Still, a lot of details are missing in the chain of our knowledge.

Unlike vitamin C, for instance, we do store vitamin D in our bodies, and so it is possible to take too much of it. You'd have to be pretty silly to overdose yourself with the vitamin; still, some people think that if a little is good, plenty must be even better. That may be true for other things, including some vitamins, but certainly not for D.

Dr. Benjamin Kramer of the Department of Pediatrics of the State University of New York in Brooklyn, together with Dr. Donald Gribetz of the Department of Pediatrics at Mount Sinai Hospital in New York City, contributed a paper on vitamin D deficiency effects in human beings to the noted scholarly reference book *The Vitamins*. I'd like to quote their definition: "The pathological changes in human beings resulting from deficiency of vitamin D are almost entirely confined to the skeleton. Here, there develops a distortion of bone growth that gives rise to the clinical picture that we designate rickets. The primary disturbance responsible for this distortion is a failure to mineralize new formed osteoid [bony] tissue and cartilage matrix. Hence, the unusual softness of the bone which under the stress and strain of weight bearing and locomotion gives rise to the characteristic deformities of the disease."

Drs. Kramer and Gribetz are writing on vitamin D deficiencies because both are pediatricians, children's doctors, and rickets is originally and basically a children's disease. Its history is that of children who grew up in airless and sunless cities, or in valleys that get little sun during the year. One oddity is that in traditional India, where women were condemned to purdah —complete withdrawal from life after the death of their husbands—these widows developed ricketslike conditions, because they were locked away from the sun, living totally indoors.

Sun for Babies

One basic lesson is this: let the babies have some sun; let the little creatures run around at the seashore, or on your terrace; don't have them swaddled in all kinds of garments, even in the winter. Even during apparently sunless days, ultraviolet rays will make their way through the cloud cover, as anyone who gets a sunburn on a cloudy day at the beach can testify. Again, this does not mean toasting the kid to a crisp, but it does mean getting an infant or child out of the house, into the backyard, on the terrace or the street. That's what I meant when I said, at the beginning of this chapter, that we take much of our vitamin D not by mouth but by skin.

The discovery of vitamin D was hampered by the curious and seemingly unrelated facts that children recovered from rickets when they were (a) exposed to sunlight, and (b) given cod-liver oil. It made no sense. What do sunlight and cod-liver oil have in common? It took a long time to find the common denominator: the body's need for vitamin D. To this day, no one really knows how the factor that is present in ultraviolet rays gets into oily fish. There are all kinds of hypotheses—some sea species float to the water's surface, soak up sunlight, are then eaten by other creatures, and eventually pass the vitamin D on to such fish as cod—but no one is quite sure.

In nutrition, as you know by now, there are a lot of argumentative people. It is nice, therefore, to find total agreement that our diet needs supplementation by vitamin D, because we, and our children, just don't get enough sunlight all year round. That's why our milk has vitamin D added. The background to this was published in the *Journal of the American Medical Association* (November 5, 1955) on behalf of its Council on Foods and Nutrition. The AMA recalled that infantile rickets had been reduced almost to the vanishing point in the United States and called this development "a modern miracle." It noted that bowed and otherwise deformed legs, deformed pelvises, crooked backs, and other defects caused by rickets in infancy and early childhood were still common in the U.S. in the 1920s, which in the 1930s led to the program of adding vitamin D to milk. The AMA added:

"Children beyond the age of infancy require vitamin D for normal growth. Adults, especially pregnant and lactating women, also need vitamin D. The importance of an automatic source of vitamin D, ingested regularly with milk, is great indeed. Infantile rickets would be prevalent within months if all preventive measures suddenly were abandoned. Four hundred U.S.P. [United States Pharmacopoeia] units of vitamin D to the quart of reconstituted milk is fully adequate to prevent rickets and to satisfy the needs for growth if milk so fortified is given in the customary amounts. Because of these considerations, the Council reaffirms its policy of recommending fortification of milk with vitamin D at this level. It is fortunate that a high proportion of bottled milk and practically all evaporated milk is fortified to the recommended level today, and it is urged that the program be continued."

The AMA's Council on Food and Nutrition believes that, in addition to conforming to the appropriate federal, state, and local regulations, vitamin D whole milk should meet the following specifications:

1. It should conform to the U.S. Public Health Service recommendations for grade A pasteurized whole milk.

2. It should contain 400 USP units of vitamin D per quart.

3. It should be checked at least twice yearly for vitamin D potency by analyses of surprise samples performed by a recognized independent laboratory.

Concerning evaporated milk, the AMA Council believes it should meet the following specifications:

1. It should contain 25 USP units of vitamin D per fluid ounce (equivalent to 400 USP units per quart when diluted with an equal amount of water).

2. It should be checked at least twice yearly for vitamin D potency by analyses of surprise samples performed by a recognized independent laboratory.

Vitamin D in Milk

There is no doubt whatever that the addition of vitamin D to milk in the United States is an outstanding nutritional development. It recognizes the fact that our children just don't get enough natural sunlight early in life, if only because the human race has migrated northward in its evolution and away from much of the life-giving environment that is the cradle of mankind.

Now that we are all sweetness and light on vitamin D, what is there left to argue about? Doesn't it all come up roses? Well, not quite. We've got the D in the milk, but do we have the milk in the kids? Do we have it, in sufficient amounts, in adults? This is important, because bones aren't just pieces of a woodlike, solid matter that holds up our bodies like the beams of a

house. Bones and teeth are delicate structures, forever wearing away and forever being renewed. And
it is this renewal process, this continuous rebuilding
of all our body cells, that affects bones and teeth.

Vitamin D is essential to a continuous supply of
calcium and inorganic phosphorus in our blood and,
as Kramer and Gribetz put it, "presumably in the
tissue fluids, thus in a large measure insuring a constant and adequate supply of these elements for mineral-
ization of newly formed cartilage matrix and osteoid."
It isn't enough that the body takes in calcium—it also
has to absorb it properly through the gastrointestinal
tract. Vitamin D is instrumental in overcoming inter-
ference with this absorption process, as can "adequate
irradiation with ultra-violet rays of the corrected wavelength."

Kramer and Gribetz report that "in the absence of
vitamin D, less that 20% of ingested calcium is absorbed from the gastrointestinal tract," while "an adequate intake of vitamin D assures that from 50 to 80%
of the calcium is absorbed." This is true not only for
children, the most obvious targets for rickets or ricketslike bone and teeth problems, but presumably also for
adults. The Indian women in purdah, who never
ventured out of their homes, today have their equivalent in much of the elderly population anywhere. People we call "shut-ins" are more and more prevalent
in Western civilization, as older people become isolated from their families, are shunted off into nursing
homes, or live lonely lives in our cities. We often
hear of elderly people who break a hip or a leg and
are unable to move for weeks and months because
their bones heal more slowly than those of younger
folk—and these are the people who don't go out and
play in a sandbox or a basketball court, who are shut
off from sunlight most of the year. Do they get
enough vitamin D?

The elderly don't drink much milk, and they are
the least likely to spend a Sunday at the beach. At
best they sit on a park bench or take a short walk. With
the increasing fear of muggings and other assaults, our

Golden Age population has turned into a beleaguered minority, often locking itself into houses and apartments, behind minifortress arrangements, with windows shut and the blinds drawn. How many of them suffer a vitamin D deficiency?

Vague Symptoms

One of the difficulties in detecting vitamin D deficiency is the very vagueness of its symptoms. In three cases of osteomalacia (softening of the bones) reported by prominent English physicians in *The Lancet* (December 12, 1964), patients complained of no more than the creeping weakness and muscular stiffness common to old age. One elderly woman complained of low-back pains and aching thighs that had plagued her for years. She lived alone in a small, dark cottage and seldom left the house. Her daily diet was two slices of bread and butter, a cracker, and thirteen cups of tea, for which she used half a pound of sugar. Her pains became so severe that she was unable to walk without help. Bone samples, viewed under a microscope, revealed advanced calcium deficiency.

Before 1962, only three cases of nutritional osteomalacia had been reported in Great Britain and America. But when three showed up at the British Royal Infirmary within a twelve-month period, doctors began to suspect that the condition was widespread among the elderly. When one considers the poor eating habits of the aged, doctors may well be treating as symptoms of old age what in reality is a deficiency. Osteomalacia in the elderly corresponds to rickets in children. A survey of five-year-old children from a cross section of society revealed that 95 percent of those in Portland, Oregon, and 73 percent of the children in San Diego had four or more signs of rickets.

One cause is relative lack of sunlight. Chicago, which is probably typical of the whole temperate zone, receives light in December the shortest wavelength of which is near 3,050 Å; in May, 2,990 Å; and in summer, 2,900 Å. Only a small fraction of the sun's ultraviolet rays possess antirachitic properties (those between 3,130 Å and 2,900 Å). Since the rays at 3,130 Å are 100 times less effective than those at 2,950 Å, in Chicago there is practically no antirachitic factor in even bright sunlight in late autumn, winter, and spring. Add to this the industrial pollution, rain, dust, and smog that are ever-present in our big cities, and the amount of antirachitic sunlight that penetrates the atmosphere to the earth's surface is severely reduced.

The first man to realize that sunlight was a cure for rickets was Dr. T. A. Palm in 1890. His researches had shown him that signs of rickets were not to be found upon the skeletons of Egyptian mummies. This led to the conclusion that in countries where the sun was strong, rickets were scarce.

Two years later, Niels Finsen, an Icelander, sat watching a cat sleeping on a sunlit roof. Each time the shadows of the building crept over him, the cat rose and moved back into the sun. He speculated that sunlight must be more than merely a source of warmth for cats, it must also contain an element that keeps them healthy. His researches into ancient cultures made clear that early man had cured many ailments, especially skin disorders, by exposure to the sun. He learned, too, that in 1815 Loebel of Jena had fashioned a glass box, which he called a heliothermos, that refracted and intensified light, causing "miraculous cures" of the patients placed within it.

In 1893, Finsen discovered that sunlight had harmful as well as beneficial effects: smallpox victims exposed to the sun were left with scars, while those shielded by red curtains, which permitted the penetration of red rays but screened out blue, violet, and ultraviolet rays, were left without scars.

In the years that followed, Finsen made hundreds of experiments, curing by means of quartz light, X (and other) rays, and founding the sciences of heliotherapy and phototherapy. He had proved that sunlight cured rickets, along with numerous other ailments, but no one knew why it did so.

Sunlight and Cod-Liver Oil

The mystery merely deepened with the discovery by an English surgeon, Bland Sutton, that the monkeys, lions, birds, and bears in the London Zoo could be cured of rickets by generous doses of cod-liver oil. Since fish are never exposed to sunlight, what connection could there be between sunlight and cod-liver oil?

It was a chemical characteristic of vitamin D, its resistance to oxidation, which led to its discovery in 1922 by Dr. Elmer McCullom's group at Johns Hopkins University. McCullom eliminated vitamin A from a sample of cod-liver oil by oxidation and named the undestroyed element vitamin D. This was later identified as a group of sterols varying in potency. In the form of a crystal it is white and odorless, but all forms are soluble in fat and organic solvents, but not in water. Being heat stable, they are not easily oxidized.

The two D vitamins most important in human nutrition are D_2 and D_3. D_2 is formed by irradiating the provitamin D_2 (ergosterol) that is found in ergot and yeast. The irradiated product is known as calciferol or viosterol.

While vitamin D_2 is man-made, vitamin D_3 occurs in fish-liver oils (and also in human skin). Provitamin D_3 (7-dehydrocholesterol) is converted to the active form by sunlight.

Vitamin D occurs naturally (mainly in fish oils and a little in egg and milk; the sunflower seed is the only plant source), and in foods irradiated by ultraviolet rays. Apart from fish-liver oils, all of these foods are rather poor sources of the vitamin D. According to Dr. Gilbert B. Forbes, in *Present Knowledge in Nutrition,* "mammalian liver contains 1 to 4 I.U. per gram, egg yolk 1 to 5 I.U. per gram, and milk 3 to 100 I.U. per liter." Even these foods do not commonly form a part of the daily diet of millions of our citizens.

Writing for *Prevention* (September, 1972), Jane Kinderlehrer, in "Heart and Nerves Need Vitamin D," says: "And while Vitamin D deficiencies are still responsible for rickets, and an ever-increasing docket of osteomalacia and unstable heart rhythms, doctors have a blind spot when it comes to recognizing them. They have been taught that there is no such thing as Vitamin D deficiency in this country because the milk is irradiated. They do not consider the fact that most adults and many children are unable to tolerate milk, while of the remainder enough are cholesterol-conscious to avoid milk or use the fat-free variety which provides no fat and no Vitamin D with which to utilize the calcium in the milk."

Regarding sunlight as a source of vitamin D, Dr. W. Farnsworth Loomis said, in *Science* (August 4, 1967), that black or brown skin allows only 3 to 36 percent of ultraviolet rays through the overlying stratum corneum, the skin's outermost horny layer, while white skin allows 53 to 72 percent. It was further estimated, in an abstract that appeared in *The Medical Journal of Australia* (August 24, 1968), that 1 square centimeter of white human skin could synthesize 18 IU of vitamin D in three hours. In effect, sunlight remains for most of mankind the only adequate source of vitamin D, and many of us are simply not aware of this vitally important fact in nutrition, biochemical balance, and general health.

As I've said right along, vitamin D is full of surprises, both good and bad. It interacts with vitamin A in many ways, and you will find that supplementary capsules usually combine the two vitamins. It also shares with A the quality of being absorbed by mineral oil. Anyone suffering from constipation is making a mistake when taking mineral oil with any kind of frequency. Mineral oil should not be taken with food, because the A and D content of food will be neutralized by the oil. Absorption of A and D is hindered by such diseases as celiac syndrome, sprue, and colitis.

Another thing: don't think sunlight creates a synthesis of vitamin D *under* the skin; instead, it appears to take place right *on* the skin. When you are out in the sun and then hop into the water, you are literally washing the ultraviolet effect away from yourself.

Moral: Don't go swimming after a sunbath—loll in the sun after your swim!

After being produced on or in the skin, vitamin D is absorbed through the skin and carried to the liver and other organs for use. A relatively small amount is stored in the liver, compared to the liver's much larger capacity for vitamin A storage. Vitamin D is excreted from the circulating blood by way of the bile.

Calcium in Bones

Research made public at the Second Drummond Memorial Lecture held at University College, London (October, 1970) indicated that vitamin D is not only necessary to build up calcium in the bones, but is an essential ingredient to permit the calcium to be withdrawn again, when the body so requires it. As we know, our bones are not, as was once thought, solid and stable, but, as with tissue, in a constant state of being destroyed and rebuilt.

In the Drummond Lecture, Dr. E. M. Lawson, of the Dunn Nutritional Laboratory of the University of Cambridge, stated: "The function of vitamin D is two-fold, being required for the proper mobilization of bone, for example calcium acquisition and, in addition, for the mobilization of calcium into blood." Vitamin D is required for the body's proper utilization of calcium from the moment it is taken into the body until it is finally deposited. Dr. Lawson continued: "The balance of calcium between the plasma and bone is maintained by vitamin D, calcitonin, and parathyroid hormone, with the latter hormone only able to act in the presence of vitamin D."

From these facts it is clear that vitamin D is not only effective with regard to rickets and similar diseases, but affects every function of the body that requires calcium. No matter how much calcium we consume, our system does not absorb it without vitamin D. Thus, any calcium deficiency disease may well be caused by lack of vitamin D.

Vitamin D depends for its effectiveness upon a balance between itself and calcitonin and thyroid hormone; any imbalance, whether caused by a lack or an excess of vitamin D, may cause serious problems. When the body has too little vitamin D, calcium and phosphorus are not absorbed into the blood but are excreted from the body, so that much of the calcium in milk and greens is lost, and teeth and bones become soft.

Vitamin D also seems to play a role in citrate metabolism. Citrates are important organic salts and esters involved in many metabolic functions, including use of minerals from bone tissue and removal of calcium from the blood. The removal of calcium has an anticoagulant effect. This effect gives vitamin D a useful role in producing blood plasma and serum for medical use. In animal experiments, doses of vitamin D have produced increases in the citrate levels in bone, blood, kidney, heart, and the small intestine. Moreover, some investigators have even cured human rickets with citrate therapy alone. Orange juice given at the rate of 600 to 700 milliliters daily also proved effective therapy for rickets.

Although vitamin D has been used successfully for treating a distention of the cornea of the eye (keratoconus), vitamin research and therapy are growing so quickly that it will be difficult to make any final assessment of its value in the field for several years. With regard to chronic conjunctivitis, the vitamin D and calcium therapy of Dr. Arthur A. Knapp, whose paper recommending this remedy first appeared thirty years ago, is now becoming recognized. In dosages large enough to be effective but moderate enough to avoid toxicity, vitamin D can achieve lasting results. Over a four-month period, twenty of Dr. Knapp's forty-one patients treated experienced complete relief from conjunctivitis and another eleven showed remarkable improvement. The *Journal of Allergy* wrote of Dr. Knapp's experiment: "The 25 patients who primarily had received other treatment all felt that their improvement was far greater with vitamin D and calcium."

Despite such improvement, the question of whether the relief obtained was permanent or temporary was not answered until the following spring and summer: five of seven patients in a second experiment were found to remain free of symptoms. (These results found corroboration in the later experiments of Dr. Saleh Ali Ibrahim, recorded in his monograph on "Vitamin D in Certain Ophthalmic Cases.")

When vitamin D is not present in sufficient quantity in the bloodstream, calcium cannot be withdrawn from the bones to come to the aid of the heart. When the calcium supply to the heart becomes low, the heart will flutter and fibrillate (twitch) and signal for more calcium. Apart from its function with regard to bone building, vitamin D is thus of service to the heart. It is the parathyroid hormone that brings about the release of calcium from the bone into the bloodstream and causes the kidney tubules to retain the calcium, which would otherwise be lost in the urine, and return it to the bloodstream. Calcitonin controls the level of calcium in the blood at any given time, thus balancing the parathyroid hormone. Both are essential to the body's utilization of calcium, and vitamin D is essential if these compounds are to perform their functions.

Not Too Much!

Unlike other vitamins, but similar to hormones, too much vitamin D can be as injurious as too little. When too much calcium and phosphorus accumulate in the bloodstream, they are deposited in the soft tissues and cause calcification. This can be a serious disorder when it occurs in vital organs, such as lungs and kidneys. However, according to several researches, calcium in the blood acts as a "cutoff" for the production of parathormone and vitamin D tends to cause the presence of calcitonin, which inhibits bone resorption. This self-regulating safety system is not infallible and, as Dr. DeLuca tersely put it, "the end-effect of vitamin D is calcification."

Any of the functions vitamin D performs can be overdone. This would be the case if the calcium involved were not accompanied by sufficient phosphorus and magnesium, which are indispensable to control of the calcium level in the bloodstream. Vitamin D taken in excess is not eliminated, but stored in the liver, harmlessly, until it is needed—unless the amount is so great that it affects the calcium metabolism. In that case, it could theoretically lead to calcification of bones, hardening of the arteries, and mental retardation of children, a matter that, although not fully understood as yet, seems connected with high levels of calcium in the blood of the pregnant woman. Excesses lead to unnatural deposits in the fetus; yet, pregnant mothers do require adequate calcium.

Since vitamin D is difficult to take into the human body, except through sunlight and oily fish, the danger of an overdose from natural sources is remote. Cod-liver oil is not the sort of thing to invite addiction. But the U.S. Food and Drug Administration, mainly concerned about the impact of too much vitamin D on the mental and physical development of children, restricts the sale of the vitamin in strengths above 400 International Units to doctors' prescriptions. The ruling, which has been in effect since October 1, 1973, makes it possible to buy vitamin D supplements up to this strength as freely as most other vitamins—except for A, which is similarly restricted.

What, then, is the correct amount of vitamin D intake on a daily basis? Difficulties in establishing requirements for vitamin D arise from the limited food sources available, from lack of precise knowledge regarding the body's needs, and, last but not least, because of discoveries about the vitamin itself. Even the degree to which the body is able to produce vitamin D in response to irradiation is not fully known.

Another variable is that a person's life-style usually determines his exposure to sunlight, and this is decisive for an individual's need for vitamin D. A cliff dweller, living in a New York, Chicago, or Los Angeles high-rise apartment or in a tenement, and working in an office, would need more than a Midwest farmer who works out of doors all day.

Government recommendations have changed in recent years, and they call for intelligent individual appraisal. The Recommended Daily Allowances (RDA) issued in 1968 specified 400 International Units of vitamin D for everybody except men between the ages of twenty-two and fifty-five. The revised chart, U.S. Recommended Daily Allowances (U.S. RDA) of 1973, switched to a recommended daily "optional" average of 400 International Units only for adults and children over four years of age. The U.S. RDAs are probably based on the assumption that added vitamin D in milk and other sources is adequate, as there are no references to infants and small children; pregnant and lactating mothers are also not mentioned. The recommendations make no provisions for the elderly or shut-ins.

Self-medication is particularly ill advised in the case of vitamin D, as in A. Too many factors are involved. Go to your doctor, make him listen patiently, and do what he suggests.

P.S. Walk on the sunny side of the street.

XV

Vitamin E: Your Heart's Good Friend

"It will help you grow hair. Cure your skin problem. Ease your arthritis. Prevent ulcers. Make you sexually young." These, according to the magazine *FDA Consumer* (July-August, 1973) are "a smattering of claims made for vitamin E." The periodical, published by the U.S. Food and Drug Administration, ended its article on "Vitamin E: Miracle or Myth?" with the conclusion that the FDA "sees no reason for persons in good health and eating a well-balanced diet to use a dietary supplement."

The claims which the FDA magazine played up are, of course, irresponsible exaggerations based on such data as isolated research incidents of hair growth in rats or of reduced sexual potency in experimental animals where Vitamin E was seriously deficient. The FDA conclusions were hedged with the usual key words, "a well-balanced diet," which is becoming more and more difficult to achieve in this age of advancing food technology.

This overstatement by the FDA did not really surprise me, because a writer learns a good deal about a subject on which he does extensive research, usually much more than he can put into a book. That happened to me when I was writing *The Truth About Vitamin*

E (Bantam), published in 1972. The final proof was, literally, in the eating; ever since I wrote this book, I have taken 400 International Units of E daily. Should any illness arise that might require a higher dose, I will go to my doctor for his diagnosis and suggestions. In any event, if the proof of the pudding is in the eating, the proof of a researcher-writer's reaction to a subject is, ultimately: what does he do about it? Well, even before getting into my chapter on vitamin E, you know how I feel about it!

You can imagine, of course, how I felt when my wife handed me *McCall's* magazine for March, 1972, and showed me the pages that are called "McCall's Monthly Newsletter for Women." There, like a newspaper headline, it said, *Scientists Put Down Vitamin E.* It also had a cartoon drawing of a vitamin capsule, making it look half-Superman and half-Popeye. The report started by saying: "When Nobel Laureate Linus Pauling hailed vitamin C as a cure for the common cold, a faithful band of followers rushed out to buy it. Now another vitamin—vitamin E—is being promoted as a cure for everything from sexual problems to aching feet."

After this lively beginning, the story quoted the St. Louis biochemist Dr. Max K. Horwitt as critical of public enthusiasm for vitamin E. By now, his statement sounds familiar: "You can't live without vitamin E, but you get enough of it without trying." The article did cite Dr. Wilfred Shute as noting the correlation between modern milling techniques, which rob grain of vitamin E, and the increase of reported heart disease, which is now a major problem in our society.

The Shute Research

As it happens, I have kept in touch with Dr. Evan Shute of London, Ontario (Canada), who is a practicing physician, and Dr. Wilfred Shute of Port Credit, Ontario, who only recently retired after a lifetime of medical practice. These brother-pioneers of vitamin E are no-nonsense doctors of the old-fashioned type who watch what happens to individual patients and draw conclusions from their observations of significant cases. As a result, the younger of the two brothers, Dr. Wilfred Shute believes that vitamin E is "such a potent drug" that "it is an absolute necessity in the armamentarium of every doctor, whatever his speciality or type of practice." In his book *Vitamin E for Ailing and Healthy Hearts,* he writes that doctors can successfully use the vitamin in dealing with acute kidney inflammation, acute rheumatic fever, and acute thrombophlebitis (blood clots) in forty-eight to ninety-six hours. In such cases, Dr. Shute maintains, the illness "will be, by all criteria, laboratory and clinical, completely cured in two to four days!"

The linkage between vitamin E and various heart conditions is based on observations that have shown the vitamin to be effective in treatment. At the University of Alabama's Department of Oral Medicine, for example, Drs. E. Cheraskin and W. M. Ringsdorf treated 299 persons suffering from cardiovascular symptoms. These symptoms might have been related to conditions of the heart itself or of the vessels conducting blood into and out of the heart.

Over a period of one year, according to Cheraskin and Ringsdorf, the cardiovascular symptoms were reduced. All but a few of the subjects, between thirty and sixty years old, were dentists and their wives. The experimental treatment began with an analysis of the participants' diet. Next came a "food frequency" questionnaire that everyone had to fill out. The data were analyzed by computer, so that the experimenters were able to determine the average daily food intake and its nutritional value.

Cheraskin and Ringsdorf concluded that symptoms of heart disease grow more noticeable with advancing age. But, while "cardiovascular findings do indeed increase with age," they do so "only in those subjects consuming sub-optimal amounts of vitamin E." After one year's observation, the two experimenters found that those who increased their vitamin intake experienced a "decrease in cardiovascular symptoms and signs." Those who did not increase their vitamin E intake "did not improve with regard to the clinical picture."

Vitamin E is a versatile vitamin. As we have seen in the case of vitamin C, people find it difficult to accept the fact that one vitamin can have so many different uses. But we must keep in mind that such vitamins as E and C are utilized in many parts of our bodies. Moreover, anything that is related to the heart and capillary systems is automatically effective in a great variety of physiological and even emotional directions.

The dilemma this creates has been recognized by Dr. Evan Shute. He wrote in *The Heart and Vitamin E* that "no substance known to medicine has such a variety of healing properties" as E, and that this very adaptability has been a major problem. Shute feels that the vitamin is just "too useful for too many things." To accept that a biochemical substance might prevent miscarriages, help burns, have certain anti-aging qualities, and, above all, influence the functions of the heart and blood vessels, Shute says, is simply "asking too much."

One of the last discoveries concerning vitamin E illustrates its fascinating future potential. Lung damage due to pollution and smoking is one of the most serious health problems in our generation. The body has to fight off the destructive, oxidizing, burning impact on the delicate membranes of our lungs day and night. In our cities, along highways, and even in much of the countryside, automobile fumes and industrial smoke cannot be avoided. And even those of us who do not smoke cannot escape the smoke-filled rooms of restaurants, terminals, and private homes. Anything, therefore, that strengthens our lungs in their continuous fight must be of value.

But one can't really make experiments with human lungs that will have statistical significance. It would mean subjecting a large number of people to damaging fumes, giving half of them no treatment while putting the other half on vitamin E therapy. The Alabama researchers mentioned earlier worked with persons actually suffering from symptoms of heart disease. Statistically valid experiments would have to induce illness, or danger of illness, and then seek to cure it.

Throughout the history of medicine, experiments with laboratory animals have filled this gap. The book *Air Pollution,* edited by A. C. Stern and published in 1968, contained a paper by H. E. Stockinger and D. L. Coffin that maintained that vitamin E and vitamin C are among nutrients that counteract oxidant damage to lung membranes. Since then, a series of experimenters have had results that confirm that conclusion. As summarized by Dr. A. L. Tappel of the Department of Food Science and Technology, University of California at Davis, studies have shown that rats who are given vitamin E have a higher resistance to smog than those that do not receive the vitamin.

Dr. Tappel, in a paper on "Lipid Peroxidation and Fluorescent Molecular Damage to Membranes," showed that rats exposed to nitrogen dioxide suffered lung damage. However, "by prior treatment of exposed animals with large doses of vitamin E," the smog effect could be "partially prevented." A later experiment, reported by E. Menzel in the *Annual Review of Pharmacology,* showed that "rats deficient in vitamin E were damaged more by ozone and nitrogen dioxide than were animals supplemented with the vitamin." A follow-up research project, by B. D. Goldstein and others, reported in *Science* (1970), illustrated that "vitamin E is important" in reducing the impact of damage to lung membranes, because "rats deficient in vitamin E were more susceptible to lethal levels of ozone than were vitamin E-supplemented rats."

Here you have a good example of scientists doing their thing: repeating—or, as they like to call it, "replicating"—each other's experiments to make sure of their findings. Dr. Tappel himself, in cooperation with B. L. Fletcher, found in 1971 that there does exist a relation between vitamin E in humans and rats exposed to air pollutants. Their research suggested that people who live in polluted air should at least get the daily 30 International Units of vitamin E recommended by the Food and Nutrition Board. Tappel and Fletcher had given rats the equivalent of a human diet containing polyunsaturated fats. They gave some of the rats the equivalent, in body weight, of vitamin E, while others were fed a diet deficient in the vitamin. Tappel wrote: "In each experiment the greatest number of deaths occurred among animals fed the vitamin E deficient diet. . . . Although death is a limited index, the results show the increased sensitivity to ozone of the animals fed lower levels of vitamin E. Death from acute edema correlated with the inverse of the vitamin E in the diet."

Tappel reports that lung damage in laboratory animals showed "the critical importance of vitamin E in protection of the lung against oxidants like ozone." Actually, "the animals fed very low vitamin E showed highest lung edema." The researchers strongly favor an adequate daily intake of vitamin E, "particularly for persons exposed to smog oxidants." They conclude: "Placing an emphasis on the recommendations of the Food and Nutrition Board for 30 I.U. of vitamin E per day per adult seems both conservative and appropriate. It appears to be of immediate practical concern that large segments of the U.S. population are exposed to oxidant smog and at the same time have an intake of vitamin E below the recommended levels."

I have cited this series of experiments in some detail. The conclusions, and the methods used to arrive at them, are as up-to-date as they are important. We are not here dealing with isolated, fragmentary research. Nor are these studies made to examine the uses of vitamin E in cattle or chicken breeding (of which there are hundreds that show the importance of the vitamin), but we are concerned with projects specifically designed to test the impact of a modern condition: man's existence in a polluted environment.

How Much Is Enough?

At the beginning of this chapter I quoted from *McCall's* magazine. A similar report, "The Facts About Those Special Claims for Vitamin E," appeared in *Good Housekeeping* (July, 1972), which said that the "myths" about the vitamin "probably come from mistaken interpretations of test results of the vitamin in animals." But how else can one interpret the Tappel results, which were presented in detail at an international conference on vitamin E at Minneapolis in September, 1973? They are as clear as bright daylight. He gave the rats diets equivalent in weight to human diets. Some of the rats got the equivalent of 30 International Units of vitamin E, and others received a diet deficient in the vitamin. Those whose diet was deficient in E, when exposed to smog-type oxidants, became very ill or died. All you have to do is multiply the body weight of the laboratory animals, the food, and the vitamins, and you have a human equivalent. No one claims that the respiratory system, the lung structure, or the membrane texture of such animals is basically different from that of man. Rat experiments are at the basis f thousands of biochemical discoveries that are firmly established in the history of modern pharmacology.

Good Housekeeping quoted the standard view that Americans are getting "a sufficient amount f the vitamin in their food if they are eating a balanced diet." Again, the two magical words "balanced diet" appear as a means of saying something quite firmly while leaving a loophole as large as Boulder Dam. Dr. Tappel, who reported his findings on smog and vitamin E at a nutrition conference in Davis, California (May 1, 1971), mentioned research indicating that a large percentage of the population receives only one-fourth of the conservative dose of vitamin E recommended by the Food and Nutrition Board. The *Sacramento Bee,* summarizing the Tappel research (April 30, 1971), stated that other researchers shared his concern "for the apparent insufficiency of vitamin E in the American diet."

The newspaper also cited Tappel as reporting on other research undertaken by him and his associates: evidence that very high levels of vitamin E and other antioxidants may retard the aging process. The paper summarized Dr. Tappel's experiment as follows:

"Three groups of male mice were fed varying amounts of vitamin E. After 1.2 years, extracts of their testes were studied for the presence of fluorescent pigments. Testes are tissues showing considerable deposition of age pigments, Tappel explained. Extracts of testes from mice on the high vitamin E diet had an average of 44 percent less age pigments than those of mice on the lowest level vitamin E diet. The high vitamin E group was 'significantly lower,' Tappel said. Dr. Tappel added that 'much more research must be completed before any human recommendations can be made regarding vitamin E and aging.'"

There is a good deal of evidence available, even now, that would support Dr. Tappel's work from experiments undertaken by other researchers. In the Soviet Union, Dr. Olga Lepeshinskaya has found vitamin E to have "an enormously beneficial effect on the diseases of old age, specifically in combination with vitamin A." In her book *Life, Age and Longevity*, Dr. Lepeshinskaya added: "The rejuvenating property of these vitamins has a direct effect on the sex glands. They also strengthen the ability of the tissues to absorb oxygen, restore impaired circulation in blood vessels, especially the small capillaries, and help to restore the normal permeability of the blood vessels."

The experiments to which Lepeshinskaya refers were undertaken by the Institute of Biochemistry at the Soviet Academy of Science. Their parallels to the findings by Dr. Shute and other researchers on vitamin E are striking. Still, it is unlikely that even the most dedicated student of vitaminology will ever seek to replicate the Tappel mice experiments in aging with actual human subjects. Somehow, it seems unlikely that volunteers will be found to submit having extracts made from their testes. This, I presume, will perpetuate the attitude among critics of this work who speak contemptuously of "mistaken interpretations of test results" with animals.

Russian Research

The Tappel experiments concerning smog did have several forerunners in addition to those already cited. Interestingly enough, as the Russian report indicates, a good deal of research on vitamin E is going on in the Soviet Union and its neighboring countries, particularly Poland, Romania, and Czechoslovakia. Romania is also a stronghold of high-powered research on anti-aging elements in human biochemistry.

In Hungary, Dr. F. Gerloczy of the University Medical School, Budapest, traced several disorders to lack of vitamin E. Among those he pinpointed was scleroderma, a water concentration in body tissues that can cause swellings, as well as abnormally slow growth in children. Dr. Gerloczy's studies indicated that premature babies are particularly prone to E deficiency. Of 320 cases of death among premature babies, 75 percent were due to scleroderma. When the Hungarian physician used vitamin E, he was able to reduce the death rate to 27 percent.

Naturally, I would like you to read my book *The Truth About Vitamin E*, but I do want you to know the nine major areas of vitamin E impact, as I list them in that book. They provide a useful overall view of the truly remarkable versatility of the vitamin. Here they are:

1. Because it reduces the amount of oxygen required by body tissues, vitamin E is of use in treating gangrene, coronary and cerebral thrombosis, diabetes mellitus, arteriosclerosis, congenital heart disease, as well as threatened miscarriage, and all forms of emotional or physical strains that may create breathing problems.

2. It helps to melt blood clots and thus is essential in the treatment of situations where thrombosis is a danger, during and after coronary infarctions, childbirth, and operations.

3. It expands blood vessels and capillaries, where there may be inadequate blood supply, thereby improving circulation and combating arteriosclerosis and thrombosis.

4. It strengthens the walls of blood vessels and capillaries and so it is useful in the treatment of nephritis, rheumatic fever, purpura, retinitis (inflammation of the retina), miscarriage, and premature detachment of the placenta.

5. By dilating capillaries, which bring blood and oxygen to the skin tissues, it contributes significantly to the treatment of burns, wounds, chronic ulcers, and some types of skin disease.

6. As further consequence of these actions, vitamin E serves to impede the formation of scar tissue, internally and externally, and on some occasions to remove it; this is especially important in the treatment of certain heart diseases, where damage to the heart tissue may have occurred.

7. It increases the number of healthy platelets in the bloodstream, essential in the normal blood-clotting process, and so is of value in the treatment of thrombosis.

8. In 25 percent of the diabetic patients who suffer from blood vessel problems in their extremities, such as the threat of gangrene, vitamin E reduces the need for insulin.

9. It regulates the metabolism of fats and proteins, and so has a profound effect on all the bodily processes.

Among the authorities quoted by Dr. Tappel, who did the research on vitamin E, smog, and lung disease, was Dr. David Herting, who has alerted scientists and laymen to unacknowledged or unrecorded vitamin deficiencies in the American population. While we are supposed to get the vitamin in vegetable shortenings, margarine, and oils, processing and storing tend to cut its effectiveness before it reaches our tables or our lips. Herting believes we may suffer from vitamin deficiencies without being aware of them. We may simply ascribe symptoms to job difficulties, family problems, a "general rundown feeling," or to the multitude of aches and pains that seem to be part of modern civilization.

But Herting told me that unrecognized deficiencies may be frequent, and that he sees the most promising current research on vitamin E in two main areas: the problem of malabsorption, the body's impaired ability to absorb nutrients into its system as food passes through the digestive tract; and the importance of the vitamin in advancing knowledge of anemia specifically and blood research generally. Herting believes that E, like vitamin C, is influential in the body's absorption and use of dietary iron and plays a role in maintaining normal blood levels.

Vitamin E has been recognized as a major nutritional factor only during the past two decades. "Since its discovery," Dr. Herting said in a talk, "literally thousands of investigations involving vitamin E have been reported in laboratory and domestic animals. These have concentrated primarily on physiologic, pathologic and anatomic manifestations of a deficiency of vitamin E and have revealed perhaps the largest variety of disorders associated with the nutritional deficiency of any single vitamin."

Supporting Dr. Tappel's research concepts, Dr. Herting noted that "vitamin E deficiency affects the reproductive system, with syndromes such as degeneration of the testes and defective development of the embryo." He added: "It affects the muscular system, with skeletal muscular dystrophy, cardiac necrosis and fibrosis, and ceroid pigment in smooth muscle; the circulatory system, with exudative diathesis, erythrocyte hemolysis and anemias; the skeletal system, with tooth depigmentation; and the nervous system, with encephalomalacia, axonal dystrophy, and depositions of a yellow-brown pigment called ceroid."

Against "Toxic Agents"

That is quite a collection of symptoms and illnesses, and it should go far to dispel the notion that vitamin E research is, at this point, either unsophisticated, fragmentary, or unprofessional. Dr. Herting also noted that vitamin E deficiency shows itself "by a number of other conditions, such as discolored adipose tissue, liver necrosis, lung hemorrhage, kidney necrosis and post-mortem autolysis and creatinuria." Had enough? Just one more tie-in with Dr. Tappel's findings; Herting says: "It is also pertinent to note that vitamin E has been found to ameliorate the adverse effects of various toxic agents and a number of suboptimal dietary and environmental conditions." Among such environmental conditions is, of course, air pollution.

As in nutrition generally, there are specific periods in our lives when we need vitamin E quite badly. In our current life pattern, chances of having a truly "balanced diet" are limited. During life's crucial transition periods, when our body demands extra vitamin bolstering, we stand even less of a chance. Pregnancy, lactation, early infancy, puberty, and advanced age are the obvious milestones in our need for vitamins generally and vitamin E in particular. But where E is concerned, careful attention obviously must be paid to premature infants.

Dr. Herting mentioned that a certain type of anemia among premature infants "responds dramatically to vitamin E supplements." In the *International Journal of Vitamin Research* (Vol. 40, 1970), Drs. M. A. Chadd and A. J. Fraser of Wales urged that "vitamin E deficiency be considered in any very small infant who has an anemia within a few weeks of birth." The little things cannot get vitamin E through the placental barrier from the pregnant mother; so they may suffer vitamin deficiency from birth.

Talking of babies brings us to sex. The relationship between sexuality and vitamin E has been sensationalized and distorted—on both sides: the people who talk about the vitamin as if it were an aphrodisiac; and those who disdain it as something vaguely related to sterility in rats, and no more. As I have quoted two women's magazines that were critical of vitamin E in a superficial, slapdash fasion, it is only fair to cite a well-balanced interview with Dr. Evan Shute that appeared in the *Ladies' Home Journal* (April, 1972). The author, Geri Trotta, taped Shute's replies. He came right to the point:

"It is simply not true that vitamin E increases male potency. But it *will* increase fertility. It is said to increase the sperm count. I can't vouch for that, but it does increase the sperm *quality*. We try to give it to the husband before conception occurs, especially when we see couples plagued by habitual abortion. So many women are given a conception they cannot carry. Treating women who tend to abort is not only a matter of securing conception, it is a question of having the pregnancy carry on for nine months, which is an altogether different thing. That is why vitamin E is so useful. It is important that the best possible sperm should fertilize the best possible egg. Now, the egg is inaccessible and, anyway, the female body produces just one or two a month. During that same month, the sire produces billions of sperms. Cutting down the number of defective sperms is the real approach, I think, to preventing miscarriages."

Contraceptive Pills

Several researchers advocate that women taking the Pill against conception should make sure they are getting an adequate supply of vitamin E. The reason is relatively simple. There is estrogen in the Pill, and this can cause phlebitis, blood clots in the vessels. Apparently, among vitamin E's cardiovascular uses is that of counteracting phlebitis. Dr. Evan Shute believes that vitamin E will protect users of the Pill from the clotting influence of the estrogens. He watches patients who go on the Pill for the first time very carefully to see that they do not develop phlebitis. If they do, he stops the

Pill and administers vitamin E only. The same thing applies for people who use the Pill after they have had chronic phlebitis for years. Phlebitis can flare up during use of the Pill, and vitamin E can protect against that, too.

You can see by now that the many uses of vitamin E have common bases. Foremost is the vitamin's apparent ability to keep the blood vessels open, to permit the flow of blood to proceed unhindered through the body's network of capillaries, including the vessels underneath the skin. The vitamin appears to be able to aid in the healing of wounds, such as burns, through its ability to eat away any new thrombi when they form in the veins. If taken in time, vitamin E clears them up quickly. According to Dr. Evan Shute, the vitamin makes bypasses around old blocks in the circulation by calling into play collateral circulation. In patients suffering from hypertension (high blood pressure), vitamin E may be needed either for recovery from existing strokes or as a preventive against future strokes, but this must be done under careful medical supervision—because some rare cases actually show a sharp rise of blood pressure when vitamin E is taken.

I made a passing reference to polyunsaturated fats before. We are eating more of them, because we have been told to stay away from animal fats. The very increase in our consumption of polyunsaturated fats demands an equal increase in the consumption of vitamin E. Although all vegetable oils contain some tocopherols (vitamin E), quite a few do not contain enough of it. This cuts down the body's E supply and actually creates a deficiency by internal attrition. As we use these very useful oils in our salads or in polyunsaturated margarine, we are likely to deplete our vitamin E supply unknowingly, thus weakening our bodies against all kinds of disorders.

There is evidence that vitamin E counteracts certain deposits in our blood vessels, thus counteracting arteriosclerosis. This is, of course, of great importance to a large part of the population. Ceroid pigment, which tends to harden the arteries, is even deposited in the arteries of children. With advancing age, this causes lack of flexibility in the arteries. It gets worse as we grow older and is apparently irreversible. Vitamin E deficiency can contribute to his condition, some research indicates. Dr. Herting comments, "Because it does appear to be irreversibly deposited, such pigment may be an important contribution to the development of atherosclerosis. Be alert."

This situation is typical of our increasing understanding of vitamin E. While ceroid pigment in nerve cells accompanies aging, and because vitamin E appears to counteract such deposits, it would be easy to go one step further and say that the vitamin counteracts aging or is rejuvenating. The truth is more subtle: vitamin E cannot, it seems, *reverse* something that is already established; but it does seems capable of *delaying* the aging process. If you want to push that conclusion one step further and speculate that vitamin E thereby prolongs life, you're quite welcome to do so—and you may well be right.

XVI

Vitamin F: Essential Fatty Acids

Maybe the reason you're overweight is that you don't get enough fat. Surprised? Hard as it may be to believe, after much indoctrination to the contrary, fat has many beneficial roles to play in the maintenance of the body. One of them is maintaining the membranes that enclose every living cell. If such a membrane is damaged or collapses, the contents of the cell, much of which is liquid, are released. Hence, many people who are overweight, or appear to be from swollen tissues, are simply waterlogged. Also, when fat is undersupplied, the body changes sugar to fat much more rapidly; this makes blood sugar plunge downward, which in turn makes you very hungry. Consequently, you eat more. And last, fats are more satisfying than other foods, so that if you cut them out of one meal you are so starved at the next you eat twice as much.

Tissues other than cell membranes that rely on fat for health are the sheathing of nerves, the thyroid gland, the kidneys, and the skin. Fat combines with oxygen in the cells to furnish energy and with cholesterol to form a combined fatty substance that is further broken down into forms used for growth, energy, and skin health.

147

Are You Fat Deficient?

It's easy enough to tell if you are deficient in fat. Symptoms are: frequent and long-lasting colds; dry skin, acne, or eczema; brittle, lusterless, falling hair and/or dandruff; brittle nails; kidney disease; or thyroid disorder.

Now, don't race right out and consume a side order of greasy french fries or a container of buttered popcorn. All fats are not alike, and you must be selective. Fats are broken down in the body into fatty acids (vitamin F), most of which your body can produce if they are under-supplied. There are three that cannot be produced: linoleic acid, linolenic acid, and arachidonic acid. These are called the "essential fatty acids," and it is these you must be sure to obtain.

You can expect to get little vitamin F from margarine, hydrogenated cooking fats, or animal fats, such as butter, cream, fish-liver oils, and fat meat, especially beef and lamb. You will have to rely primarily upon cold-pressed, dehydrogenated vegetable oils: safflower, corn, soybean, cottonseed, peanut, and wheat germ are the best sources. And if the label doesn't say "cold-pressed, dehydrogenated," it isn't.

The reason that no other kind of oil is as good, regardless of what the label says about "polyunsaturates," is that it is produced in a way that renders it nutritionally useless. Processed food in general is bad for this reason. Here's the story.

As it happens, wherever vitamin F occurs in nature, usually in grains, vitamin E can be found also. Vitamin E prevents vitamin F from combining with oxygen in the air and becoming rancid. Most vitamin E is contained in the germ of the grain, which is very difficult to work with, so when food is processed, the germ, thus the E, is usually discarded. This leaves the vitamin F prone to becoming rancid very quickly. The part of vitamin F that is beneficial, linoleic acid, is also most likely to become rancid; so to preserve the shelf life of their product, food processors usually extract the linoleic acid, leaving the product drastically reduced in its nutritional value. However, at this point it can still be labeled "rich in polyunsaturates." *But* in addition, as a final measure, a preservative called an antioxidant is added to prevent the remaining F from combining with oxygen.

The problem with this is that the anti-oxidant cannot be separated from the F in the body; the F cannot combine with body substances (pure oxygen and cholesterol) and do its work. It is simply stored as fat, which most of us don't need, or discarded. So food processing, in effect, renders the fatty acid content of a product useless. Grocery stores are full of such products. You may have to resort to a trip to the health food store for your vitamin F needs.

Avoid Shortening, Lard

Now is a good time to urge you to never again touch those solid cooking fats—shortening or lard—or anything that's been cooked in them. They are totally useless as anything but lubricants to keep heated foods from sticking to the pan. They only add pounds. Also, stay away from mineral oil. It absorbs vitamins A, D, E, and K, producing deficiencies.

Avoid rancid fats of any kind. They quickly destroy vitamins A, B, E, and K in food, in the intestine, or in the blood itself. You may think that no one in his right mind would knowingly eat rancid fat, but the truth is, many of us do unknowingly. It's very easy to overlook slight rancidity in bacon fat that's been near the stove for days or in a packaged pie crust mix that's been in your pantry for months. Throw away anything questionable. Keep those unrefined oils you paid so much for in the health food store in the refrigerator.

The best way to ensure adequate intake of vitamin F is to: have salads daily with dressings made from unrefined oils; try munching whole grains, beans, and seeds; cut down on beef and lamb (high saturated fat) and eat more fish and fowl (low saturated fat); and stay away from mineral oil, rancid fats, and processed foods. If you want to be sure, take a supplement rich in linoleic acid, fortified with vitamin E.

XVII

Vitamin H (Biotin):
Trouble with Raw Eggs

Biotin, or vitamin H, is needed in your diet—but in such small quantities that we are all probably getting quite enough of it, at all times. The Vitamin Information Bureau says that the sources of biotin are so "varied and abundant" that biotin deficiency can only arise "under exceptional circumstances, such as treatment with intestinal sulfonamides and poisoning by egg white."

How does one get poisoned by egg white? Not under normal conditions. It is true that people have come to realize that egg yolk is high in cholesterol but that they may eat egg white without worrying about cholesterol content, but few people are likely to eat large quantities of raw egg whites.

Biotin wasn't really isolated and named until 1936. It was discovered that, in addition to obtaining it in food, the body can produce biotin in large quantities in the intestinal flora. The egg-white substance—*raw* egg white, at that—can prevent intestinal biotin from being absorbed by the body. Researchers at the University of Wisconsin reported in the *Journal of Biochemistry* (March, 1937) that experimental animals that had been fed raw egg whites, amounting to about half of their total food intake, began to suffer from baldness, skin trouble, redness of the eyes, ears, paws, and mouth. A study of infants, published by E. Uroma in the *Acta Societatis Medicorum* (1939), who had fed one raw egg daily to forty-eight babies between the ages of one week and seven months, showed that only two infants developed eczema on the face and neck, which lasted a few weeks.

In 1942, researchers at the University of Georgia's School of Medicine used seven volunteers, who were given no biotin whatever in their diets. They consumed only refined rice, flour and farina, refined sugar, lard, butter, and beef. They also received a complement of vitamins and minerals—except biotin. About one-third of their food was raw egg white. Four of the volunteers stayed on this mixture, and by the fourth week their skins had developed scaliness, by the seventh week one of them had a skin rash and eruptions on neck, hands, arms, and legs. By the eighth week, all the human volunteers had been drained of color of their skins and mucous membranes, and their skins were very scaly.

By the tenth week, their emotions began to be affected. According to a report in *Science* (February 13, 1942), every one of them suffered from "depression which progressed to extreme lassitude, sleepiness and in one instance, a mild case of panic. All experienced muscle pains, excessive sensitivity to touch and localized sensations such as numbness, tingling and 'pins-and-needles.' After the tenth week they began to lose their appetites and feel nauseated. Two of the volunteers complained of distress around their hearts, and an electrocardiogram revealed that their hearts were not normal. The blood of all showed a decrease in hemoglobin (the red pigment that carries oxygen to the cells) and in red blood corpuscles, even though their diet was planned to prevent anemia. The cholesterol content of their blood was also very high. When biotin was given to them, the symptoms disappeared within several days."

A Mysterious Vitamin

Why should egg whites be harmful? Several theories have been put forth, but it is not known why this should be a law of nature. One supposition is that it is a means of preventing eggs from being eaten by other animals before the young can develop, and thus keeps up the bird population. However, animals fed this substance in experiments showed no signs of refusing it as harmful.

Biotin remains a somewhat mysterious vitamin, whose full power and properties have only recently come under examination. It is possible that further discoveries will be made, leading to new uses for this substance. The connection between biotin and the genetic factor RNA, in particular, could have far-reaching consequences when fully understood. The association of biotin and the rate of metabolism, too, could prove important to medical science.

For the average person, biotin is one vitamin that is unlikely to be missing from the diet. During mental, physical, or emotional stress, larger amounts of all B vitamins are needed. However, even in this situation it is very unlikely that any deficiency of biotin would occur.

XVIII

Vitamin K: Needed for Blood Clotting

The five-day-old baby had been under Dr. Herbert J. Goldman's care for dehydration, caused by diarrhea. The New York pediatrician put the infant on a milk-substitute diet, but a week later the baby had convulsions and a tendency to bleed. Could the child, of all things, suffer from a vitamin K deficiency? Dr. Goldman was aware that such a deficiency is regarded as extremely rare. Still, as reported in *Family Health* (March, 1973), he "decided to trust his instinct—fortunately so." After a week of vitamin K therapy, all the symptoms of disorder had disappeared.

Since that time, the magazine reported, Goldman has treated scores of other babies suffering from what he calls "one of the most overlooked diseases of infancy: vitamin K deficiency." Dr. Goldman keeps in mind that diet and intestinal flora are "man's major sources of K," and when the body's natural production center of the vitamin, the flora of the intestines, is "knocked out of commission by diarrhea or antibiotics and there isn't a corresponding increase in the diet, there is unquestionably a very real likelihood that a vitamin K deficiency will result."

Vitamin K is added to substitutes that are used, in place of milk, for dehydrated babies. But Dr. Goldman feels that a great deal of K deficiency goes unnoticed, in infants as well as adults. He regards this as a worldwide problem that hasn't been recognized as such. Goldman said, "I'm trying to stimulate awareness of the idea. I believe it's vitally important that a daily minimum requirement of vitamin K be discovered and set as soon as possible." The United States Recommended Daily Allowances, published by the Food and Drug Administration in 1973, do not include vitamin K, presumably on the assumption that enough of the vitamin is available in commonly used foods.

Why do we need K? The case of the dehydrated baby illustrates the need. When it lacked the vitamin, it bled and apparently the bleeding was not easily controlled. When a cut or wound bleeds without quickly drying up at the skin level, lack of vitamin K may well be the cause.

When we cut ourselves with a clumsily handled knife or razor, we are not unduly alarmed to see blood flowing from a small wound in our flesh. We mop up the blood with a tissue, calmly stick a Band-Aid over the cut, and that is that. Even if we haven't got a Band-Aid available, we know the bleeding will stop in a minute or two and we take this whole fortunate process very much for granted. But why should our blood, running through our veins in a liquid state, coagulate on exposure to the air outside the body and form a sort of seal or stopper that allows the healing process to begin? None of the workings of our bodies are haphazard or random and the coagulating process is no exception to this rule. The blood contains two ingredients, known as prothrombin and thromboplastin, that combine with calcium to make the enzyme thrombin. Thrombin then reacts to yet another constituent of the blood, fibrinogen, and this leads to clotting. Coagulation is possible only when all these substances are present in the blood.

In 1935 a Danish scientist, Henrik Dam, discovered the fact that vitamin K was necessary in order to produce prothrombin, and that without prothrombin blood clotting could not take place. The reason that the vitamin was given the name of K is that coagulation is spelled *Koagulation* in Danish. From that time on, new discoveries were made about vitamin K each year, but a great deal is still unknown regarding its properties.

Normal Body Product

One of the most important discoveries has been the fact that vitamin K is normally produced in our bodies by our intestinal bacteria regardless of the amount supplied in the diet. This means that normally healthy people do not have to worry whether they are obtaining vitamin K or not, as their own bodies are supplying it. After vitamin K is produced in the intestine, the bile acts upon it to absorb the substance along with soluble fats. The vitamin then passes to the liver, which manufactures the necessary blood coagulant factor. However, there are some internal conditions in which vitamin K cannot be produced automatically by the liver.

First, if, because of jaundice, gallstones, or other defects, the liver is not producing enough bile, then vitamin K cannot be absorbed.

Second, if the walls of the intestines are damaged as a result of bad attacks of diarrhea or colitis, then again absorption is hindered.

Third, when a liver is diseased and thus not able to function properly, then there is difficulty in forming thrombin.

And, finally, there is the action of antibiotics, which are used more and more against infections and viruses. These antibiotics temporarily kill off all bacteria, including the helpful bacteria in the intestines, and so prevent the formation of the blood-clotting vitamin.

Early experiments were carried out on chicks, since birds, unlike human beings and animals, take vitamin K directly from their food instead of manufacturing it in their bodies. First it was found that chicks fed on a diet containing dried skim milk, hog-liver fat, and green leafy vegetables did not begin to hemorrhage when metal tags were put on their legs. At the University of California, two researchers, Walter Holst and Everett

Halbrook, further discovered that when fishmeal (usually fed to chicks) was left to putrefy, bacteria could be taken from it that caused intense blood-clotting activity. By 1939 two kinds of vitamin K had been produced: K_1 from alfalfa and K_2 from the putrefied fishmeal.

Hemorrhage is also very common in newborn babies, because of their thin capillaries. This tragic cause of death in the newborn was written up in a medical treatise as far back as 1694. In 1937, Drs. K. M. Brinkhouse, E. D. Warner, and H. P. Smith discovered that although when a child is born the prothrombin is usually at a normal level, it then decreases very quickly and stays at a dangerously low level for several days. During this time bacteria are developing in the intestine, which will then be able to synthesize vitamin K. When a baby has diarrhea or other gastric trouble, the danger of hemorrhage becomes greater if bacteria-killing drugs are administered. As a result of these discoveries, tiny doses of vitamin K are now automatically given to newborn babies.

Pediatrics (November, 1969) contained a report by Dr. Herbert J. Goldman, with Peter Amadio, on hemorrhages in babies who were at least ten days old. They found that a combination of lack of vitamin K in the diet and slow-developing bacteria in the intestine led to this uncontrollable bleeding. They also found that even tiny hemorrhages in babies could affect important parts of the body such as the brain. The result of their research was a recommendation that 10 micrograms of vitamin K per kilogram of body weight be present in the baby's diet.

Thirty-one Babies

In *The Lancet* of February 24, 1951, there appeared a report of an experiment in which thirty-one mothers were given vitamin K before their babies were born. In every case the prothrombin level of these infants was as high as that of a baby given vitamin K after birth. This was a very important step forward, since giving vitamin K directly to newborn babies can cause a disease called kernicterus. The vitamin K that had been given via the mother was believed to have had all the dangerous elements filtered out by the placenta. Again, according to *The Lancet,* in 1942, Dr. Pancher wrote, "It can be definitely stated that if oral preparations of vitamin K are given to a normal pregnant woman 12 to 24 hours before she goes into labor, or if vitamin K is administered daily before delivery, the prothrombin time of the infant will be normal and there will be no untoward effects on the mother."

It was also found that infants suffering from liver damage and thus producing reduced amounts of vitamin K did better on cow's milk (which has 6 micrograms of vitamin K per liter) than on human milk (which has only 1.5 micrograms of vitamin K per liter). Much more vitamin K is needed during times of fast growth, and of course, a child grows more rapidly during the first year than at any other time.

Pregnant women have also benefited from treatment with vitamin K. In November, 1952, an article in *The Practitioner* reported an experiment designed to prevent vomiting and nausea caused by a factor in the placenta of pregnant women. Seventy women suffering from these symptoms were given 5 milligrams of vitamin K and 23 milligrams of vitamin C daily. After only seventy-two hours of this treatment, sixty-four of them were completely free of symptoms, three still felt nauseated, and three showed no improvement. It was noted in this experiment that the two vitamins, C and K, had to be given together in order to obtain any results. As a result, doctors now recommend that pregnant women keep up their supplies of vitamin K by eating a diet rich in the natural vitamin as found in green leaves, spinach, alfalfa, and green cabbage.

Vitamin K has proved to be of great assistance in heart conditions, where anticoagulant drugs are much used to prevent blood clots. These blood clots could shut off the flow of blood to the heart, but the drugs taken to prevent them often present a danger of hemorrhage. In March, 1964, the *Journal of the American Medical Association* recorded an experiment involving a group of heart patients. These patients, all of whom were taking anticoagulant drugs, were given large amounts of spinach and other green vegetables. After two weeks "free prothrombin had returned to normal," and the risks caused by the anticoagulants had disappeared.

Dr. Armand Quick, of Marquette University, reported, "While it is well-known that vitamin K given by injection strikingly reverses the action of the coumarin (anticoagulant) drugs, the effect of the vitamin content of the diet has been given little consideration." Now that anticoagulant drugs are being prescribed more and more frequently, we see that there is a great need for more knowledge about vitamin K. It is vital to ensure that the diet of heart victims is adequate enough to provide this vitamin.

The condition of high blood pressure, or hypertension, is, of course, related to heart disease. According to the *Proceedings of the Society for Experimental Medicine and Biology* (March, 1944) rats, put into a state of hypertension by artificial means, were used in an experiment. It was found that when they were given vitamin K their blood pressure was lowered in much the same way as it was when kidney extract was administered.

Against Snakebite

Vitamin K is useful in treating snakebite. Although most of us are unlikely to be bitten by the snake called the American pit viper, we would find, if we were, that the venom was very dangerous. As it traveled through our veins it would act in the same way as a strong anticoagulant drug and cause hemorrhaging. Vitamin K given to these snakebite victims prevents the venom from having possibly fatal results.

Another most interesting role vitamin K can play is that of a painkiller. During experiments on mice, Yugoslavian researchers found that vitamin K has a more calming effect than morphine. They then gave 20 to 30 milligrams of vitamin K, by injection, to 115 patients suffering from terminal cancers. An amazing 75 percent of these patients declared themselves completely free of pain.

Further experiments were made with a compound of vitamin K in radioactive form. A total of 102 patients with inoperable cancers were given the substance and positive results were obtained. The cells of the tumors absorbed the radioactive compounds and the life of the patients was much prolonged, especially those suffering from cancer of the bronchial tubes.

Science (1940) reported the possibility of a link between cancer prevention and levels of prothrombin. Coal tar, known to induce cancer, was completely neutralized by prothrombin. Heavy smokers, therefore, should give some thought to the amount of vitamin K provided by their daily diets.

Older persons, in particular those with serious disease, are very likely to be lacking in vitamin K. An experiment on these lines was carried out by two researchers, K. Hazell and K. H. Baloch, at St. Mary's Hospital, Colchester, England (*Gerontologia Clinica* [*Basel*], 1970). They first examined 110 patients whose ages were from 56 to 100 years, measuring the level of prothrombin in their bloodstreams. They then found that eighty-one of these aged people had lower-than-normal ability to coagulate blood. They gave all the patients vitamin K and after two weeks all except nineteen had improved considerably. The nineteen old people who did not improve were not able to absorb the vitamin K properly because of liver damage, or because they were taking bacteria-destroying drugs.

In 1938 Drs. H. R. Butt, A. M. Snell, and A. E. Osterberg of the Mayo Clinic made an investigation into the treatment of patients who had had operations for obstructions of the bile duct. This operation is very often followed by hemorrhage, and massive blood transfusions are usually needed. They gave eighteen such patients 200 milligrams of vitamin K and 75 to 100 cubic centimeters of bile mixed with pineapple juice daily, both before and after the operations. There were no incidents of hemorrhage after these operations had been performed, which was very unusual.

Preserving Food

Another interesting property of vitamin K is that it can preserve food without affecting its taste. It is completely nontoxic, in contrast to sulfur dioxide, which is often used for food preservation. Also in contrast to this substance, vitamin K has no odor, does not produce a strong gas, keeps its strength for months, and does not alter the color of fruits and berries. It would seem that the commercial world of food manufacturers might do well to look into this aspect of vitamin K.

How much vitamin K does a normal person need? In 1967, P. G. Frick, G. Riedler, and H. Brogli (*Journal of Applied Physiology,* 1967) gave vitamin K to four patients who had a deficiency of this substance, in order to find out how much was needed for blood coagulation. "The minimum daily requirement was taken as that dose of vitamin K which elicited a sustained elevation of clotting factors sensitive to vitamin K. This effect was achieved by a dose of 0.03 milligrams of vitamin K_1 per kilogram of body weight."

However, synthetic vitamin K can be toxic in large doses, and for this reason, it is a vitamin that should be taken only under strict medical supervision. Since it concerns such a vital area as your blood and whether it will clot too quickly and cut off supplies to the heart, or too slowly with the resultant danger of hemorrhage, no risks should be taken.

In any case it seems that natural foods can provide you with all the vitamin K you need. Dr. John Udall, of Phoenix, Arizona, reported in the *Journal of the American Medical Association* (October 11, 1965) on an experiment carried out with a group of volunteers. He gave them a diet of polished rice, black coffee, sugar, and a multivitamin tablet for three weeks. Their blood-clotting time rose appreciably. When he added liver and spinach to their menu their prothrombin time fell almost to normal. Dr. Udall writes, "Foods, rather than bacterial synthesis, probably provide most vitamin K for humans."

All this means that in certain conditions you should take particular care to see that vitamin K is contained in your diet. These who are taking strong drugs of any kind should be wary, especially if they are elderly. Two doctors, Hazell and Baloch, have said, "Antibiotics should not be used for long periods in the elderly without a thrombo-test being given. Anticoagulant therapy, in particular, is extremely risky and extremely unstable when factors are present suggesting vitamin K deficiency. Careful consideration should be given to all these factors before using anticoagulant drugs in patients over 60, and the sooner they are abandoned in the elderly, the better." Even aspirins can affect your vitamin K production, and you don't have to be elderly to suffer from taking a prolonged course of antibiotics.

In any case of excessive bleeding, which often shows up first as bruising, you should consult your doctor, and possibly have a thrombo test made. But if you just want to keep your blood-clotting mechanism working smoothly, and you are in normal health, then see that you get sufficient quantities of vitamin K in your diet. And that means ensuring that you eat plenty of fresh vegetables, especially spinach and other leafy green vegetables, pork liver, and egg yolk.

XIX

Vitamin P (Bioflavonoids):
A Taste for Orange Peel

Vitamin P is really a complex of nutrients called the "bioflavonoids." Some of these are "rutin," "citrin," and "hesperidin." But at this point, so little is known about them individually that there is no need for you to learn all their names. Some researchers suspect that the good effects of the bioflavonoids are not due to themselves alone but to some other as yet undiscovered nutrient associated with them. Research with this complex is still in its infancy, and it may be some years before we know the story.

A curious thing about vitamin P is that wherever it occurs in nature vitamin C can be found also. This is one reason some people argue for natural vitamins as opposed to synthetic ones. In this case, when you buy natural vitamin C, you also get vitamin P, which is not the case when you buy synthetic vitamin C. It may be no accident that the two occur together in nature.

There are a number of ailments that neither vitamin C nor vitamin P can help very much if given singly, but the two may work wonders if given together. An example of this is capillary fragility, a condition in which the walls of the body's millions of tiny veins become weak and are apt to collapse, or hemorrhage, causing sometimes serious internal bleeding.

There have been a couple of studies in which vitamins C and P have been given together to prevent miscarriages due to capillary fragility. Women who had never been able to carry their children and bring them into the world alive have had successful pregnancies and deliveries when given enough of these two vitamins. But these are isolated cases, and medical scientists are reluctant to generalize from them.

Certain heart and vascular diseases cause the blood to "coagulate," or clot, too easily; so patients with such disorders are given drugs called "anticoagulants." The problem with these drugs is that they may cause hemorrhaging in some patients. In one study, when patients who were hemorrhaging because of anticoagulants were given vitamins P and C, the hemorrhaging areas cleared up quickly.

The most encouraging research with vitamin P has been done with the common cold and influenza. Drs. Morton S. Biskind and William C. Martin published in the *American Journal of Digestive Diseases* (July, 1954) a study done with a number of people with various grades of these kinds of infections. They found that in almost every case doses of vitamin P and C together speeded up recovery. The optimum dosage of vitamin P, they feel, is 200 milligrams three times a day. They also believe that the vitamin is effective no matter at what stage of the infection dosage is started.

Watch That Orange!

The next time you eat an orange, try not to peel away the white skin and segment part of the fruit, because that's where the vitamin P is. If you don't eat fresh citrus (rose hips, lemons, apricots, black currants, grapes, grapefruit, cherries, blackberries, cabbage, plums, parsley, or prunes), you may get no vitamin P at all, because it occurs only in these and, in small amounts, in a few other foods.

Technically, the term *vitamin P* is outdated. The Joint Committee on Biochemical Nomenclature of the American Society of Biological Chemists and the

American Institute of Nutrition have decided that *bio-flavonoid* is more appropriate; however, the letters of the alphabet have a known image, and the term vitamin P continues to be used. Dr. Philip L. White, nutrition authority of the American Medical Association, says in his book *Let's Talk About Food* that "to date, there is no evidence that the nutrient is required by man" and that "no significant therapeutic effects of this vitamin have been discovered and confirmed."

XX

The Very Latest: U.S. RDA

What's that you're eating? What's in it? Will it add up to a proper daily vitamin and mineral intake?

You should be able to answer these questions as the food industry complies with the latest rules of the Food and Drug Administration. One by one, the food packers are putting labels on the packages you find on super-market and grocery shelves, showing the nutritional composition of each product. These figures are on small segments of the label that the FDA calls "information panels" and should usually be found "immediately to the right of the principal display panel," which gives you the name and category of the food, as well as such data as weight.

The FDA announcement on new labeling appeared in the *Federal Register* (January 19, 1973). It made it clear that compliance is up to the individual marketer. "Except for some standardized foods," the FDA said, "the decision to add a vitamin or mineral to or make a nutritional claim for a food is entirely voluntary." Still, considering that nutrition information is something the consumer wants to have, competition in the food industry makes it likely that most major companies will tell you what vitamins their products contain.

The FDA insists that producers should be specific

when they do make a nutritional claim. It doesn't like it when a company simply says it has "added" such and such a vitamin. In effect, the FDA says, "If so, how much?" It wants the food company to either give detailed figures or not make any nutritional claims at all. Here is the passage from the FDA ruling, although you may have to read it twice to understand it fully:

"The Commissioner has therefore concluded that, when a nutrient is added to a food, e.g., the addition of vitamin C to a breakfast drink, or a claim or information with respect to a nutritional properties of a food is included in labeling or advertising, e.g., the amount of vitamin C in orange juice, or the fact that orange juice is a good source of vitamin C, or a general or specific reference to the caloric or fat content, or any other representation that a food is useful in the daily diet because of any of the nutrient qualities covered in this regulation, the full nutrition labeling established in this regulation must be utilized."

Got that? The companies shouldn't just say something like "vitamin C added," but should say how much has been added. The FDA regards incomplete claims as "confusing or misleading." Such claims could "deceive" us about "the true nutritional value of the food, its overall nutritional contribution to the daily diet, and its nutritional weaknesses as well as strengths." Rather pointedly, the FDA adds: "A manufacturer who does not wish to use nutrition labeling need not add nutrients to his products or refer to their nutritional properties in labeling or advertising."

The FDA also decided to abandon the MDR, or Minimum Daily Requirements. As we have noted in earlier chapters, the MDRs are just enough to keep the average person from getting scurvy, beriberi, or any of the other serious illnesses caused by vitamin deficiency. The FDA considers the MDRs "outdated" and the old Recommended Daily Allowance (RDA) as too complicated and not really useful to non-average people, such as infants and pregnant women. We now have new standards: the United States Recommended Daily Allowances, or U.S. RDA.

The FDA also acknowledges that biotin, pantothenic acid, copper, and zinc "are now recognized as essential to human nutrition." This is a point that such pioneer researchers as Henry A. Schroeder, M.D., who wrote the Introduction to this volume, have been pressing for a number of years. The FDA adds that these four vitamins and minerals are "so widely distributed in conventional foods that it would be difficult to select a diet in which they would be deficient," but that they are essential and therefore included "as optional nutrients in dietary supplements" and should be listed on labels.

Negative Labeling

None of this is final, because research continues and new findings are accepted year after year. For this reason, the FDA's conclusions will be "amended periodically" to conform with "major changes that may be made" in the U.S. RDA values of the National Academy of Sciences and the National Research Council. When the FDA held hearings to get the view of the food industry and of consumer groups, it found the industry resistant to food labels that would say that certain nutrients were "not present." Some consumer representatives would have liked such "negative labeling" to show how empty of nutrients some foods really are. The FDA decided that where there is just a fraction of a nutrient in a food, the package should state that it "contains less than 2 per cent of the U.S. RDA of . . ." This would apply to any of seven nutrients.

A special problem arises with manufactured foods that are usually eaten together with something else—such as a breakfast cereal that is commonly mixed with milk or fruit. The cereal itself may have little nutritional value, acting more or less as the depository of something more nutritious. Some manufacturers would have preferred saying only what vitamins and minerals are in their product once it has been mixed with something else, rather than reveal the bareness of its nutrition value. The FDA decided that they should say both: with and without the admixtures.

As the Pillsbury Company was among the manufacturers who sought to comply with the FDA labeling concept immediately, they provided several examples of such labeling. One of these is the mix for a banana cake. The "information panel" on the Pillsbury Banana Cake Mix box says that it "provides you with energy," and adds: "Serve with a glass of milk for more protein, minerals, and vitamins, or top with your favorite ice cream." Under the heading "Nutrition Information," right underneath this suggestion, you can read the following: "When prepared according to the suggested basic recipe, each serving (3-inch square) of unfrosted cake contains approximately the following nutritional values: Calories 200, Protein 3 GMS, Fat 5 GMS, Carbohydrate 35 GMS, Sodium 290 MGS." The abbreviations refer to grams and milligrams. Underneath these figures the label says, "Percent of Recommended Daily Allowance ** per serving," and this refers to a table that looks as follows:

	Mix	Prepared with Eggs and Water
Protein	*	5
Vitamin A	*	*
Vitamin C	*	*
Thiamine (B_1)	5	5
Riboflavin (B_2)	*	5
Niacin	*	*
Calcium	*	*
Iron	*	*
Phosphorus	5	5

The label explains the stars on the package as follows: " *Insignificant quantity; less than 5% RDA. **Standard Recommended Daily Dietary Allowance adopted by U.S. Food and Drug Administration." As you can see, the Pillsbury people made up these boxes on the basis of a 5 percent rather than a 2 percent minimum of a nutrient, and based on the old RDA instead of the new U.S. RDA. The chart shows that the mix, by itself, contains only 5 percent of the RDA of B_1 and 5 percent of phosphorus. When you add egg and water, you get an additional 5 percent protein and 5 percent riboflavin. Small wonder they tell you to drink a glass of milk with the cake, or put some ice cream on it, if you want more proteins, minerals, and vitamins. Incidentally, if you look at the list of "Contents" in this so-called Banana Cake Mix, you will find no bananas listed. Instead, it says, "Artificial Flavoring and Artificial Coloring." Underneath the large letters of Banana Cake Mix, it says, "Artificially Flavored."

Yes, They Have No Bananas!

In other words, it really is a Cake Mix with Artificial Banana Flavor. If it had real banana in it, you'd also have more vitamins. One banana contains between 200 and 250 IU of vitamin A, between 25 and 30 IU of vitamin B_1, close to 1 milligram of vitamin B_2, and 6 to 8 milligrams of vitamin C. To really make the cake mix nutritious, you could, of course, cut a banana into it!

Now, back to the FDA's rules and regulations. It notes that "some foods currently available to consumers have added nutrients at levels of 50 percent or more of the U.S. RDA per serving, are promoted as a form of dietary supplements," and should therefore show labels "as related to vitamins, as well as conforming to the requirements of nutrition labeling relating to nutrients other than vitamins and minerals." The Commission received comments on the "possible abuse of nutrition labeling by the use of labeling claims for specific properties of a food in the prevention or treatment of diseases or disorders, or suggesting that conventional foods in the U.S. diet, as usually prepared, are different and better than vitamins chemically produced or in isolated form."

On these rather crucial questions, the Commission concludes that a food would be violating its rulings if its labeling "represents, suggests or implies" the following:

"1. That the food, because of the presence or absense of certain dietary properties, is adequate or effective in the prevention, cure, mitigation, or treatment of any disease or symptom.

"2. That a diet of ordinary foods cannot supply adequate amounts of nutrients.

"3. That the lack of optimum nutritive quality of a food, by reason of the soil on which that food was grown, is or may be responsible for an inadequacy or deficiency in the quality of the daily diet.

"4. That the storage, transportation, processing, or cooking of a food is or may be responsible for an inadequacy or deficiency in the quality of diets.

"5. That the food has dietary properties when such properties are of no significant value or need in human nutrition. Over the years there have been a number of ingredients or products marketed as nutrients and nutritional supplements which have not been shown to be essential in human nutrition. This point was discussed in considerable detail during the 1968–70 Special Dietary Food Hearings. Among ingredients or products of this type are rutin, other bioflavonoids, para-aminobenzoic acid, inositol, and similar ingredients or products. These ingredients or products have frequently been combined with vitamins and minerals or otherwise represented as a type of nutritional supplement. In these situations, there is a false representation that these ingredients or products have nutritional value. The Commissioner has concluded that for ingredients or products of this type there may not properly be made direct or implied nutritional claims, and that in no instances can these ingredients or products be represented in any way that suggests a nutritional value. Combining these ingredients or products with added vitamins and/or minerals in any food, or adding these ingredients to any food for which nutrition labeling is used, or calling attention to these ingredients or products in a manner which would be considered to imply some nutritional benefit, is inherently misleading. Labeling of such ingredients or products may not state that their usefulness in human nutrition has not been established or otherwise disclaim dietary or therapeutic value since such statements are also misleading. The Commissioner recognizes that there are individuals who desire to purchase ingredients or products of this type for various reasons. These individuals have a right to obtain these ingredients or products as long as they are truthfully labeled. Thus, ingredients or products of this type may properly be marketed as individual ingredients or products or mixtures thereof, provided that no nutritional or dietary supplement claims or disclaimers are made.

"6. That a natural vitamin in a food is superior to an added vitamin, or to differentiate in any way between vitamins naturally present from those added."

If you have read this book this far, you know by now that these views of the Food and Drug Administration are, at least in part, being challenged by some prominent people in the nutrition field. The FDA says that among items that have "not been shown to be essential in human nutrition" are "rutin, other bioflavonoids, para-aminobenzoic acid, inositol, and similar ingredients or products." But it also grants people "the right to obtain" them as long as they are "truthfully" labeled. We have quoted the FDA's six points in full, because they are important. It is not clear, for instance, whether the fourth point is a basic conclusion of the FDA, or whether it only does not like to see labels that suggest that foods lose nutritional value in storage, transportation, processing, or cooking. True, the FDA is mainly concerned with labeling, in this instance, but nutritional losses from the farm to the dinner plate would seem to be too firmly established to be in doubt.

In setting down labeling standards, the FDA rules that protein content is to be listed first, followed by information on vitamin A, vitamin C, thiamine, riboflavin, niacin, calcium, and iron, in that order. The statement adds: "The following U.S. Recommended Daily Allowances (U.S. RDA) and nomenclature are established for these vitamins and minerals, essential in human nutrition:

Vitamin A, 5,000 International Units.
Vitamin C, 60 milligrams.[1]
Thiamine, 1.5 milligrams.[1]
Riboflavin, 1.7 milligrams.[1]
Niacin, 20 milligrams.
Calcium, 1.0 gram.
Iron, 18 milligrams.
Vitamin D, 400 International Units.
Vitamin E, 30 International Units.
Vitamin B_6, 2.0 milligrams.
Folic acid, 0.4 milligram.[1]
Vitamin B_{12}, 6 micrograms.
Phosphorus, 1.0 gram.
Iodine, 150 micrograms.
Magnesium, 400 milligrams.
Zinc, 15 milligrams.
Copper, 2 milligrams.
Biotin, 0.3 milligram.
Pantothenic acid, 10 milligrams.

[1] The following synonyms may be added in parentheses immediately following the name of the vitamin:

Vitamin	Synonym
Vitamin C	Ascorbic acid.
Folic acid	Folacin.
Riboflavin	Vitamin B_2.
Thiamine	Vitamin B_1.

The FDA does not want a manufacturer to claim that a food is "a significant source of a nutrient" unless this nutrient is present in the food at a level of at least 10 percent of the U.S. RDA in a serving. Also, a food should not be claimed to be "nutritionally superior" to another food, unless it contains at least 10 percent of the U.S. RDA of "the claimed nutrient" per serving.

Definitions of Standards

In its obvious effort to standardize and police the production, sale, and promotion of vitamin supplements, the FDA applies what it calls "Definitions and Standards of Identity for Food for Special Dietary Uses." These dietary supplements may come in powdered, granular, or flake form, or in the physical form of conventional foods. They "purport to be or are represented" to supplement the human diet "by increasing dietary intake of one or more of the essential vitamins and/or minerals" listed by the FDA. They should either be "all vitamins and minerals," or "all vitamins," or "all minerals," or "all vitamins and the mineral iron." There are special references to vitamin D, biotin, pantothenic acid, copper, and zinc. Liquid vitamins that don't contain folic acid should specifically say so.

On p. 174 is the table the FDA has drawn up as "permissive qualitative and quantitative composition of dietary supplements of vitamins and/or minerals":

If nothing else, the Food and Drug Administration's initiative has served to alert the food industry to the need for telling the public what, exactly, our foods consist of. It is now up to us to check the things we buy and to act as our own expert guides. Surveys of supermarkets that engage in unit pricing (which enables the consumer to compare prices and quantities of one unit with another) have shown that the so-called "educated" and "affluent" are more likely to buy carefully than others. Be that as it may, a woman with a baby in her shopping cart, one kid tugging at her skirt, and the third roaming through the aisles has little time to look at percentage figures in small print. But when she gets home, she should take time out to look at labels carefully: The health of her family is in her hands. She may do better, next time.

The FDA says over and over again that the standards it sets are subject to revision, as the Federal Nutrition Board gains new insights into our nutritional needs. But we are, after all, responsible for our own health. It is good that Washington tries to help, establishes labeling standards that are fairly uniform and understandable—but the final decision is yours.

U.S. GOVERNMENT RECOMMENDED DAILY ALLOWANCES (U.S. RDA's) AND PERMISSIBLE COMPOSITIONAL RANGES FOR DIETARY SUPPLEMENTS OF VITAMINS AND MINERALS

Unit of measurement	Infants and children under 4 years of age			Adults and children 4 or more years of age			Pregnant or lactating women		
	Lower limit	U.S. RDA	Upper limit	Lower limit	U.S. RDA	Upper limit	Lower limit	U.S. RDA	Upper limit
Vitamins, mandatory:									
Vitamin A ------- International units	1,250	2,500	2,500	2,500	5,000	5,000	5,000	8,000	8,000
Vitamin D[1] ------- do	200	400	400				400	400	400
Vitamin E ------- do	5.0	10	15	15	30	45	30	30	60
Vitamin C ------- Milligrams	20	40	60	30	60	90	60	60	120
Folic acid[2] ------- do	0.1	0.2	0.3	0.2	0.4	0.4	0.4	0.8	0.8
Thiamine ------- do	0.35	0.7	1.05	0.75	1.5	2.25	1.7	1.7	3.0
Riboflavin ------- do	0.4	0.8	1.2	0.8	1.7	2.6	1.7	2.0	3.4
Niacin ------- do	4.5	9.0	13.5	10	20	30	20	20	40
Vitamin B6 ------- do	0.35	0.7	1.05	1.0	2.0	3.0	2.0	2.5	4.0
Vitamin B12 ------- Micrograms	1.5	3	4.5	3	6	9	2.6	8	12
Optional:									
Vitamin D ------- International units				200	400	400			
Biotin ------- Milligrams	0.08	0.15	0.22	0.15	0.3	0.45	0.3	0.3	0.6
Pantothenic acid ------- do	2.5	5.0	7.5	5.0	10	15	10	10	20
Minerals, mandatory:									
Calcium ------- Grams	0.125	0.8	1.2	0.125	1.0	1.5	0.125	1.3	2.0
Phosphorus[3] ------- do	0.125	0.8	1.2	0.125	1.0	1.5	0.125	1.3	2.0
Iodine ------- Micrograms	35	70	105	75	150	225	150	150	300
Iron ------- Milligrams	5.0	10	15	9.0	18	27	18	18	60
Magnesium ------- do	40	200	300	100	400	600	100	450	800
Optional:									
Phosphorus ------- Grams									
Copper ------- Milligrams	0.5	1.0	1.5	1.0	2.0	3.0	1.0	2.0	4.0
Zinc ------- do	4.0	8.0	12	7.5	15	22.5	7.5	15	30

1 Optional for adults and children 4 or more years of age.
2 Optional for liquid products.
3 Optional for pregnant or lactating women.

XXI

Adding It All Up: Your Vitamin ABC

Most of us know about vitamins from TV commercials that say "with vitamin D added" or talk in general terms about foods that have been "enriched" with vitamins. Friends have their favorite vitamins; cosmetics now come with vitamin E; and A, B, C, or other letters of the alphabet appear on labels of multivitamin tablets and other products. Then there are strange-sounding names for vitamins that appear without alphabet identification and often sound rather forbidding, such as folic acid and pantothenic acid.

On the next few pages you will find an alphabetic listing of major vitamins, together with identification. This is not a complete list, because there are vitamins that for one reason or another have not gained much prominence outside biochemical laboratories. This is simply a listing, for quick reference, of the vitamins that have been discussed in separate chapters of this volume.

VITAMIN A. Among the functions of vitamin A is the maintenance of the body's thin coverings, the membranes, including the skin. People used to associate vitamin A with night vision, saying, "Eat plenty of carrots, so you can see in the dark!" It is quite true that carrots contain the kind of carotene that goes to make up vitamin A, and lack of it can cause inability to adapt to dim light. The vitamin is needed for the health of the outer membrane of our eyes, just as it is needed in the mucous linings of the gastrointestinal and urinary tracts, bones, teeth, hair, gums, and several glands.

Your best sources of vitamin A are not only carrots but all yellow and green leafy vegetables. Among the dark green vegetables that should be in your diet to make sure you are getting vitamin A, as well as other vitamins and minerals, are spinach, kale, chard, turnip greens, mustard greens, brussels sprouts, broccoli, and kale. Beet greens generally are a good source of the vitamins. Among yellow vegetables and fruits that contain vitamin A are squash, rutabagas, sweet potatoes, pumpkins, apricots, and cantaloupes. It is also contained in butter or margarine, egg yolk, liver, and milk.

VITAMIN B COMPLEX. We have become so used to associating the word *complex* with something complicated or unwieldy (a complex problem, a building complex, an Oedipus complex) that it would be better to call this category simply the "B vitamin group," because that's what it is. The trouble started when scientists thought they had found just one vitamin they could call B, but then discovered that it was a whole group of vitamins. So they started to number them, dividing them up into subcategories that now have such labels as "acid" this or "acid" that, or "factor" this or that. We'll take them one by one.

VITAMIN B₁ (THIAMINE). When modern eating habits prompted people to discard the thin film covering from such grains as rice, they became ill with beriberi. This disease, which still occurs in the Orient and among severely malnourished populations elsewhere, emaciates people, makes their legs grow numb and their calf muscles painful. They may grow partially paralyzed, and their hearts suffer. In another form of this illness, the body swells up. When you see photographs of starving children's bodies, these often show symptoms of beriberi. White sugar, refined flour, and polished rice have vitamin B_1 refined out of them and must therefore get it back later by being "enriched." No one is likely to get beriberi in the United States these days, but there are earlier symptoms of B_1 deficiency.

You get vitamin A in whole-grain, enriched bread and cereals, as well as in brewers' yeast, fish, lean meats, and such foods as liver, kidneys, sweetbreads, poultry, pork, milk, peanuts, and lentils.

VITAMIN B_2 (RIBOFLAVIN). Vitamin B_2 enables the body to utilize fats, proteins, and carbohydrates. It aids in releasing energy to body cells. When it is lacking, skin and tongue are likely to be affected, and possibly the eye, which can become itchy and bloodshot. Persistent cracks at the corner of the mouth may be due to lack of vitamin B_2.

You get B_2 in whole-grain, enriched bread and cereals, in the best greens we've listed under vitamin A, in brewers' yeast, liver, lean meats, eggs, green leafy vegetables, and in milk.

VITAMIN B_3 (NIACIN). The body needs vitamin B_3 to avoid pellagra, which affects the central nervous system, the skin, and the gastrointestinal tract. Various forms of subclinical pellagra seem to occur when there is a lack of niacin. These may be psychological or physiological in nature. Experimental and individual treatment of seemingly retarded children has involved relatively high doses of the vitamin, and it is being used in the treatment of some schizophrenics.

Niacin is to be found in green leafy vegetables, fish, lean meats, milk, wheat germ, brewers' yeast, kidney, liver, and eggs.

VITAMIN B_5 (PANTOTHENIC ACID). This vitamin has many functions designed to help us withstand stress. It is required for the formation of certain hormones and nerve-regulating substances. As an aid to body metabolism, it functions in the changeover of proteins, fats, and carbohydrates to meet the body's molecular needs. B_5 is needed to maintain the proper level of blood sugar. In recent years, much attention has been paid to hypoglycemia cases (instances of low blood sugar), and some of these may be due to lack of pantothenic acid. Among the vitamin's functions in stress resistance is maintaining the body's ability to counteract infections and to resist low temperatures.

Vitamin B_5 is found in green leafy vegetables, eggs, nuts, liver and kidneys, lean meats, poultry, potatoes, and tomatoes.

VITAMIN B_6 (PYRIDOXINE). Vitamin B_6 plays a key role in assuring a chemical balance in blood and tissue. It influences the body's metabolism, particularly in the formation of certain proteins and the utilization of fats. Pyridoxine assists in the smooth functioning of the nervous system and helps retain salt and water balances within the body. When B_6 is lacking in infants, symptoms may include convulsive seizures. In adults, a pyridoxine deficiency may result in a variety of symptoms, including emotional fluctuations and loss of hair. One of the key functions of B_6 is control of the cholesterol level.

You get B_6 in green leafy vegetables, lean meats, whole-grain cereals, soybeans, wheat, liver, eggs, milk, and nuts.

VITAMIN B_{12}. Vitamin B_{12} is essential in the treatment of pernicious anemia and is thought to be important for growth. It helps in the building of vital genetic substances, the nucleic acids, for the cell nucleus and in the formation of red blood cells. B_{12} aids the body's utilization of proteins, fats, and carbohydrates. When the vitamin is used in the treatment of anemia, it has to be injected, as the illness is linked to an inability of the body to absorb B_{12}.

Vegetarians, who avoid meat and fish, run the risk of vitamin B_{12} deficiency, because it is mainly found in foods of animal origin. Its major sources include beef, liver, kidney, saltwater fish, oysters, and milk.

FOLIC ACID. Like several other vitamins, folic acid acts best in conjunction with related nutrients. It is useful in fighting pernicious anemia, but most effective when functioning together with vitamin B_{12}. It plays an important part in the body's use of substances that contain carbon, one of the most important elements in organic molecules. Folic acid is essential for the function of the four oil-soluble vitamins, A, D, E, and K. Basically, aid in forming certain body proteins and genetic materials for the cell nucleus is the overall role of folic acid.

We get folic acid, as we do many other nutrients, in green leafy vegetables, but also to a high degree in liver. Milk and meat are also good sources of this vitamin.

CHOLINE, which belongs to the B complex, is needed by the body in such large quantities that some people doubt whether it should be regarded as a vitamin at all. Biochemists and nutritionists really don't know very much about it. They assume that people get enough of it, or of the nutrients that the body can turn into choline, not to have to worry too much about it. The body uses choline to take fat deposits and put them to use; it also facilitates the use of certain amino acids in the body and is required in liver development and to repair kidney damage.

You get choline from organ meats, such as liver, in egg yolk, peanuts and peanut butter, whole grains, green leafy vegetables, and various seeds.

INOSITOL, like choline, is as yet little explored in human body chemistry. Lack of it causes loss of hair, at least in experimental animals, and it may have some significance for human hair growth as well. It appears to be useful in resisting cirrhosis of the liver. Inositol interacts well with other vitamins, such as E.

The foods that give you choline in most cases also provide inositol; it can also be found in many fruits, including those of the citrus family.

VITAMIN C is a vitamin of major importance. Although it has received a great deal of publicity because of its apparent use in checking the common cold among some people, that is far from exhausting its uses. It helps to hold the body's cells together; strengthens blood vessels and thus, among other things, checks internal bleeding; is effective in wound healing; and aids in maintaining the solidity of bones and teeth.

Major sources of vitamin C are oranges, grapefruit, lemons, and limes. It is also present in green leafy vegetables, in broccoli, cauliflower, cantaloupe, strawberries, apples, tomatoes, and potatoes.

VITAMIN D is traditionally known for preventing rickets in children. But it generally functions in the body's use of calcium and phosphorus in building bones and teeth. Vitamin D is added to milk, so that children will get a sufficient supply: It is known as the "sunshine vitamin," because our body absorbs it from the ultraviolet rays of sunlight. We do not get enough sun on our bodies, in temperate zones, to go without substantial D in our diet.

In addition to enriched milk and enriched cereals, vitamin D is available in egg yolk, liver, fish-liver oils (including cod-liver oil), and in such oily fish as herring, salmon, and canned tuna.

VITAMIN E, another major vitamin, may well serve a crucial function in keeping the blood supply flowing through the heart, by benefiting the condition of the blood itself as well as of the arteries that carry it. As it is found in all body tissues, it is obviously essential to their health and function: to muscle cells, and to a general control of the unsaturated fatty acids in our diet; it counteracts rancidity in fats.

Corn oil, cottonseed oil, wheat germ, and peanuts

are among sources of the E vitamin. It is also present in whole-grain cereals.

VITAMIN F. Into this category fall the so-called "essential fatty acids," which are: linoleic acid, linolenic acid, and arachidonic acid. If you can't spell them, pronounce them, or tell them apart, don't worry! But do remember that they are essential to provide the body with fats in a manner that can be nutritionally well utilized. If you lack them, your skin will get dry, and you will be bothered with acne, eczema, and possibly more serious disorders.

As the role of these acids is specific and complex, but relatively little known, make sure to read the chapter on vitamin F. Meanwhile, when you buy vegetable oils, be sure the label reads "cold-pressed, dehydrogenated," not just "polyunsaturated." The best sources are safflower, corn, soybean, cottonseed, peanut, and wheat germ oils.

VITAMIN H (BIOTIN) is essential in the workings of the body's chemical systems, with the specific ability to synthesize the lipids (fats) in the liver. It has been labeled the "anti-egg-white-injury factor," because it neutralizes the effect of avidin, found in egg whites and capable of creating severe allergies. Biotin works to provide energy from the metabolism of glucose (sugar). Severe deficiency can cause a variety of physical and emotional symptoms, ranging from loss of hair to feelings of depression.

You get biotin in green leafy vegetables, eggs, liver, and kidney, as well as in meats.

VITAMIN K. The function of vitamin K is easy to understand: it is essential for the clotting of blood. Without it, our blood would keep flowing from any cut or wound; with it, the flow dries up, clots, heals over. Vitamin K helps the liver to develop a protein named prothrombin, which eventually turns into the fiber required to create a blood clot. Outright K deficiency is thought to be rare, although some new-born babies may need an extra dose of the vitamin.

Our trusted standbys, the green leafy vegetables, are sources of vitamin K. It can also be found in root vegetables, cauliflower, and various fruits and seeds.

VITAMIN P is a catchall name for the bioflavonoids. We know about as little about them as we do about choline and inositol. Vitamin P is found with vitamin C, and the two seem to operate in tandem in such actions as strengthening blood vessels. The partnership between C and P may carry over into preventing the common cold and influenza, but knowledge of this field, too, is limited.

Vitamin P is present in a select group of fruits and vegetables. There include the citrus fruits, apricots, cherries, blackberries, grapes, black currants, plums, and prunes, as well as cabbage and parsley.

XXII

You've Got to Look Out for Yourself!

Well, what does it all add up to? From 1955 to 1970, the number of Americans eating a good diet had dropped by 10 percent. The figure is based on a study by the U.S. Department of Agriculture, and its standards are probably more lenient than those of strict nutritionists. I am not assuming that you, the readers of this book, are actually among those who are eating a poor diet. But none of us has completely escaped, for ourselves or other members of our family, the trend away from fresh fruits and vegetables toward the multitude of snacks, soft drinks, frankfurters, and other convenience foods.

Of course, we can't devote our lives to constant measuring of nutrients, spending our days in nutritional self-consciousness. A milligram here, a milligram there —it gets to be a nuisance to ourselves and others. What does count is getting into basically good eating habits. We've just got to be our own masters when it comes to picking food. This simply calls for a maturity and independence of mind that go counter to many TV ads, lures in the supermarket, and all those luscious sweets and refreshing drinks.

We are still the prisoners of an age that not only regarded cleanliness as next to godliness, but felt sure that the only good food is one that has been thoroughly boiled. One summer I found a can of sour cherries on a kitchen shelf; leading a summer bachelor's life, I decided to eat it, although it was leaking—a dangerous sign. I emptied the cherries into a pan and boiled them unmercifully. Then I let them cool down and placed them in the freezer section of the refrigerator. There they stayed for at least a week. Then I began to eat the cherries as a frozen desert. What I had done, of course, was to kill just about every vitamin that had remained in the can, together, as I can now testify, with any dangerous bacteria that might have been lurking in the can.

Must You Boil It?

If we want to eat right, we must deal more gently with vegetables and fruits. We should put such things as raw cauliflower and spinach leaves into our salads, because the vegetables we boil lose vitamin content with every water bubble that rises to the top of the pot. At the same time, we can't avoid washing vegetables and fruit, because remnants of pesticides might be on an apple. We are forced to perform a daily juggling act between what is nutritionally desirable and what is possible.

Throughout this book, I have said that the best way to get your vitamins is in the food itself, not in pills or tablets. Still, many of us have reached the point when we frankly doubt those easy reassurances that we need no supplements if we eat a "balanced diet." Chances are we just can't eat a balanced diet, given the production and distribution methods of the food industry and storage and cooking methods in our own homes. In Appendix A to this book, you will find the full text of an industry memorandum on handling, storing, and preparing fresh fruits and vegetables. One of the points quoted in it is the three Rs: Reduce the amount of water used in cooking vegetables and fruits, reduce the length of the cooking period, and reduce the amount of surface area exposed. Vitamins escape food as quickly and sneakily as a cat winding its way through a partly opened door to the backyard. You have to be alert to keep vitamins trapped in your food.

Modern civilization has given us convenience, accessibility, and variety in foods—at the cost of their nutritional value. The University of New Mexico in Albuquerque, in a survey announced December 10, 1972, found that parts of the native Indian population were malnourished because they, too, had been caught up in food technology. William Elliott, director of the University's nutrition improvement program, reported that "Indian native foods, when consumed in their natural form, such as kernels of corn leached with lime and ground to make bread or tortillas, are quite nutritional." The trouble starts when these foods are commercialized. When the Indians abandon "their indigenous staples for convenience foods," Elliott said, "the nutritional value goes way down and health suffers."

We have all heard, over and over again, that the stresses of modern civilization are responsible for a good deal that plagues our physical and mental health. Our bodies and minds just haven't had a chance to adapt to the rapid changes imposed by contemporary living patterns. In food, this is even more obvious. We have seen that vitamin C is being produced in the bodies of most animals, including our house pets. Except for the big apes and a few odd creatures, man is the only one who has to consume vitamin C constantly to keep his body supplied. The big apes can, to this day, reach up and get an orange off a tree and so get vitamin C in its natural state. Only we can't, because we have migrated north in the relatively short period of human history—give or take a few tens of thousands of years.

But the really big change in human nutrition came, in terms of man's existence, practically yesterday afternoon: during the last century, or even just the past fifty years. Of course, the conquest of illness had a great deal to do with it. Louis Pasteur (1822–1895), the brilliant French chemist, discovered that bacteria floating around in the air could cause milk fermentation. Now we have "pasteurization," which enables us to store milk without its going sour. Also during the last century, medicine was faced with ravaging cholera epidemics that traveled from Asia to Europe and North America. One of the ways in which cholera is transmitted is in raw food, and we have inherited from our grandparents the attitude that raw meats, fish, and vegetables are somehow unclean.

Pure, Not Sterile

When you destroy bacteria, you are likely to destroy vitamins with them, and so we are faced with the dilemma of keeping our food pure but not sterilized into a state of zero nutrition. We are indebted to primitive man for butter, because making it was his trick of preserving milk. Otherwise, the old methods of keeping food were drying, salting, or smoking. Vitamins disappear rapidly with such preservation methods. As fruits and vegetables are at their best, most attractive, and most nutritious just before they are ready to wilt, go bad, and eventually decompose, they have a relatively short span of being just right and good to eat.

Basically, anything that doesn't spoil rather quickly has, so to speak, been immunized. This is certainly true of bread produced by factory-type bakeries. If you get fresh bread from a neighborhood baker who does not add chemicals against spoilage, keep it in the refrigerator (wrapped carefully so it doesn't dry out too fast). Generally speaking, get your food fresh, don't let it lie around too long, and do only a little boiling, sautéing, steaming, or whatever before eating it. Things kept in a freezer don't lose vitamins quickly, but you may find that their taste suffers. Again: look at Appendix A, which deals with fruits and vegetables.

Getting into the habit of guarding against vitamin deterioration of foods will probably take you a while. Still, it can become a conditioned reflex, like looking left and right before crossing a street; and it, too, is life-preserving. Now we come to the tricky question of vitamin supplements to your diet, even that "balanced diet" we're supposedly eating in these enlightened days. Should you, or shouldn't you?

With due respect to those authorities who still tell us that we'd get all the vitamins we need if we only ate just right, let us not shy away from taking vitamin supplements, in addition to daily foods, in moderate amounts. Large doses, or megavitamins, are not so much a nutritional as a therapeutic factor. You shouldn't try to imitate the megavitamin therapists by self-medication. You will just have to try and find a physician who is nutrition oriented, should you feel the need to deal with an apparent vitamin deficiency on a long-term, professional basis. It may take a good deal of effort on your part to find a doctor who has the knowledge and insight to see vitamins in the same light as do some advanced nutritionists.

The AMA Position

Appendix G of this book contains the full text of a statement by the American Medical Association, together with a table of the Recommended Daily Allowances prepared by the Food and Nutrition Board. The AMA statement is extremely cautious, but you should read it, nevertheless, with objective attention. It goes counter to many of the arguments I have cited throughout this book; yet, as laymen, we must listen to both sides of the argument with equal alertness: it is our health that is at stake, and we can't ignore an argument between sincere professionals.

The AMA statement on *Vitamin Supplements and Their Correct Use* (Appendix F) says that "a diet selected from the variety of foods available can supply all the vitamins a person needs." Available where? To whom? To Americans on all levels of society, income, education, and geographical location? Next, the AMA tells us that the Recommended Daily Allowances "are daily nutrient intakes recommended to assure good

nutritional status in healthy persons." Of course, these
are vague phrases. It would be difficult to define someone's "good" nutritional status precisely, or to say just
what, exactly, is meant by a "healthy" person. Our own
personal health changes constantly—if not from week
to week, certainly from month to month and year to
year.

Do read the AMA's suggestions concerning use of
the four food groups: the milk group, the meat group,
the vegetable-fruit group, and the bread-cereals group.
The medical association states, again in a very general
way, that "an adequate intake of vitamins is assured
when one consumes a proper variety of foods in
sufficient amounts." Of course, if you eat the right
quantities of the proper food, you'll be all right! But
we have become aware that modern food processing
and storing can severely reduce the vitamin content of
the food we eat. The AMA concedes that "there might
be times" when "supplementation is necessary." It
adds:

"Supplementation is useful when a person is unable
or unwilling to consume an adequate diet, as during
illness, allergy, or emotional upsets. Vitamin supplementation augments the diet but does not replace it.
The physician is trained to determine the most beneficial supplement and also to help the patient remove
disturbing factors causing poor eating habits."

The AMA is an association of doctors, and you can't
blame them for suggesting that the doctor knows best
what's good for you. Nutrition, however, is an everyday activity, and one would have to be old-time
royalty, with a court physician always in attendance,
to live up to the demand that our food and vitamin
intake be constantly guided by a doctor. Most doctors
are likely to regard anyone who takes such advice
literally as a nutritional hypochondriac, a waiting-
room addict, a pest.

The AMA has further words of caution, which you
can find in Appendix F. They particularly warn
against too much vitamin A; we have spoken of this
before. They also caution against too much vitamin

D. And again, the AMA says: "The decision to employ vitamin preparations in therapeutic amounts clearly rests with the physician." They seem to regard as "therapeutic" any amount of vitamins that exceeds the Recommended Daily Allowances. Yet, to use these RDAs and assume that any variation above them can only be made at a doctor's suggestion doesn't seem realistic. The RDAs are based on average needs, and you and I aren't average—that is a statistical, across-the-board formula. Roger J. Williams writes in *Nutrition Against Disease* that "if we think in terms of 'average' diet we might infer that everyone gets more than the minimum daily requirement of every known nutrient." He refers specifically to the RDAs, pointing out that "too little is known about the variations in human needs for specific nutrients."

Minerals Are Essential, Too

Because I set out to answer the question "Which vitamins do you need?" in writing this book, I have not included material on minerals. As it is, the names and numbers of all the known vitamins are enough to tax the average person's memory. But minerals are an essential part of nutrition. The foods we have discussed, such as the fresh fruits and vegetables, include a variety of needed minerals. The U.S. Recommended Daily Allowances list the major minerals: calcium, phosphorus, iodine, iron, and magnesium as "mandatory" and phosphorus, copper, and zinc as "optional." You will find them in well-rounded multiple-vitamin tablets. Basically, what goes for vitamins also goes for minerals: eat those green vegetables every day— raw, if you can manage, or cooked as little as possible; eggs and nuts are among good mineral sources.

There is one basic theme we need to emphasize in this final chapter: *practice preventive medicine through proper nutrition*. The word *medicine* actually does not fit into this context. It sort of smells of disinfectant. What we need to do more of is simply to live right. And that calls for a much better understanding of the relationship of the things we eat to our physical and mental well-being. If you look at the word *disease,* you will see that it originally meant "dis-ease," lack of "ease" or of a general relaxed well-being. The basic idea is not to need medication, to keep the "dis" out of "disease," to use common sense in food and drink.

But common sense is a rare commodity. We have permitted ourselves to accept standards of food consumption that are a foolish kind of social climbing. The rare steak has become the food equivalent of the Lincoln Continental, the smoke-filled nightclub, and the fashionable shoe that is likely to distort your bones. Isn't it curious that we look upon the drink-in-hand and cigarette-in-mouth image as something worth imitating, when we know full well that alcohol and nicotine are poisonous? The French aristocracy, eager to dramatize its distinction from the peasant masses, began to cover its foods with fancier, more and more intricate sauces. Anyone who would have admitted that, in a sauce with twenty-three ingredients, your taste buds are totally lost would have been disdained as some low-life country bumpkin. Because of quirks in culinary culture, these overbred sauces became symbols of that much revered *haute cuisine,* which, among other things, cooks large amounts of vitamins out of everything it touches. This is the very opposite of good French country cooking—where you may get a piece of fresh fish from the nearby brook, done in equally fresh country butter, with a glorious and enticing fresh salad on the side.

The vitamins you need, in other words, are part of your life-style. Not caviar, but dark green leafy vegetables are the height of sophistication. As we have moved away from the basics of life, and into year-round air-controlled houses and offices, so we have moved away from the foods that come from natural and healthy soil. This is something we must learn ourselves and pass on to our children.

How can we teach our youngsters the need for vitamins, for good nutrition, for that elusive aim, a "balanced diet"? The schools aren't doing it. They don't teach children how to change a fuse or why a savings bank pays 5 percent interest; nothing as practical as nutrition, certainly. Homer's *Odyssey* is shoved down their reluctant throats, but the everyday task of properly selecting and preparing foods is way down the line somewhere. There is no use lecturing children on their eating habits, either. If their crowd goes for pizzas and cola drinks, that's what they'll eat. Chances are that forcing green leafy vegetables on them will turn them away for life.

What can we do? We can set a good example, that's what we can do. Without fuss, without lectures. Later, they may come to look back on Ma's cooking with nostalgia: those wonderful salads, the rich and ripe tomatoes in slices with a touch of oregano, the string beans cooked so that they had some of that crunchiness left, the bowl of fruit out in the hall, just asking to be raided! Certainly, there is a strong trend toward health foods of all sorts, toward organically grown foods. There is new nutrition conciousness. But it is important for these things to be more than passing fads—a basic attitude, a vitamin awareness must develop that will become conditioned, automatic, second nature.

Eating right is a delicate high-wire act. The Medical Establishment stands on one end of the trapeze and the vitamin hucksters on the other. Then we also have to put up with friends, neighbors, relatives, restaurants, airlines, TV commercials, supermarkets, and others who pull us back and forth. Still, eating right need not be a constant battle. To become vitamin conditioned should be no more difficult than learning to drive a car. After a while, you no longer know precisely why you are selecting one kind of food over another, cook it this way instead of that way. When you drive a car, you exercise exactly the kind of automatic judgment you need in eating right.

Beware the Vitamin Freak

There's also no sense in becoming a nutrition addict,

a Vitamin Freak. Being aware of vitamins should be a natural part of living, like getting dressed or taking a bath. It isn't a religion, although the passion with which the pro- and antivitamin partisans argue sometimes resembles religious fanaticism. At the beginning of this book I quoted a Food and Drug Administration poll that spoke of people who think vitamins will give them more pep, making it sound as if vitamins were pep pills. True, there are occasionally claims that a vitamin will give new zing to your sex life. To the degree that sexuality is part of general health and well-being, nutrition does have an effect on it. But claims for sexy vitamins are usually based on some unromantic laboratory experiment that showed rats having trouble breeding when a particular vitamin was removed from their food. Exaggerated claims are about as bad as uninformed negation. The vitamin freak and the vitamin bore are part of our society right now, but that merely illustrates that everything can be a passing fad, including the simple art of eating.

It is regrettable that the nutrition controversy has driven a wedge between people and their doctors. We don't really gain much by disillusionment with the medical profession. They do know more about diseases than we do; it's their job. Unfortunately, medical schools teach young doctors more and more about technology and research and little about men, women, and children. I have talked to several young doctors who became so disillusioned by the lack of human contact in everyday medicine that they went into psychiatry. I wonder, of course, whether psychiatric training by now includes courses in the biochemistry of human emotions. The impact of nutrition on the human mind is an embattled research frontier.

One doctor, an M.D. in psychiatry, surprised me recently when he said that patients are beginning to have a strong impact on medicine. I had been under the impression that most people are cowed by their doctors, reluctant to take up their high-priced time, and afraid to look foolish when they ask questions or make suggestions. Are individual doctors, or the medical profession as a whole, really becoming responsive to their patients' ideas? If so, we are coming full circle. In Old China, doctors undertook to keep their patients well, while we are heirs to a European tradition that put physicians into a superior social position from which to cure rather than prevent ills. The four stages—complaint, diagnosis, treatment, and cure—are standard in therapy. Prevention is far less dramatic than successful treatment through medication or surgery. As patients, we frequently do not even adhere to the obvious pattern of seeing our dentist twice a year, and annual checkups have grown more prevalent but far from universal among business executives.

Primitive man and people on certain social levels today appear to live so much in the present that they cannot plan the future. This shows up in their handling of delicate machinery: they seem to have little sense of continuity, of the need for constant maintenance (such as lubrication), of anticipating that equipment wears out and should be repaired or replaced before it brings the whole mechanism to a halt.

Although most of us have developed a maintenance-conscious approach to our automobiles, with regular tune-ups and checkups, we often abuse the machinery of our body until it creaks and groans. And then we run to the doctor. Living sensibly, above all eating sensibly, is certainly something most of us have yet to learn. In Germany, an experimental chain of preventive examination clinics closed down in 1972 for two reasons: the patients' ingrained habit of waiting until they became ill, and the medical profession's lack of enthusiasm for the concept behind these clinics. No doctor, we may be sure, prefers people to be sick instead of healthy, but the medical profession doesn't really put much emphasis on health education, including nutrition, and other aspects of prevention.

Every Time You Lift a Fork

In the end, it is up to you to look out for yourself. Your life is in your own hands, every day: every time you cross the street and, to a lesser degree, every time you lift a fork or spoon to your mouth. Although doctors can help you, it is you who selects the doctor, tells him your symptoms, adheres to his instructions and medications correctly or incorrectly. The extent to which people will take pills improperly is astonishing. They may neglect them in the morning, and then take more in the evening. They are forever acting on the assumption that if a little does some good, twice as much will be doubly health giving. One statistical observer of the pill scene has concluded that some people will take any kind of pill, as long as it hasn't been prescribed.

Vitamin pills have certainly been overused, or used wrongly by many people. The main reason is, of course, the incredible jungle of different brands, combinations, and doses in vitamins on the market. I hope that the information on categories and doses, provided earlier in the book, will help you avoid pitfalls. The most important decision concerning vitamin supplementation of your food is selection of a well-constituted multivitamin. Those on the market vary greatly in combinations and dosage, but there are widely marketed multivitamins that have much in common. Here is the kind of formula you may want to aim for:

Vitamin A 10,000 USP Units
Vitamin D 400 USP Units
Vitamin B_1 (thiamine) 2 milligrams
Vitamin B_2 (riboflavin) 3 milligrams
Vitamin B_3 (niacinamide) 100 milligrams
Vitamin B_6 (pyridoxine) 2 milligrams
Vitamin B (pantothenate) 20 milligrams
Vitamin B_{12} (cyanocobalamin) 5 micrograms
Choline 100 milligrams
Inositol 100 milligrams
Vitamin C (ascorbic acid) 100 milligrams
Vitamin E (tocopherol) 100 milligrams

Many well-rounded multivitamin capsules also contain a cross section of minerals. Vitamin E may not be found in standard multivitamin capsules, and certainly not in doses advocated by such authorities as Drs. Evan and Wilfred Shute. Similarly, vitamin C is likely to be found in capsules in doses of 50 milligrams or less. If you wish to add these or others, on top of what should be a general diet rich in vitamins and minerals, you should certainly, regardless of the controversial nature of vitamin supplements, consult a nutrition-minded physician. Check with your doctor to make sure vitamin D is all right for you.

This kind of regimen is a form of insurance. It is no substitute for the complex chemical combinations found in foods. There may even be vitamins or other nutrients in foods that have not yet been isolated. That is the most convincing argument against dependence on vitamin pills. Still, if you look upon your well-rounded multivitamin as a sort of insurance, to which you may wish to add, on your physician's advice, then you are on firm ground. Because that's what it all comes down to: the maintance of a healthy body through nutrition, with vitamins used as insurance against the body's chemical reactions to modern food technology.

XXIII

How to Read the Vitamin Labels

You have by now read a lot about vitamins and know pretty well what each does for you and what its absence could do to you. You are convinced that, for the sake of your family's health, you need to pay closer attention to their daily vitamin intake.

You've taken the time to go over your week's menus and figured out what you can expect everyone to get from the food you prepare. By now, the meals you serve are better balanced than they've been in the past. Everyone will get plenty of protein from the meats, fish, cheese, eggs, and milk you've included, and a good start on the required vitamins from fresh green and yellow vegetables, fruits, whole grains, and oils.

But even with the well-balanced meals, you're concerned that the family may still not be getting enough. How long were those fruits and vegetables around before they got into your shopping cart? What if there is some preservative you can't avoid? And anyway, the U.S. Recommended Daily Allowances may not go far toward overcoming present deficiencies and ensuring good health. And what about your husband's night blindness and your son's acne? Can you do something about them? You decide a trip to the local health food store for supplements is in order.

But don't go unprepared, or you may find it a confusing and frustrating experience. It takes some knowledge of standard measures and abbreviations to read a label intelligently and in terms of your family's nutritional needs. The worst pitfall of vitamin shopping is the bewildering variety of ways of measuring vitamins. For instance, B_1 is usually sold in "mg.," B_{12} in "mcg.," D in "USP," and E in "IU." It seems wild, but there are good reasons for it.

Activity and Quantity

Vitamins are measured by two standards: activity and quantity. Vitamins A, D, and E are measured by activity, and the reason is that different forms of each carry different potencies—physical quantity has no bearing on how strong a dose is. Activity is measured in two units: International Unit (IU) and United States Pharmacopoeia Units (USP). The difference between the two is so small that you can use the two units interchangeably.

Other vitamins are measured by quantity because they have standard strengths. There are two ways of measuring quantity: the metric and the apothecaries' systems. The metric system is based on meters (distance), liters (liquid), and grams (weight). We're concerned with the gram: a microgram, used to measure vitamins of which we need only microscopic traces (for instance, B_{12} and biotin), is equal to 1/1,000,000 gram; a milligram, used to measure vitamins of which we need moderate doses (like B_1 and B_2), is equal to 1/1,000 gram. Larger dosages are measured by the apothecaries' system. The unit most often used in vitamin labeling is the grain (gram), equal to about 65 milligrams or 1/15 gram. Liquids, such as wheat germ oil, are usually measured in the apothecaries' system too, and the unit most often used is the minim (min.), equal to about one drop of water.

Keeping all these bases of measurement straight will at first be quite a chore. You may have to take this book along to remember it all, but with practice it will become easier. You should make your own list: all you need to know is the total amount of vitamins (and minerals) necessary each day and the amount you expect to get from foods. The difference is what you need to buy in the form of supplements. Remember that no amount of supplements takes the place of sensible eating.

Other abbreviations you have to deal with are MDR, AMDR, and U.S. RDA. MDR and AMDR stand for, respectively, Minimum Daily Requirement and Adult Minimum Daily Requirement. These are minimum averages set by the government, which, it is estimated, will ensure protection from deficiency (probably not an accurate estimate of how much you should take, since none of us is average and most of us want more than minimum protection). RDA, or Recommended Daily Allowance, is a more generous estimation of what you need to maintain good health. There are vitamins and minerals for which neither MDR nor RDA has been established, but there surely is need for them. These have been superseded by the U.S. RDA, first announced in 1973, but it may take a while before everyone has become aware of this.

No doubt you will be confronted with the terms *organic, natural, artificial,* and *synthetic. Organic* and *natural* are almost synonymous. A natural product is part of the make-up of plant or animal matter, and if it is also organic, it was produced without use of man-made chemical fertilizers or preservatives in any form at any stage of production. Artificial substances are those that are not found in nature and are foreign to our bodies and food. Synthetic substances are those produced in the laboratory and may be either natural or artificial or a combination.

What Is "Organic"?

A note of caution about the word "organic" as it applies to fresh fruits and vegetables. Inspection of some foods sold with this label has shown that even carefully grown produce may contain residual pesticides and chemical fertilizers. No matter how careful a grower may be, chemicals used by a neighboring farmer can, through wind or water, find their way to his crops.

The argument for synthetic vitamins is that they are cheaper. The argument for natural vitamins is that they are more likely to contain additional, as-yet-unisolated nutrients. You must decide which is more important to you.

What about economy? There are a couple of rules of thumb. Concentrates of A and D are inexpensive, while concentrates of B and C cost a good deal. If you buy a preparation containing all, you are likely to be buying a large amount of A and D and a small amount of B and C. Also, it is not really to your advantage to stock up on vitamins during a sale. Most have a shelf life of about six months and, after opening, should be refrigerated for preservation. It serves no purpose to save money by buying a lot, only to have your supplements lose potency before you can use them.

Abbreviations, Weights, Measures

Although the terms, abbreviations, and figures you encounter on food and supplement labels may, at first glance, look confusing, you will find that there are actually only a few·of them, and these are constantly used. As you may want to tear out this page we have nothing printed on the back.

Abbreviations

U.S. RDA	United States Government Recommended Daily Allowance
RDA	Recommended Daily Allowance (superseded by U.S. RDA)
MDR	Minimum Daily Requirement (superseded by U.S. RDA)
USP Unit	United States Pharmacopoeia Unit of Measurement
IU	International Unit of Measurement (established by League of Nations)
mg.	milligram; 1,000th of a gram
mcg.	microgram; 1,000th of a milligram
gm.	gram
gr.	grain

Conversion Factors
1 gram equals 15.4 grains
1 grain equals 0.065 grams (65 milligrams)
1 ounce apothecary equals 31.1 grams
1 fluid ounce equals 29.6 cc.
1 fluid ounce equals 480 minims

Metric Measures
1 kilogram equals 1,000 grams
1 gram (gm.) equals 1,000 milligrams (mg.)
1 milligram equals 1/1,000th part of a gram
1 microgram equals 1/1,000th part of a milligram
1 gamma equals 1 microgram

Avoirdupois Weights
16 ounces equal 1 pound
7,000 grains equal 1 pound
453.6 grams equal 1 pound
1 ounce avdp. equals 437.5 grains
1 ounce avdp. equals 28.35 grams

Liquid Measures
1 drop equals 1 minim
1 minim equals 0.06 cc.
15 minims equals 1.0 cc.
4 cc. equals 1 fluid dram
30 cc. equals 1 fluid ounce

Household Measures
1 teaspoon (tsp.) equals 4 cc. equals 1⅓ fluid dram
1 tablespoon (tbsp.) equals 15 cc. equals ½ fluid ounce
½ pint equals 240 cc. equals 8 fluid ounces

APPENDICES

A. How to Preserve the Vitamins in Fresh Fruits and Vegetables

This text, prepared for the United Fresh Fruit and Vegetables Association by R. A. Seeling, was originally published under the title "Conserving Nutrients in Handling, Storing and Preparing Fresh Fruits and Vegetables." It contains general information on vitamin maintenance, trimming, temperature control, and ripening, as well as specific instructions on how to handle and prepare individual categories of fruits and vegetables. The text is reprinted here by the Association's permission.

The nutritive value of fruits and vegetables is not measured by their cost or the quantity brought home but on how much of the food purchased is actually eaten and the nutrients this portion contains. Nutrients begin to be lost as soon as fruits and vegetables are harvested, and whether or not they are processed, although in exceptional instances, there is an actual increase in certain nutrients in the fresh, still living, unit. There are ways of keeping losses to a minimum and especially of insuring the preservation of a high percentage of the ascorbic acid (vitamin C) and carotene (pro-vitamin A) of which fruits and vegetables are the principal dietary sources. They supply more than 92%

of the vitamin C and 59% of vitamin A, as well as many other nutrients including iron and folic acid. This report deals only with conserving nutrients in the fresh products.

Enemies of the Nutrients

The enemies of fruit and vegetable nutrients—generally speaking—are time (because if there are losses, they usually are progressive with time), heat, enzyme activity, invading micro-organisms, direct contact with water, mechanical or chemical injury of the cellular structure, oxidation, light in some instances, excessively dry environment and waste.

Conversely, factors favorable to conserving nutrients are rapid harvesting, cooling, packing, transporting and marketing; gentle handling; early consumption of purchased produce; use of properly controlled temperatures and humidity until the food is served; avoidance of soaking in water; rapid cooking; use of liquids in which vegetables are cooked; avoidance of light while cooking and also in storing certain vegetables; conservatism in paring and coring; conservatism in chopping and mashing; and preparing amounts fairly close to what will be consumed so there are not large quantities of leftovers.

Freshness and Nutrients Are Companions

A study of the technical literature made for the United Fresh Fruit & Vegetable Association by the medical research firm of L. G. Maison & Co., Chicago, showed that "a close correlation usually holds between good retention of vitamin values of fresh fruits and vegetables and good retention of their quality values (such as color, flavor, aroma and texture). Conditions that make for retention of freshness also make for retention of the vitamins."

It was also concluded that "the deteriorative changes in the fresh fruits and vegetables improperly cared for in the home or in dining establishments may be more serious than the sum total of the deteriorative changes during the entire course of the products from the field to the retail market."

It is evident, therefore, that buying fresh, high quality fruits and vegetables means buying more nutrients per dollar than when poor quality produce is purchased. Buying for quality also conserves nutrients by eliminating or reducing the number of units discarded; and permits use of the product with a minimum of trimming or paring.

Aroused Appetites Avoid Waste

Serving these foods in attractive forms that stimulate the family appetite also saves nutrients by encouraging consumption of what might otherwise be rejected. No matter how many milligrams of vitamins and minerals are in a vegetable, they are useless if the food is so poorly cooked or otherwise prepared that it is left on the plate. Ascorbic acid, the major nutrient in fruits and vegetables, is more subject to loss than any other vitamin or mineral. Therefore, if this vitamin is guarded, it is quite likely other nutrients will be preserved also. While the compound is fairly stable in acid solution, it is readily destroyed under non-acid conditions, especially when heat is applied, which speeds up oxidation. (It should be noted that oxidation does not necessarily require a supply of oxygen, as from air.) To a large extent the vitamin can be conserved by refrigeration under humid conditions; cooking for as short a time as possible or using without cooking; utilizing the cooking water or other liquids in which some of the ascorbic acid would be dissolved; avoiding keeping food hot (as on a steam table) for long periods; avoiding long exposure to air especially when the food has been chopped or mashed, thereby greatly increasing the surface reached by air; and using the produce within a reasonable time. Ascorbic acid is soluble in water as are also the B vitamins.

Vitamin A Oxidized

Vitamin A, on the other hand, is not soluble in water, nor is carotene, the vitamin A precursor, the compound found in fruits and vegetables. Heat, of itself, does not destroy vitamin A but heat and air cause rapid oxidation and destruction. For example, aeration of heated cod liver oil causes complete loss of vitamin A activity. The same safeguards that apply to ascorbic acid apply in general to vitamin A except those that apply to solubility in water.

The minerals are not destroyed by heat and age but though present in their original quantities in an old, withered fruit or vegetable, they are not of value to the purchaser since the item will be discarded. Minerals are water soluble and can be leached out in soaking or cooking. Consequently, an excessive amount of cooking water should not be used; and the cooking liquid should be consumed if palatable.

The Three R's

The three R's of cooking to preserve nutrients, as given by Dr. Bernice K. Watt and associates of U.S. Department of Agriculture are: Reduce the amount of water used; reduce the length of the cooking period; and reduce the amount of surface area exposed.

A Word About Trimming

Trimming of vegetables may be necessary to remove damaged leaves or inedible material, but should be held to a minimum. As a general principle, outer leaves, if good should be used, because they generally are dark green and contain more nutrients than inner leaves. Fibrous parts of leaves such as stems and ribs generally are not only less palatable but have less nutrients than the leaf blade. It is reasonable, therefore, to discard these parts if desired. The leaf blades of collard greens, for instance, have 30 times as much vitamin A as an equal weight of the midrib.

Temperature Control

All fresh fruits and begetables should move to market under temperature control, suited to the particular requirements of each, and most of them are so transported. Conservation of nutrients starts at shipping point when field heat is quickly removed, units are washed or otherwise cleaned, vegetables are trimmed and all are packed and either stored at suitable temperature and humidity or loaded for rapid movement to market. Proper refrigeration is so important that fruits and vegetables shipped long distances under proper temperature conditions are likely to be in better condition and be more nutritious than local commodities sometimes marketed without pre-cooling and subsequent refrigeration.

The table (opposite) provides a broad, general guide on desirable temperature and humidity for specific fruits and vegetables. Since few institutions have enough storage boxes and refrigeration equipment for maintaining a variety of temperatures, all the fruits and vegetables have been split into two groups, the 32° group and the 50° group. There is also a list of commodities requiring special conditions. This data is from a paper "Maintaining the Fresh Quality In Produce in Wholesale Warehouses" by Bogardus and Lutz of USDA in Agricultural Marketing Dec. 1961.

Proper Ripening Is Important

Most non-citrus fruits and most melons may be ripened to eating stage at room temperature, considered to be 65–80° F., then should be refrigerated. Citrus fruits, however, are ripe as received, and can be refrigerated at once. The same is true of grapes. Holding an unripe fruit or melon at low temperature delays ripening. Obviously, if a melon or other fruit is served before it is ready for eating, it will not be liked and the fruit will not be consumed.

In the case of vegetables (other than tomatoes) ripening is not a factor. Keeping vegetables in covered

Maintaining the Fresh Quality in Produce in Wholesale Warehouses

Fresh Fruits

Store at 32° F. and 90% Relative Humidity

Apples	Figs	
Apricots	Grapes	
Blackberries	Nectarines	Pomegranates
Cherries	Oranges	Prunes
Coconuts	Peaches	Quinces
Cranberries	Pears	Raspberries
Dates	Persimmons	Strawberries
Dewberries	Plums	Tangerines

Store at 50° F. and 80-85% Relative Humidity

Avocados	Olives
Grapefruit	Papayas
Lemons	Pineapples
Limes	
Mangoes	
Melons	

Commodities Requiring Special Conditions

Bananas for ripening: 58° to 68° F., 90 to 95% relative humidity.

Bananas, ripe (for holding): 55° to 60° F., 75 to 90% relative humidity.

Fresh Vegetables

Artichokes	Cauliflower	Horseradish	Radishes
Asparagus	Celeriac	Kohlrabi	Rhubarb
Beans, Lima	Celery	Leeks, green	Rutabagas
Beets	Corn, Sweet	Lettuce	Salsify
Broccoli	Endive	Mushrooms	Spinach
Brussels Sprouts	Escarole	Onions, green	Squash
Cabbage	Garlic, dry	Parsnips	*(yellow summer)*
Carrots	Greens *(general)*	Peas, green	Turnips

Beans, green	Okra	Potatoes	Sweet potatoes
Cucumbers	Onions, dry	Pumpkins	Tomatoes *(ripe)*
Eggplants	Peppers, sweet	Squash *(hard shell)*	

Green tomatoes, for ripening: 55° to 70° F., 85 to 90% relative humidity.

Pears, for ripening: 60° to 65° F., 85 to 95% relative humidity.

containers or film bags helps to prevent evaporation and withering.

Data by Commodities

Following is nutrient retention data on various commodities, based on USDA and private studies in our files. Space does not permit listing data on all fruits and vegetables.

FRUITS (general) There has been little or no evidence that fruits lose carotene (pro-vitamin A) in the ordinary processes of handling and marketing where temperature and humidity are controlled and light excluded. Fruits largely retained their ascorbic acid content during 7 to 10 weeks of storage and in some cases much longer.

VEGETABLES (general) Cooked vegetables show losses of ascorbic acid that progress with the length of time that they are kept. They have about 75% as much ascorbic acid after one day in the refrigerator as when freshly cooked. They have about 66% as much after two days. Reheating takes another toll of ascorbic acid, so that cooked vegetables reheated after 2 or 3 days in the refrigerator can be counted on for only 33% to 50% as much ascorbic acid as when freshly prepared.

Green vegetables contain an enzyme which oxidizes the vitamin, but the enzyme only comes into contact with it when the leaves wilt or are crushed. The vitamin will be oxidized, however, even in the absence of the enzyme, when conditions are alkaline or when traces of copper are present. Being water-soluble, vitamin C rapidly diffuses into the cooking water. Vitamin C is best preserved if the vegetable is not allowed to wilt before cooking. It should be cut sufficiently to allow it to be cooked quickly, but not chopped up so fine that the enzyme has easy access to the vitamin. To avoid alkalinity and consequent destruction of vitamin C, soda should not be used.

APPLES stored for 6 months at 32° F. showed virtually

no loss of vitamin C. Storage for 3 months at 45° resulted in loss of about 17% of the vitamin C content, and in 6 months resulted in 25% loss. By contrast, apples stored in a cellar until spring retained only half as much ascorbic acid as apples stored under refrigeration.

ASPARAGUS refrigerated at ice temperature lost less than 20% of its original ascorbic acid in 5 days, whereas when cut and kept in a warm kitchen or in a store without refrigeration, it may lose 50% of its original vitamin C the first day; and by the second day have lost almost 80%.

BANANAS lost some ascorbic acid (sometimes 25%) during ripening as compared with the content of the fully green fruit, but when fully ripe the ascorbic acid remained constant until complete browning of the peel.

BEANS Both snap beans and shelled lima beans retained 90% or more of their original ascorbic acid when refrigerated for a week.

BLUEBERRIES lost 7% of their ascorbic acid in 2 days at 41° F. and 14% in four days.

BROCCOLI cooked quickly in a small amount of water loses only half as much vitamin C as when cooked in excess water. Broccoli retains ascorbic acid well under refrigeration.

CABBAGE is a stable source of ascorbic acid. In cold storage, the whole heads retain 75% or more of their vitamin C as long as six months. It should not be allowed to dry out. The outer dark green leaves are the most nutritious, being high in vitamins, so trimming should be conservative. Cabbage cooked quickly in about a third as much water as cabbage retains nearly 90% of the vitamin C it had when cooking starts, but when cooked in four times as much water as cabbage, it retains less than half of this vitamin.

CANTALOUPES retained almost all their ascorbic acid for seven days in a refrigerator but lost 50% at room temperature. (However, ripen at room temperature.)

CARROTS generally increase in carotene content during storage. There is large loss of ascorbic acid during long storage, but carrots are not important for this vitamin. Carrots showed no marked loss of thiamine even in seven months storage. Removing the tops does not affect the vitamin value of this vegetable.

CITRUS fruits have a high initial content of vitamin C and it is well retained under many conditions. These fruits, when whole, keep well several days without refrigeration. The edible yield of the orange as strained juice is only about 66% to 75% as much as that of the orange eaten by sections. Since citrus fruits are rarely cooked, almost the full amount of the vitamin in the fruits is available, if eaten out of hand.

CORN stored at room temperature lost 45% of its total sugar content in the first 24 hours and an additional 4% in the succeeding 24 hours; but ears stored at 32° were still sweet and in good marketable condition after 10 days. Refrigerated corn lost little or none of its ascorbic acid after 7 days but corn at room temperature lost half its vitamin C after 4 days and in any event was no longer edible.

GREENS of all kinds have a high content of vitamin C and vitamin A. To keep it, they need to be refrigerated near 32°. However, the ordinary household refrigerator may be around 40° in the general food compartment. Tests show that greens refrigerated at 40 to 50° F. for 5 days lost about half their ascorbic acid. The thin part of the leaf may contain 20 times as much vitamin A, many times more vitamin C and 2 to 4 times more iron than the midribs, which are more fibrous and consequently less edible.

LETTUCE The dark green outside leaves have as much as 30 times more vitamin A than the inner bleached leaves, yet the darker leaves may make up only 10% of the weight of a head. So discard only discolored and damaged outer leaves. Lettuce loses ascorbic acid rapidly at room temperature but refrigeration favors retention of the vitamin.

ONIONS stored at not over 55° F. lost no appreciable amount of either ascorbic acid or thiamine in 6 months.

PEARS retain ascorbic acid well. When stored in closed containers near freezing they still had half their original ascorbic acid after 7 months.

PEPPERS retain ascorbic acid well under refrigeration. They may lose only around 10% in a week.

POTATOES retain their most important nutrients quite well outside the refrigerator if kept fairly cool, and inclosed so as to prevent withering. Freshly dug potatoes are highest in ascorbic acid, and immature potatoes have more than those more mature. The loss of ascorbic acid is progressive throughout the storage period, but is most rapid during the early weeks. About half is left after 3 months storage. Potatoes still retain about a third of their original vitamin C after 6 months storage. Chilling potatoes below 40° F. does not impair their nutrient content but causes them to develop an undesirable sweetness. For vitamin C value, potatoes should be freshly cooked. Potatoes baked, broiled or pressure cooked and then stored in a refrigerator for 24 hours contained only about a third of the vitamin C in the freshly baked product.

STRAWBERRIES, an excellent source of ascorbic acid, lose much of it if capped or stemmed, or if their tissue becomes bruised. They should be kept cold, dry and whole to retain maximum nutritive value.

SWEETPOTATOES retain their most important nutrients reasonably well out of the refrigerator if withering is prevented. The carotene content of sweetpotatoes is initially high and increases during the usual period of storage. The carotene content drops gradually after 6 months storage, but few sweetpotatoes are kept that long. Ascorbic acid is lost more rapidly in early months of storage and more slowly later. At the end of 3 months in storage, when about half of the crop has reached the consumer, 50 to 70% of the ascorbic acid remains. By the end of 6 months, 40 to 60% remains.

TOMATOES picked before they turn red develop highest nutritive value at a temperature between 60 and 75° F. which means they should not be refrigerated until all red. Neither should they be exposed to high temperatures, such as 85°. Tomatoes grown outdoors have about twice as much vitamin C as tomatoes grown in greenhouses in winter. In fact green tomatoes just beginning to turn color, if they have been exposed to full sun, may have more vitamin C than red tomatoes ripened with less sunlight. Firm-ripe tomatoes can be held at room temperature for several days, probably a week, without loss of ascorbic acid. They lose vitamin C value rapidly as soon as they become over-ripe. So when ripe, refrigerate. Green fruit has been shown to increase in ascorbic acid as it ripens. Cooking tomatoes causes significant loss of ascorbic acid, and the longer they are cooked, the greater the loss.

B. Vitamins, Minerals, and the FDA

The following article, explaining the U.S. Food and Drug Administration's rulings on vitamins and minerals, appeared in the government agency's magazine FDA Consumer *(September, 1973). The magazine's editors noted that "no program in recent FDA history has generated as vocal a public outcry" as these regulations, and added that "a good deal of the protest is based on misinformation which in turn rose from misinterpretation of the proposals." The article was designed to explain "what the new rules will do, what they won't do, and why they are necessary."*

The Food and Drug Administration has spent the past decade investigating consumer needs and the FDA role in regulating vitamins, minerals, and food supplements. This study included two years of formal hearings on every aspect of the various issues. Industry, science, medicine, and consumers participated.

The FDA has published new regulations based on this study. The FDA aim is to protect the consumer against proven hazards from toxic amounts of nutrients and to require accurate labeling, honest promotion, and rational formulation of vitamins and mineral products. The FDA believes that with full and valid information

214

the consumer will be better able to make informed decisions about personal nutrition practices.

The new regulations have been the subject of much misinformation and some misrepresentation. Here, to set the record straight, is what the Agency is trying to do and why.

FDA's regulations begin with a series of basic definitions:

• The term *"United States Recommended Daily Allowance"* or *U.S. RDA* describes a new and more effective system for measuring human nutritional needs. Based on continuing study for many years by the National Academy of Sciences, the system represents the best available scientific judgments on the daily intake of vitamins and minerals needed to maintain a positive state of health. It replaces the old and generally lower *Minimum Daily Requirement* or *MDR* which was based on the minimum intake necessary to prevent deficiencies and related illness. With adoption of the U.S. RDA standard, the FDA is recommending generally higher daily intake of essential vitamins and minerals.

• Products supplemented with up to 50 percent of the vitamins and minerals needed to maintain health (U.S. RDA) are *general foods.*

• Products supplemented with 50 percent to 150 percent of the U.S. RDA are *dietary supplements.* The term "dietary supplement" is limited to the use of vitamins and minerals by well and healthy individuals seeking "insurance" against irregular or poor eating habits. The term does not cover the use or promotion of vitamins or minerals for the treatment of any disease or medical condition.

• Products containing more than 150 percent of the U.S. RDA are *drugs.* Any vitamin or mineral used at any dosage for therapeutic purposes is a drug and should be understood by the consumer, regulated by the FDA, and marketed by industry as such. This definition implies no automatic restriction on public availability any more than does the FDA designation of aspirin as a drug.

High-potency nonprescription vitamin-mineral products have been available for many years, and FDA does not intend to require all high-potency vitamin-mineral products to be sold on prescription. This point has been broadly misunderstood and broadly misrepresented to the public.

Another major misunderstanding concerns the broad range (50–150 percent) allowed for the definition of dietary supplement products. Although 100 percent of the U.S. RDA is sufficient to meet the nutritional needs of essentially any healthy individual, FDA has provided for an additional 50 percent of the U.S. RDA in these products in recognition of the possibility that the nutritional needs of some individuals may vary greatly. Thus, the permitted range covers the dietary supplement needs of all individuals except for circumstances where consultation with a physician is appropriate.

The single most important purpose and effect of the new FDA regulations is to require full and honest labeling as well as promotion of vitamin and mineral products, whether marketed as foods, dietary supplements, or as drugs. The regulations redefine and clarify FDA's intentions to act against false labeling or deceptive promotion of such products.

In general, the regulations seek to protect the consumer against promotional claims for dietary supplements so low in potency as to be nutritionally ineffective or so high as to exceed any reasonable definition of a dietary supplement.

Specifically, the regulations seek to protect the consumer against unfair or deceptive promotional claims by requiring that:

1. No food or dietary supplement because of the presence or absence of certain vitamins or minerals may claim or suggest it is sufficient in itself to prevent or cure disease.

2. No food or dietary supplement may imply that a balanced diet of conventional foods cannot supply adequate nutrients or imply that transportation, storage, or cooking of conventional foods may result in an inadequate or deficient diet, thus suggesting that everyone needs a dietary supplement.

3. No food or dietary supplement may claim that inadequate or deficient diet is due to the soil in which a conventional food is grown.

4. All dietary supplements must list the source of their ingredients, but no supplement may claim superiority for either a natural or synthetic source. Rose hips, a part of the rose blossom, for example, cannot be promoted as a better or safer source of vitamin C than ascorbic acid tablets. (Vitamins and minerals are the same in chemical structure regardless of natural or synthetic origin.)

5. No nutritional claims may be made for ingredients such as bioflavonoids, rutin, inositol, and similar ones having no scientifically recognized nutritional value. Such unproven ingredients may continue to be marketed as food items, but they may not be combined with essential nutrients in products labeled for dietary supplementation.

In these five requirements, FDA is *not* saying there is no loss of nutrients from cooking, storage, or transportation of conventional foods.

The Agency is *not* saying that soil composition does not cause variation in the nutritional content of food.

The Agency is *not* seeking to limit personal choice between the natural and chemical forms of supplementary nutrients.

The Agency *is* saying that in terms of overall diet, today's general food supply can provide adequate amounts of all nutrients necessary to good health.

The Agency *is* saying that it will prohibit unsupported generalizations about nutrient losses because of soil, transportation, and processing when such generalizations are used to frighten or mislead consumers about their need for dietary supplements.

The FDA responsibility for the vitamin and mineral regulations is assigned by the Congress. The basic Federal Food, Drug, and Cosmetic Act of 1938 requires that FDA act as it has to insure safety, honesty, and full consumer information about such products.

In the 1940's, it was generally thought that vitamins and minerals were such innocuous substances that excessive quantities would merely be excreted. FDA regulations at the time reflected this view and were sufficient to the needs and to the knowledge of the day.

This is no longer true. Even though a number of vitamins and minerals are essential to human nutrition, we know, for example, that excessive and prolonged vitamin A intake can cause serious problems, including pressures within the skull that mimic a brain tumor. This in turn may raise the danger of serious operations for brain tumors that do not exist.

Excessive and prolonged doses of vitamin D can cause calcification in soft tissues and bone deformity in adults as well as children.

Vitamin C in very high doses can cause diarrhea. High doses of this vitamin have been used in Russia to induce early abortion.

Iron toxicity is a well established cause of accidental poisonings in children. Iron as well as all other minerals essential to human nutrition are toxic at some level.

On the basis of increasing knowledge, the thinking of the 1940's is obsolete today. The view that unlimited quantities of vitamins and minerals are innocuous is today not only obsolete but dangerous. The evidence of this is so clear on vitamins A and D, for example, that FDA is recommending that high-potency doses be taken only under physician guidance. Nevertheless, both A and D will continue to be available, either in nonprescription strengths up to the U.S. RDA or in higher potency forms under physician prescription.

Other than vitamins A and D, all vitamin and mineral products in excess of 150 percent of the U.S. RDA and now available without prescription may continue to be sold singly or in combination formulas as nonprescription drugs. They are, nevertheless, drugs and not dietary supplements. These products eventually will be reviewed by experts who will judge their safety and effectiveness as drugs and advise FDA on appropriate labeling. As a general rule, FDA will continue as in the past to presume a drug acceptable for nonprescription use unless it is unsafe to use except under supervision of a physician.

FDA knows of no economic hardship on consumers or manufacturers that could result from handling high-potency vitamin-mineral products as drugs. Indeed, this will clearly work an economic benefit for consumers, who for the first time will begin to receive accurate information on the different uses of different levels of nutrients.

In summary, the FDA will continue to act in behalf of consumer safety and better consumer information. New regulations primarily affect labeling of vitamin and mineral products and will likely require more accurate consumer information on most such products.

FDA will continue to seek out and act against deceptive or false promotions.

The Agency is not banning any vitamin or mineral from the market or forcing any manufacturer willing to provide proper product formulation and labeling out of business.

The Agency is not restricting any vitamin or mineral available without a prescription today to prescription use only. This includes vitamins A and D in doses up to the U.S. RDA.

The FDA will continue to regulate on the basis that vitamins and minerals are essential *foods* when taken according to bodily need. When taken far in excess of this need, they are *drugs* and should be treated by the consumer and by the FDA accordingly.

The term "bodily need" is not set in concrete. FDA and others are constantly monitoring research to more precisely measure the body's nutritional requirements. As a result, changes may be anticipated in the future, in some cases to lower the U.S. RDA's and in other cases to increase them.

Above all, the new regulations will not alter or interfere with the consumer's basic responsibility for deciding his own individual nutritional practices. The rules will insure more and better information to guide the consumer in making such choices.

C. Better Health Through Nutrition

By Dr. Roger J. Williams

Dr. Williams, whose experiments and conclusions have been cited in various parts of this book, was the only nonphysician on the President's Advisory Panel on Heart Disease appointed in the spring of 1972. As an outstanding biochemist and lifelong researcher in the field of vitamins, Williams submitted a Minority Report to President Richard M. Nixon, which embodied concepts not yet accepted by the medical professional generally and was critical of what he regarded as the medical profession's "shortsighted neglect of nutritional science." The following text is excerpted from Dr. Williams's Minority Report.

While no one knows why heart disease is so prevalent, it is highly probable that a primary cause lies in the fact that in our industrialized age the public chooses its food only on the basis of appearance and taste, and has not been educated to choose on the basis of nutritional value. Much of our food is processed, transported long distances and kept a long time, and the purveyors of food cater to those who want attractive and tasty foods and who pay little attention to its nutritional efficacy. Modern scientific prowess has not been utilized as it should have been. Nutrition science has lagged.

Three things in our 1972 physical environment stand out as requiring the utmost in scientific attention: air, water and food. Of these three, food is by far the most complicated and hence requires by far the most scientific attention. Food contains about 40 nutritional elements that have to be taken into our bodies daily in about the right amounts and proportions. Nature helps us immeasurably in meeting these demands, but we must learn better how to cooperate with nature. These nutritional elements enter into and become a part of what Claude Bernard, a famous 19th century French physiologist, called the *milieu intérieur* of the body. This internal environment should be of crucial concern in connection with heart disease, as I have brought out in chapter 5, "Protecting the Hearts We Have," in my new book *Nutrition Against Disease*. This chapter is documented by about 450 references to the scientific and medical literature.

Two kinds of "sins" can be committed against our internal environments—those of commission and those of omission. One flagrant sin of commission occurs when we inhale tobacco smoke. This corrupts the environments of cells and tissues and is one of the causes of heart disease, as practically all panel members would agree. But many people have heart attacks who do not smoke, so we must look elsewhere.

The sins of omission occasioned by modern industrialization of food production without adequate regard for nutritional value are many. Among the essential nutrient items likely to be deficient or out of balance in the supermarket produce commonly consumed are vitamin B_6, magnesium, vitamin E, ascorbic acid, folic acid and trace minerals. This is not a complete list, but these items all appear to be involved in the heart disease problem. All these and other nutrient items are needed to keep the cells and tissues of hearts and blood vessels healthy. When, particularly in West Germany, thalidomide, used as a medicine, was introduced into the environment of growing fetuses, deformed babies were born. This resulted from a sin of commission. Sins of omission committed in early pregnancy can have similar results. Folic acid is one nutrient that needs to be scrutinized carefully in this context.

It is highly probable that heart and blood vessel defects, which are common in the general population, arise largely because of the poor environments pregnant women furnish their growing fetuses when they eat in a careless and uninformed manner. Many heart problems arise from these defects. One responsible medical dean has written me that the reproductive record of human beings is "terrible"—much of the difficulty probably arises from poor prenatal nutrition. In a 1971 two-volume report issued by the United States Department of Agriculture, it is estimated that in the case of 13 common serious diseases, 20–90% relief can be looked for as a result of nutritional research. Some of these estimates would have been increased if the writers had been aware of some of the material contained in my book *Nutrition Against Disease*.

The President's second question, "What can be done about it?" can be answered broadly and very simply: promote nutritional science. The air we breathe and the water we use are now receiving substantial scientific attention. The food we eat requires incomparably more scientific attention, and it is not getting it. Nutritional science is underdeveloped and at a low ebb. This is primarily because medical science and education has never accepted and nurtured nutritional science and treated it as though it really belonged. This fact, and some of the historical reasons behind it, have been discussed in my book *Nutrition Against Disease*.

The situation has become so bad that Senator Schweiker of Pennsylvania has introduced the Nutritional Medical Education Act of 1972 to provide funds for developing nutritional education in medical schools. The low ebb of nutritional education was emphasized in a two-column article on "Nutritional Illiteracy" in the New York *Times* of June 14, 1972, by the industrialist and food producer, Henry J. Heinz II. As one who has spent a lifetime of study in this general area, I would say that the situation is even worse than Mr. Heinz pictures it.

If something is not done soon, our physicians are going to be *far* behind the dentists and the osteopaths in their comprehension of nutritional science. It is good for the dentists and osteopaths to forge ahead, but it is intolerable for the physicians to forge behind. A multidisciplinary approach involving not only biochemistry and physiology but also internal medicine, pathology, microbiology, dentistry, endocrinology, reproduction, and other related areas, is urgently needed. In my letter of October 9 to Dr. Millis, Chairman of the President's Panel on Heart Disease, I wrote: "I regard it as a national calamity that nutritional science has received so little attention and that physicians and other medical scientists are so inattentive to and ignorant of what might be a tremendous boon for humanity." The mere teaching of traditional "nutrition courses" will not by any means meet our needs. The strongest statement regarding nutrition in the majority report of the President's Advisory Panel on Heart Disease is on page 36, Recommendation 1.8: "The Panel endorses creation of Comprehensive Research, Training, and Clinical Cardiovascular Centers. The Panel believes that first priority should be given to support of a Center in Arteriosclerosis, including, as a very important component, studies on nutrition—a conspicuous field of ignorance and one which offers great promise for prevention."

The matter of uncertainty, ignorance and confusion in the field of nutrition cannot be overemphasized. There are, as all of us know, many conflicting ideas about nutrition afloat, and many notions of a faddist nature which gain more or less acceptance. Unfortunately, some of the most "crackpottish" ideas are promoted by licensed physicians who failed to get adequate grounding while in medical school. People's ignorance in this field is being exploited. Millions of people are grasping for help and do not know where to go for sound advice since it is notorious that most physicians know very little about nutrition. Many of them, including panel members, will freely admit that this is so. Typically, the advice patients get when they ask their doctor about their nutrition is, in effect, this: "Forget it. We are the best fed people in the world. If you want to take vitamins, they probably won't hurt you." If the physicians were well informed about the intricacies of nutrition and were to give this advice, the situation would be very different from what it is when they speak out of ignorance rather than knowledge.

The only way the uncertainties, confusion and ignorance about people's nutrition can be dispelled is through careful, comprehensive and realistic objective research to ascertain the answers to a host of questions. In one of the memoranda which I passed out to the panel, there were 36 pressing problems relating nutrition to heart disease. None of these were even discussed, and there are many more. While there is a large amount of research to be done, the picture will clear rapidly as soon as competent scientists, in sufficient numbers, put their minds to it. This at present is not being done. Many who are interested in nutrition are concerned with defending time-honored positions which are certain to become obsolete.

The only way I see out of this crippling situation is for the Federal Government to create two or more Institutes for Nutritional Science. This can be done under the *Heart, Blood Vessel and Lung Act of 1972.* One Institute could well be concerned with nutrition as it relates to atherosclerosis; the other to prenatal nutrition as it relates to congenital heart disease and cardiomyopathies. Manpower for these Institutes for Nutritional Science will present a problem, but not for long if money becomes available; for there are real problems to be solved, and keen interest can be engendered in the minds of thousands of competent scientists once support is assured.

Once nutritional science gets substantial support, it will become more evident that nutrition can play a tremendous role in the prevention of all types of disease. This is the theme of my book *Nutrition Against Disease* which has been pronounced even by some physicians as "thoroughly sound." Mental retardation, dental disease, arthritis, mental disease, alcoholism, and possibly even cancer, can be blamed on the poor internal environments which the cells and tissues of our bodies have to live with. These environments can be vastly improved by nutritional means.

The basis for wide sweeping hope for prevention of disease lies in the realization that environments are of paramount importance, and nutritional environments have not really been considered seriously. Are environments important to living creatures? The answer is obvious. Are environments important for living cells and tissues? The affirmative answer is also obvious. Do cells and tissues become deranged (diseased) when the environments are inadequate? This too can be answered with certainty. Improvement of internal environments can be accomplished through the application of technical scientific prowess—by developing nutritional science. Creation of Institutes for Nutritional Science would be an important step toward the promotion of better general health for the entire public.

In the *Heart, Blood Vessel and Lung Act of 1972* it is estimated that the potential gain from conquering heart disease would be more than 30 billion dollars per year. This figure would certainly more than double if we could conquer other diseases as well. Of course there is no magic formula for eliminating disease entirely, but we are dealing with enormous potential savings not only of money but also in terms of grief and distress. A private citizen would not hesitate to invest ten dollars per year if there were reasonable prospect of getting $30,000 per year in return. The Federal Government should not hesitate to risk 10 million dollars a year when the return to the public might well be 30 billion dollars per year.

If we reject the proposal to develop nutritional science, we are voting for ignorance. This is unthinkable in the light of the unexplored gold mine of opportunities for health betterment suggested by the U.S. Department of Agriculture's report. Surely we wish to adhere to the basic philosophy that knowledge is to be preferred to ignorance. In the field of nutritional science we cannot afford to remain ignorant. Because of decades of indoctrination, many physicians will automatically "pooh pooh" the idea that nutrition can be so important for the prevention of disease. This, in my opinion, is because they are so inexpert in the area of nutritional physiology. No physician worthy of the name, however, can take the position that ignorance about nutrition is preferable to understanding.

D. Losses of Vitamins and Trace Minerals Resulting from Processing and Preservation of Foods [1,2]

By Henry A. Schroeder, M.D.

The foods we buy for our families have, for the most part, undergone processing and preservation treatments that reduce the nutrient content. In this article, which originally appeared in the American Journal of Clinical Nutrition *(May, 1971, Vol. 24, pp. 562–73), Dr. Schroeder examines these losses in detail. The author is emeritus professor of physiology, Dartmouth Medical School, Hanover, New Hampshire, as well as director of research, Brattleboro (Vt.) Memorial Hospital. This article is reprinted here with the author's permission. Copyright © 1971 by the* American Journal of Clinical Nutrition.

The use of vitamins or vitamin-mineral supplements is widespread among certain sections of the population of the United States, although such use, except under special conditions, is not recommended by all nutritionists. So-called "health foods" are sold, usually at high prices, to many persons who believe that modern

[1] From the Department of Physiology, Dartmouth Medical School, Brattleboro, Vermont, and Brattleboro Memorial Hospital, Brattleboro, Vermont.

[2] Supported by National Heart Institute Grant HE 05076 and General Foods Corporation.

food practices of freezing, canning, processing, and refining of foods result in sizable depletions of organic and inorganic micronutrients essential to optimal health.

The Food and Nutrition Board of the National Academy of Sciences–National Research Council, in its latest publication, Recommended Dietary Allowances (1), has included vitamin B_6, with a recommendation of 2.0 mg/day for adults, 2.5 mg/day for pregnant and lactating women, and 1.4 to 2.0 mg/day for adolescents. To fulfill this adult recommendation requires a level of 2 ppm in a diet weighing 1 kg wet wt, exclusive of fluids (2). Because considerable data on the vitamin B_6 content of foods have recently been compiled (3, 4), it appeared rewarding to examine major sources of calories. The purpose of our analyses was to ascertain how many sources provided levels equal to the recommended intake, and whether or not losses resulted from storage and processing to the extent that total intake would be less than the recommended level.

Likewise, the Food and Nutrition Board has set a recommended allowance for pantothenic acid of 5.0 to 10.0 mg/day as "probably adequate," stating that usual diets furnish 6 to 20 mg. Based on the total weight of the diet, this level would require at least 5 ppm. Data are available on pantothenic acid concentrations of some processed foods (3, 4). Losses of vitamins in the refining of flour can be calculated from available data (5).

This laboratory has analyzed many foods for their concentrations of the essential trace minerals chromium, manganese, cobalt, copper, zinc, molybdenum, and selenium (6–12), and for magnesium (13). Canned and processed foods were among those analyzed, as were major sources of calories, flour, sugar, and fats. The Food and Nutrition Board has set recommended allowances for magnesium and iron, but for no other essential trace mineral (1). Dietary contents, however, are known, and in some cases, extrapolation can be made from animal requirements. Losses caused by refining flour and sugar have been ascertained (5–13).

Results

VITAMIN B₆ AND PANTOTHENIC ACID

There were 723 foods and edible products on which analyses were made (3). Levels of vitamin B_6 were ascertained on 552 and of pantothenic acid on 507. There were 83 varieties of baby foods analyzed for vitamin B_6 but not pantothenic acid. Of these samples, 47.5% had pantothenic acid concentrations of 5 ppm or more, 31.0% had vitamin B_6 concentrations of 2 ppm or more, and 28.9% of baby foods had vitamin B_6 concentrations of 2 ppm or more. Many of the foods with relatively high levels of both vitamins were seeds, nuts, condiments, yeasts, or dried meats and fish. When dried legumes, seeds, and nuts were excluded, only 77 foods, mainly raw fish and meats, had levels of B_6 over 2.5 ppm (13.9%).

Analyses had been made on 58 canned foods and 32 frozen foods and their raw counterparts. In Table 1 are shown the concentrations of vitamin B_6 in a variety of seafoods, meats, dairy products, and raw, frozen, or dried and canned vegetables. Of 10 seafoods, six had more than 2 ppm B_6 in the raw state and four had more than 2 ppm in the canned state. The mean loss was 48.9%. Of four meats, losses due to canning amounted to 42.6%. Losses in dairy products and those produced by drying meats were negligible.

Large losses occurred as a result of the canning of vegetables, ranging from 57 to 77%. Frozen vegetables showed losses of 37 to 56% in vitamin B_6. Of the nine raw vegetables with more than 2 ppm, none had this level when canned or frozen.

Table 1 also shows the losses of pantothenic acid in dried, frozen, and canned foods compared with raw foods. In canned foods of animal origin losses ranged from 20 to 35%, and in canned vegetables from 46 to 78%. Using the yardstick of 5 ppm for the mean requirement, seven of 18 animal products, and 15 of 16 vegetable foods had values below this level when canned, whereas among their raw counterparts there were three more animal and four more vegetable foods

Table 1. Losses of Vitamin B₆ and Pantothenic Acid in Frozen and Canned Foods, Micrograms per Gram

Food	Vitamin B₆			Pantothenic acid		
	Raw	Frozen	Canned	Raw	Frozen	Canned
Fish and Sea Food						
Clams	0.80		0.83			
Eel	2.30		1.23	1.50		
Turbot			0.38	2.50		7.20^a
Haddock	0.82			1.30		1.25
Herring	3.70	3.20^a	1.60	9.70	9.30^a	7.00
Mackerel	6.60	4.10^a	2.80	8.50	5.20^a	5.00
Oysters	0.50		0.37	2.50		
Roe, cod	1.65		1.40	32.00		19.65
Salmon	7.00	7.00^a	3.00	13.00	7.10^a	5.50
Sardines, Atlantic				10.90		7.00
Sardines, Pacific	2.80		2.20	10.00		6.00
Shrimp	1.00		0.60	2.80		2.10
Tuna	9.00		4.25	5.00		3.20
Mean	3.54		1.81	7.98	7.20	6.39
% Loss		17.3	48.9		20.8	19.9
Meats and Poultry						
Chicken	6.83		3.00	8.00		8.50
Pork	4.50		2.70	7.90		4.40
Ham	4.00		3.60	6.75		
Frankfurter	1.40		3.01	4.30		2.00
Tongue, Beef	1.25		2.40	20.00	5.96^a	
Mean	4.18		2.40	6.73		4.97
% Loss			42.6		70.2	26.2
Dairy Products						
Cheese, Cheddar	0.80		0.80	5.00		4.00
Cheese, Limburger	0.86		0.82	11.80		5.80
Cheese, Swiss	0.75		0.43	3.70		2.60
Milk, Whole	0.40	0.20^a	0.30	3.40		3.20
Buttermilk	0.36			3.07		
Mean	0.70		0.59	5.98		3.90
% Loss		50.0	15.7			34.8
Grains and Cereals						
Corn	1.61	2.20	2.00	5.40	4.40	2.20
Vegetables, Roots						
Beets	0.55		0.50	1.50		1.00
Carrots	1.50		0.30	2.80		1.30

Table 1—Continued

Food	Vitamin B[a]			Pantothenic acid		
	Raw	Frozen	Canned	Raw	Frozen	Canned
Potatoes	2.50		1.02	3.80	2.40	
Sweet Potatoes	2.18		0.66	8.20		4.30
Mean	1.68		0.62	4.08		2.20
% Loss			63.1		36.8	46.1
Vegetables, Legumes						
Beans, Lima	1.70	1.50	0.90	4.70	2.40	1.30
Beans, Common	5.60			2.25		0.61
Beans, Green	0.80	0.70	0.40	1.90	1.35	0.75
Beans, Yellow		0.79	0.42	2.50	1.38	
Cowpeas	5.62	1.10	0.53	10.50	4.00	1.62
Peas, Green, Young	1.60	1.30	0.50	7.50	2.15	1.50
Mean	2.43	1.08	0.55	5.73	2.46	1.16
% Loss		55.6	77.4		57.1	77.8
Vegetables, Green						
Asparagus	1.53	1.55	0.55	6.20	4.10	
Broccoli	1.95	1.50		11.70	4.50	
Brussels Sprouts	2.30	1.75		7.23	4.20	
Cabbage	1.60		1.30	2.05		0.93
Cauliflower	2.10	1.90		10.00	5.40	
Kale	3.00	1.85		10.00	3.76	
Mustard Greens		1.33		2.10	1.64	1.50
Okra	0.75	0.45		2.60	2.15	
Rhubarb	0.30	0.25		0.85	0.70	
Spinach	2.80	1.90	0.70	3.00	1.30	0.65
Squash, Summer	0.82	0.63		3.60	1.73	
Squash, Winter	1.54	0.91		4.00	2.82	
Turnip Greens	2.63	1.00		3.80	1.40	0.68
Pepper, Red				2.71		0.92
Tomatoes	1.00	0.90		3.30		2.30
Mushrooms	1.25	0.60		22.00		10.00
Mean	1.69	1.07	0.85	5.42	2.81	2.43
% Loss		36.7	57.1		48.2	56.4
Fruit and Fruit Juices						
12 varieties, mean	0.55	0.47		1.37	1.27	
% loss		15.4			7.2	
24 varieties, mean	0.57		0.35	2.00		0.99
% loss			37.6			50.5

[a] Dried.

Table 2. Losses of Vitamin B₆ and Pantothenic Acid in Processed Foods

Food	Vitamin B₆ μg/g	Vitamin B₆ % loss	Pantothenic acid μg/g	Pantothenic acid % loss
Grains and cereals				
Corn, raw	4.7	—	5.40	—
Cornmeal, white	0.6	87.2	5.80	+7.4
Cornmeal, yellow	2.5	46.8	5.80	+7.4
Corn, grits	1.47	68.7	3.40	37.0
Corn flakes	0.65	86.2	1.85	65.7
Corn, puffed	—		2.88	46.7
Rice, wild			10.20	
Rice, brown	5.5	—	11.00	—
Rice, parboiled	4.25	22.7	9.00	18.2
Rice, white	1.70	69.1	5.50	50.0
Rice, precooked	0.34	93.8	2.85	74.1
Rice, flour	1.60	70.1		
Rice, cereal	0.80	85.4		
Rice flakes	1.25	77.3	3.40	69.1
Rice, puffed	0.75	86.4	3.78	65.6
Rye, flour, whole	3.00	—	13.40	—
Rye, flour, refined	0.90	70.0	7.20	46.2
Rye bread	1.00	66.7	4.50	66.4
Oatmeal	1.40		15.00	
Oat, soy, rice cereal	6.70			
Bulgur, whole	2.25		6.60	—
Bulgur, peeled	1.88	16.7	6.08	7.9
Wheat flour, whole	3.40	—	11.00	—
All-purpose flour, patent	0.60	82.3	4.65	57.7
Bread flour	0.60	82.3	5.00	54.5
Cake flour	0.45	86.8	3.20	70.9
Bread, whole wheat	1.80		7.60	—
Bread, white	0.40	77.8	4.30	43.4
Bread, white and whole wheat	1.00	44.4	4.25	44.1
Bread, French	0.53	70.2	3.78	50.3
Bread, cracked wheat	0.92	48.9	6.67	12.2
Rolls	0.35	80.6	3.10	59.2
Rusk	0.90	50.0	—	
Crackers, saltine	0.68	62.2	—	
Spaghetti and macaroni	0.64	64.4	—	
Noodles	0.88	51.1	—	
Breakfast cereals, wheat				
Whole meal, hot	3.91	—	8.74	—
Farina, hot	0.67	82.9	5.15	41.1
Bran, 100%	8.20	+109.7	29.00	+231.8
Bran flakes, 40%	3.84	1.8	8.75	+0.01
Bran flakes	2.92	25.3	4.69	46.3
Germ, toasted	11.50	+194.1	12.00	+37.3
Puffed wheat	1.70	56.5	—	

Table 2—Continued

Food	Vitamin B6		Pantothenic acid	
	µg/g	% loss	µg/g	% loss
Grains and cereals—Continued				
Shredded wheat	2.44	37.6	7.06	19.2
Malted barley, and wheat	—		7.14	18.3
Cakes				
Chocolate	-		2.00	73.7
Plain	0.40	77.8		
White			3.00	60.0
Meats				
Pork, raw	3.50	—	6.00	—
Pork sausage	1.65	52.6	6.82	+13.7
Pork, luncheon meat	—		5.50	8.3
Salami	1.23	64.9		
Vienna sausage, canned	0.83	76.3		
Bologna	1.00	71.4		
Liver	8.40	—	77.00	—
Liverwurst	1.90	77.4	27.80	63.9
Number of samples processed	41		33	
Number < 2 or 5 ppm	33		15	
%	80.4		45.5	
Number < 1.5 or 3 ppm	15		5	
%	36.6		15.2	

Dashes indicate the raw product used as a standard.

above this level. In frozen foods, losses were also large, from 37 to 57% in vegetables and 21 to 70% in animal products.

Of the fruits and fruit juices analyzed 12 were frozen and 24 canned. Average loss of vitamin B_6 from freezing was 15.4% and from canning 37.6%. Likewise, loss of pantothenic acid were 7.2% and 50.5%, respectively, compared with the raw product. No raw fruit or juice contained the recommended concentration of either vitamin.

In Table 2 are the differences in concentration of vitamin B_6 and pantothenic acid in foods processed or refined. Losses of B_6 in corn products, rice products, breads, and flours were large, as they were in processed

Table 3. Losses of Vitamins in the Refining of Whole Wheat; Concentrations in Wheat, White Flour, Germ, and Millfeeds [a, b]

Nutrient	Wheat μg/g	Flour μg/g	Germ μg/g	Mill-feeds μg/g	Loss in flour %	Mill-feeds/ flour, ratio
Thiamin [e]	3.5	0.8	22	17	77.1	21.1
Riboflavin [e]	1.5	0.3	5.5	4.2	80.0	14.0
Niacin [e]	50	9.5	80	150	80.8	15.8
Vitamin B₆	1.7	0.5	12	7.2	71.8	14.4
Pantothenic acid	10	5	25	22	50.0	4.4
Folacin	0.3	0.1	1.5	1.1	66.7	11.0
α-Tocopherol	16	2.2	125	38	86.3	17.25
Betaine	844	650	4,825	3,546	22.8	5.52
Choline	1,089	767	3,002	1,603	29.5	2.09
Gross energy, kcal/g	4.4	4.3	5.1	4.7	2.3	1.09
Fat, %	1.61	0.87	8.03	3.7	46.0	4.25
Starch, %	57.21	68.66	18.05	22.13	+20.0	0.32
Protein, %	10.50	10.71	24.82	15.43	+2.0	1.44

[a] Data from reference 5.
[b] Milling caused no loss in energy, starch, or protein in flour.
[e] Added to make enriched flour.

pork and liver. Losses of pantothenic acid were at a lower level. Both vitamins were concentrated in wheat bran and germ. About four-fifths of the samples had levels of vitamin B₆ less than 2 ppm and nearly three-eighths had levels of less than 1.5 ppm. There was less depletion of pantothenic acid; 45.5% were below 5 ppm and 15.2% below 3 ppm.

There were adequate concentrations of vitamin B₆ in 24 baby foods that contained from 2.0 to 5.0 ppm, with three meat products having 5.3 to 8.1 ppm. There were adequate concentrations in 118 adult foods; 33 fish and seafoods, 23 meats and meat products, 19 grains and grain products, 15 legumes, 13 vegetables, 5 fruits, 3 nuts, 3 dairy products, 2 seeds, molasses, and yeast. Almost all of these foods were raw, or in the case of cereals, enriched with germ or bran. All 26 fruits and juices had inadequate levels.

Table 4. Losses of Biotin, Folacin, Choline, and Inositol Caused by Refining, Preserving, and Processing Foods, per 1,000 g[a, b]

Food	Biotin, μg	Folacin, μg	Choline, mg	Inositol, mg
Cereal products				
Corn	210	265	610	500
Cornmeal, white	66	90		510
Cornmeal, yellow		90	100	
Hominy grits	7	45		30
Corn flakes		55		
Rice, brown	120	200	1,120	1,190
Rice, converted	80	200	890	200
Rice, parboiled	100	190	980	250
Rice, white	50	160	590	100
Rice, dry cereal	13	76		190
Wheat, whole	160	490	940	3,700
Wheat, flakes		470		
Wheat, shredded		550		
Bread, whole wheat	19	300		670
Bread, white	11	150		510
Flour, whole wheat	90	380		1,100
Flour, white	10	80	520	470
Dairy products				
Milk, whole	47	6	150	130
Milk, evaporated	45	7	150	
Milk, non-fat, dry	34	2	100	
Milk, butter	0	0	50	
Meats				
Beef, round	26	105	680	115
Pork, loin	52	24	770	450
Frankfurter			570	
Sausage		115	480	
Vegetables				
Asparagus, fresh	17	1,090	100	
Asparagus, canned	17	270		
Lima beans, fresh		340		
Lima beans, canned		130		
Green beans, fresh		280	420	
Green beans, canned	13	120		
Beets, fresh	19	140		210
Beets, canned		28		
Carrots, fresh	25	80	130	480
Carrots, canned	15	33		
Corn, fresh	60	280		
Corn, canned	22	77		

Table 4—Continued

Food	Biotin, μg	Folacin, μg	Choline, mg	Inositol, mg
Vegetables—Continued				
Mushrooms, fresh	160	240		170
Mushrooms, canned	73	39		170
Cowpeas, fresh	210	410	970	2,400
Cowpeas, canned		260		
Green peas, fresh	94	250	750	1,620
Green peas, canned	21	103		
Spinach, fresh	69	750	220	270
Spinach, canned	23	490		
Tomatoes, fresh	40	80		460
Tomatoes, canned	18	37		
RDA	150	400	500	

ᵃ Data from Table 6, reference 4.   ᵇ Fresh vegetables were raw or frozen. Fats were devoid of all of these vitamins but choline.

VITAMINS IN WHEAT AND FLOUR

In Table 3 are shown the losses of vitamins resulting from the refining of wheat and the highly enriched millfeeds (left from the flour) that are fed to cattle. Losses of seven vitamins amount to 50 to 86.3% of those in the wheat. Half the pantothenic acid, 72% of the vitamin B_6, 86.3% of the α-tocopherol, and two-thirds of the folacin are removed in about 30% of the wheat, leaving a product with almost the same caloric energy. Three vitamins are restored to bread or enriched flour.

These losses in white flour reduce the vitamin B_6 concentration below the recommended level of 2.0 ppm, the tocopherol level below 25 to 30 IU, the folacin level below 0.4 ppm, and the pantothenic acid level to the minimum requirement. Choline and its precursor, betaine, were at adequate levels, above 500 ppm (2).

OTHER VITAMINS IN PROCESSED FOODS

Table 4 shows the losses of biotin, folacin, choline, and inositol in processed or canned foods as compared

Table 5. Losses of Essential Bulk and Trace Elements in the Refining of Wheat; Concentration in Whole Wheat, White Flour, Bread, Germ, and Millfeeds[a]

Element	Wheat	White flour	White bread	Germ	Millfeeds	Loss in flour, %	Millfeeds/ flour, ratio
Percent of wheat	100	72		2.5	25.5		0.35
Ash, %	1.96	0.48	2.96	3.98	2.1 to 6.5	28.0	8.95
Calcium, %	0.045	0.018	0.127	3.98	0.11 to 0.133	75.5	6.67
Phosphorus, %	0.433	0.126	0.183	0.923	0.781 to 1.57	60.0	9.33
Magnesium, %	0.183	0.028	0.034	0.268	0.23 to 0.38	70.9	11.61
Potassium, %	0.454	0.105	0.191	0.889	0.9 to 1.67	84.7	12.14
Sodium, ppm	45	9.8	8.580	23.2	3.05 to 37.2	77.0	3.45
Chromium, ppm	0.05	0.03	0.03	0.07	0.07	78.3	2.33
Manganese, ppm	46	6.5	5.9	137.4	64 to 119	40.0	14.15
Iron, ppm	43	10.5	27.3[b]	66.6	47 to 78	85.8	5.95
Cobalt, ppm	0.026	0.003	0.022	0.017	0.07 to 0.18	75.6	41.67
Copper, ppm	5.3	1.7	2.3	7.4	7.7 to 17.0	88.5	7.27
Zinc, ppm	35	7.8	9.7	100.8	54 to 130	67.9	11.79
Selenium, ppm	0.63	0.53	0.32	1.1	0.46 to 0.84	77.7	1.22
Molybdenum, ppm	0.48	0.25		0.67	0.7 to 0.83	15.9	3.06

[a] Data from references 5 and 24. Data on chromium from reference 21 and on other trace elements from references 6 to 13, which essentially confirm the data in the Millfeed Manual (5). [b] Added to flour, which is then called "enriched."

with raw foods. Biotin was reduced in the processing of corn and rice and in the canning of corn, mushrooms, peas, spinach, and tomatoes, to levels below the recommended 0.15 ppm. Folacin was reduced in processed corn and milk, and canned asparagus, beans, beets, carrots, corn, mushrooms, peas, spinach, and tomatoes, in most cases to levels below that recommended, 0.4 ppm. When measured, there was little loss of choline; inositol was lower in processed rice than in brown rice, in hominy grits than in corn, and in white flour than in whole wheat flour. Three vitamins were somewhat lower in white bread than in whole wheat bread, and these differences were greater in the respective flours.

MINERALS IN WHEAT AND FLOUR

In Table 5 are given the concentrations of 13 minerals in wheat, refined flour, bread, wheat germ, and the residue from refining, or millfeeds. From 60.0 to 84.7% of the five bulk minerals and 75.5% of the ash are removed during the milling process, with from 40.0 to 88.5% of seven essential trace metals. Refining of wheat thus provides luxus amounts of minerals to millfeeds.

In spite of these losses, white bread contains concentrations of calcium above the recommended 800 ppm, of magnesium at approximately the recommended level of 350 ppm, and of phosphorus above the recommended level of 1,300 ppm. Bread is probably deficient in chromium, but appears to have adequate levels of manganese, iron, cobalt, copper, zinc, and molybdenum. Whether or not it has enough selenium is not known; in foods, selenium is volatile (12).

TRACE MINERALS IN RAW AND CANNED FOODS

The canning of foods would not necessarily be expected to result in losses of trace minerals, except perhaps in the fluid in which the foods were kept or in the cooking water. Analyses in this laboratory of a few representative canned foods, however, have shown differences

Table 6. Essential Metals in Partitioned Foods, Parts per Million, Wet Weight

Food	Magnesium	Chromium	Manganese	Cobalt	Copper	Zinc	Molybdenum
Wheat	1,502	0.05	49.0	0.75	4.08	31.5	0.79
Patent flour	299	0.03	6.0	0.36	1.50	8.9	0.32
Gluten	18		2.25	1.46	9.63	48.5	
Rice, unpolished	1,477	0.16	2.8	0.16	4.10	6.5	
Rice, polished	251	0.04	1.53	0.10	3.04	1.6	
Corn, dry	664	0.18	4.70	0.36	1.80	18.2	
Meal	269	0.08	2.05	0.87	2.13	9.0	
Starch	22	0.05	0.34	0.55	1.25	0.8	
Oil	5	0.12	1.00	0.15	2.21	1.6	
Sugar cane	190	0.10	1.75	0.03	1.00	0.5	0.13
Raw sugar	94	0.30	1.18	0.40	3.35	8.7	0.0
Molasses	250	1.21	4.24	0.25	6.83	8.3	0.19
White sugar	2	0.02	0.13	<0.05	0.57	0.2	0.0
Raw milk	102	0.01	0.19	0.06	0.19	3.5	0.20
Skimmed milk	96	<0.01	0.0	0.36	0.29	3.0	0.02
Butter	6	0.17	0.96	0.35	3.92	1.5	0.19
Egg	113	0.16	0.53	0.10	4.10	20.8	0.49
Yolk	101		0.88	0.12	2.44	35.5	
White	103		0.43	0.06	1.70	0.3	0.12
Beef	283	0.09	0.05	0.52	0.90	56.6	0.07
Fat	5	0.23	0.03	1.94	0.88	1.5	0.0
Pork	209		0.34	0.17	3.90	18.9	3.68
Lard	5	0.07	0.98	0.20	2.56	2.0	0.0

Data from references 6 to 13.

from the raw counterparts. Canned spinach apparently lost 81.7% of the manganese, 70.6% of the cobalt, and 40.1% of the zinc found in raw spinach. Zinc losses amounted to 60% in canned beans and 83.3% in canned tomatoes. Canned carrots, beets, and green beans lots 70, 66.7, and 88.9%, respectively, of the cobalt found in the raw foods. White bread, as compared with whole wheat bread, was lower in magnesium by 40%, in chromium by 71.4%, in cobalt by 69.4%, in copper by 69.8%, and in zinc by 77.4%. It contained, however, 24.5% more manganese. Canned beets gained manganese by 226.8% and zinc by 60.0%, compared with raw beets, according to our analyses (6–13).

ESSENTIAL METALS IN PROCESSED OR PARTITIONED FOODS

When a food is divided into its component parts by refinement or extraction, a majority of the trace metals goes with one part or the other. Table 6 illustrates this point. Zinc was largely contained in the germ and bran of wheat, and the remainder appeared largely in gluten. Marked losses of all trace metals but copper occurred when rice was polished. Corn oil, compared with corn, contained little magnesium, much chromium, and retained most of the original copper. Refined white sugar had minimal amounts of chromium, cobalt, molybdenum, and zinc, compared with raw sugar or sugar cane. Almost all of the chromium, manganese, cobalt, copper, and molybdenum in raw milk appeared in the butter, whereas magnesium and zinc remained in the skim milk. Beef and pork fats also had little magnesium, and beef fat had little zinc.

TRACE MINERALS IN FOODS

In Table 7 are shown mean concentrations of seven essential trace minerals in 11 types of foods, compiled from 100 to 150 samples analyzed for each element (6–13). The best approximation of requirements is also given, taken from Recommended Dietary Allowances (2) and contents found in average diets. The level for chromium was calculated at half the requirement found for rats. Few foods fulfilled this requirement. Seven of 11 classes of foods were low in manganese, 5 low in zinc, 6 low in copper, 5 low in selenium, and 4 low in molybdenum. Manganese requirements can be met by the use of leafy and fruity

Table 7. Essential Trace Elements in Various Types of Foods, Average Values, Parts per Million [a]

Type of food	Chromium	Manganese	Cobalt	Copper	Zinc	Selenium	Molybdenum
Seafoods	0.17	0.05	1.56	1.49	17.5	0.57	0.10
Meats	0.13	0.21	0.22	3.92	30.6	1.07	0.36
Dairy products	0.10	0.70	0.12	1.76	8.6	0.02	0.15
Vegetables							
Legumes	0.05	0.44	0.15	1.31	10.7	0.02	1.73
Roots	0.08	0.78	0.13	0.69	3.4	<0.02	0.10
Leaves and fruits	0.03	3.47	0.14	0.42	1.7	<0.02	0.07
Fruits	0.02	1.0	0.14	0.82	0.5	<0.02	0.24
Grains and cereals	0.31	7.0	0.43	2.02	17.7	0.31	1.79
Oils and fats	0.15	1.83	0.37	4.63	8.4	0.72	0.0
Nuts	0.35	17.7	0.26	14.82	34.2	0.24	1.00
Condiments and spices	3.3	91.8	0.52	6.76	22.9		0.45
Beverages							
Alcoholic			0.03	0.38	0.9	0.35	0.08
Nonalcoholic		3.8	0.01	0.44	0.2	0.07	0.12
Probably required in diet	0.3	2.2	0.18	2.0	10.0		0.18
Found in diet							
Mean [b]	0.28	5.2	0.28	2.2	14.2	0.07	0.20
Range	0.20 to 0.40	3.3 to 9.3	0.16 to 0.47	0.9 to 6.2	11 to 18		0.10 to 0.46

[a] Data from references 6 to 13. [b] Data on long-term balances of five adults for 30 to 347 days, from references 14 and 15, analyzed by emission spectroscopy.

vegetables and grains, copper by meats, grains, and oils and fats; zinc by seafoods, meats, legumes, and whole grains; selenium by meats, seafoods, and grains; and molybdenum by meats, legumes, and grains. The high levels of all trace minerals in nuts are noteworthy.

Discussion

From these data, the need for a well-balanced diet in respect to vitamin B_6, pantothenic acid, chromium, manganese, and zinc is clear. Foods with excess amounts of micronutrients are needed to compensate for foods with less than adequate amounts in order that the total intake may supply the body's requirements. It is apparent that raw foods supply adequate amounts of all the micronutrients here considered. It is not apparent, however, that persons subsisting on refined, processed, and canned foods will be provided with adequate amounts, and intakes may be marginal for those receiving reducing diets and for older persons whose caloric intakes are limited.

To decide whether or not a given food is nutritionally adequate in a micronutrient, one needs to know the daily requirements for the micronutrient, its concentration in the food, and the wet weight of the diet. Selected hospital and institutional diets analyzed by this laboratory have shown that total weights varied from 1,700 to 2,500 g (10), of which approximately 800 to 1,000 were fluids. Dry weights averaged 440 g (range 348 to 533 g). Tipton et al. (14, 15) analyzed diets of five normal subjects for 30 to 347 days for 17 trace elements. Dry weights averaged 410 g and 700 g in two experiments, whereas food and milk varied from 1,322 g to 1,834 g. The mean weight of all these diets, assuming an intake of 500 g milk, was 1,014 g. Calculated consumption of food per person per day in 1955 was 1,103 g (2), excluding 508 g of liquid milk. Therefore, 1,000 g appear to be approximately the average weight of food consumed per day. On this basis, any food having a concentration in milligrams per kilogram of a micronutrient that is below the rec-

WHICH VITAMINS DO YOU NEED

ommended daily allowance can be considered to be marginal or partly deficient in that micronutrient, and any food with a concentration above the allowance can be considered adequate. When the major sources of calories consumed contain levels of a micronutrient below the recommended daily allowance, it is likely that deficiency will result in a certain fraction of the population.

The major sources of calories in this country are flour and cereal products, sugar, potatoes, and fats, making up approximately one-fourth of the weight of the diet and about 80% or more of the calories (2). In respect to vitamin B_6, and using an index of requirement of 2.0 ppm, almost all corn, rice, rye, and wheat products had lower concentrations than the required level, as did all canned vegetables and potatoes, all fresh and canned fruits except fresh bananas, all dairy products, and seven of 11 canned meats. Inadequate levels were found in all frozen vegetables. Refined sugars contain virtually no vitamins, and fats virtually no B_6. Thus, a diet consisting of those foods would be deficient, and the deficiency would be little lessened by the use of canned meats, and would not be corrected by sausages or liverwurst.

In respect to pantothenic acid, a level of 5.0 ppm was not reached in three of four canned dairy products, any canned root vegetable, legumes, and green vegetables, and any frozen vegetable but cauliflower. Levels were adequate in dried and canned fish, but not in all meats. They were inadequate in three corn products, three rice products, rye bread, most flours and breads except whole wheat, and cakes. They were adequate in some meats, cornmeal, whole rice, whole rye, oatmeal, bulgur, whole wheat, germ and bran products. Therefore, a diet without whole grains and some meats would supply insufficient pantothenic acid.

These data cast doubt on the adequacy of the American diet for vitamin B_6 and pantothenic acid. This doubt is increased by the findings of Murphy et al. (16), who analyzed 271 public school and 29 private school lunches of Type A, which include milk, meat, poultry, fish, egg, or peanut butter, two vegetables, whole grain or enriched bread, and butter or margarine. They found that more than half, or 171, of the schools did not meet the nutritional goal for vitamin B_6, and 7% served lunches with less than one-fourth of the recommended allowance. If the intakes of these two vitamins are as marginal as they appear from these data, they probably should be restored to foods from which they are removed by refining, especially wheat and corn products.

Losses of vitamin B_6 are explicable on the basis of the relative stabilities of its three components. Pyridoxine is quite stable, pyridoxal and pyridoxamine fairly unstable. More than half of the B_6 in most vegetables, fruits, legumes, nuts, grains, and cereals occurs as pyridoxine, whereas pyridoxal and pyridoxamine account for most of this vitamin in some vegetables, corn, meats, poultry, fish, milk and milk products, and eggs (3). It is likely that losses of pyridoxine occur largely from refining and losses of the other two components from processing, cooking, and storing.

Data are insufficient to draw conclusions on marginal intakes of biotin and folacin, although the results presented here are suggestive.

In respect to the essential trace minerals, chromium, manganese, and zinc are the three that require close examination as to whether or not intakes are marginal. Clinical zinc deficiency has been described only in exceptional circumstances (17), but significantly low levels of zinc in plasma have been found in a number of conditions (18). Patients with indolent ulcers of the lower extremity resulting from atherosclerosis or diabetes mellitus, chronic tuberculosis, chronic infections, and azotemia, and women who are pregnant or are taking oral contraceptives have shown decreased plasma zinc. Supplementation with large amounts of zinc has restored plasma levels and promoted healing of ulcers (19). Adequate zinc is as important to the body's economy as is adequate iron, zinc probably being the largest intracellular trace metallic component except in red blood cells. Reference Man contains 4.2 g iron and 2.3 g zinc; intakes in food are similar. Laboratory chows contain 18 to 178 ppm zinc, a level that is apparently safe. Human subjects have been given 150 mg/day for long periods. The logic of enriching refined flour and sugar with zinc is becoming apparent. Elderly persons should probably take supplements of 10 mg zinc/day until this procedure is accepted.

Human requirements for manganese are not known. Levels at which deficiency occurs in the rat, however, are similar to levels in human diets. Laboratory chows contain much larger concentrations, i.e., from 40 to 42 ppm, and millfeeds contain 64 to 119 ppm, which do not appear to be toxic. Whereas there is no clear reason at present to restore manganese to refined flour, no hazard would result. The body content of Reference Man is only 12 mg; wild and laboratory animal tissues have much higher concentrations (7).

Chromium deficiency exists in tissues of many persons from the United States but in few from foreign countries (20, 21). Deficiency in tissues increases with age. The major cause is probably low chromium levels in refined foods making up the major sources of calories, flour, rice, sugars, and fats. At this time, replacement or supplementation would have little effect, for inorganic chromium salts are poorly absorbed and their action may be slight. When the effective organic complex, or glucose tolerance factor of Mertz (22), becomes available, it may be desirable to enrich foods with absorbable chromium. Chromium deficiency is probably a factor in atherosclerosis (21, 23).

School lunches theoretically should supply one-third of the recommended daily allowances of vitamins and minerals. Murphy et al. (25), however, found that this goal in Type A lunches was not met for calcium in 14%, for magnesium in 60%, for iron for boys in 20%, and for iron for girls in more than 90% of the lunches in the 300 schools studied. Trace elements in foods usually follow bulk elements, and it is likely that marginal intakes existed in many school lunches.

Murphy et al. (26) have analyzed the same school

lunches for five essential trace metals and four nones-
sential ones. They found the diets marginal or deficient
in chromium and copper, probably deficient in manganese by most criteria, adequate in zinc, and possibly
adequate in strontium. The diets were low in cadmium and barium, and contained approximately normal amounts of aluminum and boron. The low values
of copper and manganese were unexpected.

The data on raw foods in the tables do not account
for possible losses of vitamins and minerals in home
cooking. If losses occur, they will increase the tendency to inadequacy of the diet in certain micronutrients. These data, when compared with processed,
frozen, and canned foods, are not to be construed as
meaning that identical samples were compared. Obviously they were not. Although mineral and vitamin
contents of plant foods may vary somewhat according
to area and condition of growth, it is extremely doubt-
ful that they vary enough to account for the consistent
differences found between raw foods and their processed counterparts.

From these data, it is apparent that American diets
may be marginal in respect to adequate intakes of
several micronutrients essential for optimal function.

Summary and Conclusions

Data on the concentrations of vitamin B_6, pantothenic acid, other vitamins, and trace minerals in raw
and frozen, processed, refined, or canned foods have
been evaluated in the light of probable human requirements and recommended allowances, based on a
total food intake of 1.0 kg/day, wet wt, excluding
fluids. Of 552 foods analyzed for vitamin B_6, 31.0% had
concentrations of 2.0 ppm or more and 13.9% had concentrations of 2.5 ppm or more, the approximate recommended allowances for adults and pregnant
women, respectively. Of 507 samples analyzed for
pantothenic acid, 47.5% had concentrations of 5 ppm
or more, the minimal recommended daily allowance.
Mean losses of vitamin B_6 amounting to 36.7% and

44.6% occurred in frozen vegetables and 57.1 to 77.4% in canned vegetables, compared with those in the raw state, reducing concentrations to less than 1 ppm. Losses in canned fish, seafood, meats, and poultry amounted to 42.6% and 48.9%. Mean losses of pantothenic acid due to freezing of vegetables were 36.8 to 57.1%, and due to canning, 46.1 to 77.8%. Losses in canned meat, fish, and dairy products were less.

Processed and refined grains lost 51.1 to 93.8% of the vitamin B_6 and 37.0 to 74.1% of the pantothenic acid in the whole product. Processed meats lost one-half to three-quarters of both vitamins. Seven vitamins were lost during the refining of flour to the extent of 50 to 86.3%. Biotin and folacin were also usually reduced in refined cereals, white bread, and canned vegetables.

Thirteen minerals were depleted from wheat by the refining of flour, with negligible loss of energy. Bulk minerals were lost to the extent of 60.0 to 84.7%, and trace metals of 40.0 to 88.5%. Large losses of magnesium and most trace metals apparently resulted from the refining or partitioning of foods into two or more fractions. Refined sugar was especially low in trace elements.

These data demonstrate the dietary needs for the use of whole grains and unprocessed foods of most varieties. They suggest that enrichment of refined flours, sugars, and fats with some vitamins and essential trace elements may be necessary to meet recommended daily allowances, especially of vitamin B_6, pantothenic acid, chromium, zinc, and possibly manganese.

References

1. Recommended Dietary Allowances (7th rev. ed.). *Natl. Acad. Sci.–Natl. Res. Council Publ.* 1694. Washington, D. C., 1968.
2. Food Consumption and Dietary Levels of Households in the United States, 1955. *Household Econ. Res. Rept. 6, U. S. Dept. Agr.,* 1957.

3. ORR, M. L. Pantothenic acid, vitamin B₆ and vitamin B₁₂ in foods. *Home Econ. Res. Rept. 36, U. S. Dept. Agr.*, Washington, D. C., 1969.

4. MITCHELL, H. S., H. J. RYNBERGEN, L. ANDERSON AND M. V. DIBBLE. *Cooper's Nutrition in Health and Disease* (15th ed.). Philadelphia: Lippincott, 1968.

5. *The Millfeed Manual.* Millers' Natl. Fed., Chicago, 1967.

6. SCHROEDER, H. A., J. J. BALASSA AND I. H. TIPTON. Abnormal trace metals in man. Chromium. *J. Chronic Diseases* 15: 941, 1962.

7. SCHROEDER, H. A., J. J. BALASSA AND I. H. TIPTON. Essential trace metals in man: manganese. A study in homeostasis. *J. Chronic Diseases* 19: 545, 1966.

8. SCHROEDER, H. A., A. P. NASON AND I. H. TIPTON. Essential trace metals in man: cobalt. *J. Chronic Diseases* 20: 869, 1967.

9. SCHROEDER, H. A., A. P. NASON, I. H. TIPTON AND J. J. BALASSA. Essential trace metals in man: copper. *J. Chronic Diseases* 19: 1007, 1966.

10. SCHROEDER, H. A., A. P. NASON, I. H. TIPTON AND J. J. BALASSA. Essential trace metals in man: zinc. Relation to environmental cadmium. *J. Chronic Diseases* 20: 179, 1967.

11. SCHROEDER, H. A., J. J. BALASSA AND I. H. TIPTON. Essential trace metals in man: molybdenum. *J. Chronic Diseases* 23: 481, 1970.

12. SCHROEDER, H. A., D. V. FROST AND J. J. BALASSA. Essential trace metals in man: selenium. *J. Chronic Diseases* 23: 227, 1970.

13. SCHROEDER, H. A., A. P. NASON AND I. H. TIPTON. Essential metals in man: magnesium. *J. Chronic Diseases* 21: 815, 1968.

14. TIPTON, I. H., P. L. STEWART AND J. DICKSON. Patterns of elemental excretion in long term balance studies. *Health Phys.* 16: 455, 1969.

15. TIPTON, I. H., P. L. STEWART AND P. G. MARTIN. Trace elements in diets and excreta. *Health Phys.* 12: 1683, 1966.

16. MURPHY, E. W., P. C. KOONS AND L. PAGE. Vitamin content of Type A school lunches. *J. Am. Dietet. Assoc.* 55: 372, 1969.

17. PRASAD, A. S., A. MIALE, JR., Z. FARID, H. H. SAND-

STEAD AND A. R. SCHULERT. Zinc metabolism in patients with the syndrome of iron deficiency anemia, hepatosplenomegaly, dwarfism and hypogonadism, *J. Lab. Clin. Med.* 61: 537, 1963.

18. HALSTED, J. A., AND J. C. SMITH, JR. Plasma-zinc in health and disease. *Lancet:* 1: 322, 1970.

19. HUSAIN, S. L. Oral zinc sulphate in leg ulcers. *Lancet:* 1: 1069, 1969.

20. SCHROEDER, H. A. The role of chromium in mammalian nutrition. *Am. J. Clin. Nutr.* 21: 230, 1968.

21. SCHROEDER, H. A., A. P. NASON AND I. H. TIPTON. Chromium deficiency as a factor in atherosclerosis. *J. Chronic Diseases* 23: 123, 1970.

22. MERTZ, W. Chromium occurrence and function in biological systems. *Physiol. Rev.* 49: 163, 1969.

23. SCHROEDER, H. A. Serum cholesterol and glucose levels in rats fed refined and less refined sugars and chromium. *J. Nutr.* 97: 237, 1969.

24. CZERNIEJEWSKI, C. P., C. W. SHANK, W. G. BECHTEL AND W. B. BRADLEY. The minerals of wheat, flour and bread. *Cereal Chem.* 41: 65, 1964.

25. MURPHY, E. W., L. PAGE AND B. K. WATT. Major mineral elements in Type A school lunches. *J. Am. Dietet. Assoc.* 57: 239, 1970.

26. MURPHY, E. W., L. PAGE AND B. K. WATT. Trace minerals in Type A school lunches. *J. Am. Dietet. Assoc.* 58: 115, 1971.

E. Malnutrition and Hunger in the United States

This Report of the American Medical Association's Council on Foods and Nutrition, originally published in the Journal of the American Medical Association *(July 13, 1970), pinpoints the danger of vitamin and mineral deficiencies in infants and preschool children, the elderly, and pregnant women, as well as geographical concentrations of malnutrition. It is reprinted here by permission; copyright © 1970 by the American Medical Association.*

America is now aware that malnutrition is here. Attention has been sharply focused on problems of hunger and malnutrition in the United States by the Citizens' Board of Inquiry report, "Hunger USA," and by the CBS television program, "Hunger in America." Following these reports, most major newspapers and TV companies published documentaries highlighting local or national examples of dismal poverty and malnutrition. The Senate Select Committee on Nutrition and Related Human Needs has been holding hearings for more than a year.

The Citizens' Board of Inquiry into Hunger and Malnutrition in the United States opened a Pandora's box. While its report has received criticisms because of inadequate techniques and dependence upon evidence of a subjective nature, it contains useful data and a good review of current literature. Only a few studies are available providing information on the incidence, severity, or location of malnutrition. The report also reviewed and criticized federal and state relief programs. Certain of the recommendations have resulted in new programs or made possible legislation aimed at eliminating hunger and malnutrition.

Both of these reports were particularly important in that they called attention to a national problem, but neither report presented factual information on the *extent* of hunger and malnutrition in the United States.

HUNGER AND MALNUTRITION Every society has some individuals who suffer from hunger. Although hunger (inadequate amounts of food for short or long periods of time) occurs more frequently among the poor, there has been no measure of the extent of hunger nor is it known whether hunger in our country has been sufficiently severe and prolonged to have produced physiological effects. Psychological health has undoubtedly been impaired in many people and this has great social significance.

Malnutrition is a state of impaired functional ability or deficient structural integrity or development brought about by a discrepancy between the supply to the body tissues of essential nutrients and calories and the specific biologic demand for them.

Malnutrition may be classified as primary or secondary. Primary malnutrition is defined as an inadequate (or excessive, eg, calories) intake of nutrients for the normal body requirement. This condition may be caused by faulty selection of foods, by lack of money to purchase adequate food, or by actual food shortages.

Secondary malnutrition results from factors that interfere with ingestion, absorption, or utilization of essential nutrients or from stress factors that increase their requirement, destruction or excretion. Two common examples are anemia associated with heavy infestation with intestinal parasites (particularly hookworm) in children and malnutrition resulting from chronic diarrhea.

It is important that a clear distinction be made between primary and secondary malnutrition in population surveys. Failure to recognize the conditioning factors associated with secondary malnutrition can falsely lead to the conclusion that all examples of malnutrition found were caused by dietary inadequacies.

Hunger has been reported particularly among hard-to-reach rural inhabitants of the Southeast and along the Appalachian Mountains, on Indian reservations, among migrant farm workers, and among people living in city slums. Recluses and incapacitated elderly people who must fend for themselves may also experience hunger. The Citizens' Board of Inquiry estimated that between one third and one half of the very poor may experience hunger of varying intensity and duration. There is no truly reliable estimate of the number of hungry people in our country.

In all likelihood, malnutrition is much more prevalent than hunger per se, but it is not as politically dramatic. Malnutrition producing physiological impairment is probably common. Conditions such as iron deficiency, growth impairment, and obesity are widespread. While such classical deficiency diseases as scurvy, beri beri and pellagra are rare, goiter and rickets have been reported recently in alarming proportions.

NUTRITION SURVEYS Congress directed the Department of Health, Education, and Welfare to conduct a survey to identify the incidence, magnitude, and location of malnutrition and related health problems within the United States.

Surveys have been developed to identify population groups and areas of the country where nutritional problems are likely to be most evident. For these reasons, the surveys are concentrated in areas with the lowest income; it was anticipated that census enumeration districts used in sample selections would also include some families with middle and upper incomes. Each survey includes clinical, biochemical, dental, and dietary assessments of those parameters which define nutritional status. Attention also is given to socioeconomic conditions and to environmental factors which influence nutritional status. The biochemical appraisal is the measure of tissue concentrations or urinary excretion of nutrients. Such measures permit an evaluation of nutrient concentrations which may not be sufficiently low to have produced clinical manifestations.

The National Nutrition Survey director, Arnold E. Schaefer, PhD, has presented preliminary findings from surveys in Texas and Louisiana. The general impression (as stated by Dr. Schaefer) is that the poverty groups have signs and indices of malnutrition of essentially the same incidences and severity as found in low-income Central American families.

Malnutrition from deficiency of iron, vitamin A, vitamin C, iodine, protein and/or calories seems to be a common finding among samples in Texas and Louisiana. These same nutrients are generally found to be in short supply in studies of poverty areas within American cities or among disadvantaged rural people. Appalling rates of dental decay, missing or filled teeth were encountered; dental hygiene was dismal. While all dental pathology does not result from inadequate nutrition, it is often closely associated with diet. Nearly 10% of the survey population in Texas had discernible goiters. Iodized salt was not generally used; in fact, 40% of the markets failed to stock iodized salt. An additional finding from the two surveys was low height in relation to age among preschool children. A preliminary statement of the nutrition program survey performed in Upstate New York suggests that no overt cases of malnutrition were encountered there. Studies in the other states have not progressed to the point to provide information but should be forthcoming in the near future.

USDA FOOD CONSUMPTION SURVEYS The US

Department of Agriculture conducts periodic food consumption studies of households in the United States. The most recent survey, completed in 1965, included a detailed evaluation of the dietary and food habits of 6,200 households and provided information about regional and seasonal differences in food consumption, as well as differences in consumption as related to economic status. Half of the households studied had diets that failed to meet the recommended dietary allowances (RDA) for one or more nutrients. Calcium, vitamin A, and vitamin C were the nutrients most often below the allowances. About one fifth of the diets provided two thirds or less of the RDA for one or more nutrients and were rated as poor. The significance of these findings can be questioned. An intake of nutrients less than recommended does not mean deficiency, since the allowances include a margin of safety. The US Department of Agriculture survey points out where difficulty might be expected but does not provide definitive information of its presence.

Malnutrition, because it can have so many manifestations is insidious. Depending on how it is defined, it can be found under many situations. Classical malnutrition exemplified by vitamin deficiency diseases is but a small segment of the spectrum. The less dramatic manifestations of malnutrition—growth retardation, weight loss, increased burden of chronic diseases, depression, weakness, retarded convalescence from disease and trauma, poor performance in pregnancy—are widespread and of great significance. It is not yet known whether impaired brain and central nervous system development associated with severe and early protein malnutrition (kwashiorkor) is a problem here; the possibility should not be dismissed.

The groups in danger of malnutrition are infants and preschool children, the elderly, and pregnant women—in particular when the pregnancy occurs during very early adolescence or when the pregnancies are closely spaced. In these latter instances, the health of both the mother and child is in jeopardy because of inadequate nutritional preparation for the pregnancy and inadequate nutritional support during pregnancy.

PATHOGENESIS OF MALNUTRITION In addition to poverty, causes of malnutrition are very likely factors such as illness, ignorance of the relation of diet to health, indifference to the importance of good nutritional practice, loneliness, and mental illness. Examples are numerous of malnutrition secondary to such illnesses as cancer, gastrointestinal disorders, febrile diseases, and biliary and pancreatic diseases.

The nutrition program surveys have discovered examples of almost complete ignorance regarding the need for appropriate food sources of certain nutrients, for example, table salt as a source of iodine. Ignorance, indifference, and poverty combine to expose the child to the risk of malnutrition. While he may not demonstrate clinical symptoms of malnutrition, he may have undesirably low levels of vitamins and minerals in his tissues. This is of concern because he is therefore without any significant nutrient reserve.

It has been firmly established that preschool-aged children are most vulnerable to the effects of malnutrition. The synergism between malnutrition and infectious disease is well documented. Infections in the undernourished are more devastating, persist longer, and result in a much higher death rate in malnourished children. Infectious diseases also play an important role in the initiation of malnutrition itself.

Iron deficiency is perhaps the most common example of malnutrition. It is found in large numbers of children and is very frequent among women of all ages. The deficiency in women is aggravated by menstrual losses and by the extra requirements of pregnancy and lactation. Parasitic infestation and inadequate iron intake account for some deficiencies among children in the South. Iron deficiency has been reviewed by an AMA Committee (*JAMA* 203:407, 1968). Iron deficiency requires therapy.

Obesity is also a form of malnutrition resulting from

a combination of excessive caloric intake and inadequate caloric expenditure. It has been estimated that almost 40% of the American population are obese. Ironically, malnutrition bordering on starvation has resulted from ill-advised weight reduction programs (crash programs) frequently used by adolescents and young women.

Nutrient deficiencies sometimes result from drug therapy and surgery. While this form of malnutrition is not often encountered, it does reflect the inadequate attention to nutrition and lack of awareness of nutritional complications on the part of the physician.

William J. Darby, MD, in testimony before the Senate Select Committee stated:

Although the majority of the cases of nutrition disease that we see in our hospital are those occurring with other medical conditions, practically all of the deficiency disorders would have been prevented had the patients and their physicians utilized proper understanding of nutrition and diet.

Malnutrition: Its Effects on Man and Society

The existence of hunger, in a society that can afford to abolish it, is morally and economically indefensible. A child who is hungry because his family cannot afford to buy food is a living reproof to a wealthy society's claim that it treasures human life over financial capital.

Neither can a society excuse itself from a charge of harboring hungry people on grounds that they are ignorant of proper nutritional practices. Hunger damages the moral and economic fiber of the nation, no matter what the reason for its existence. Ignorance that causes hunger should be attacked as vigorously as poverty. The reverse side of the coin, malnutrition, may be just as damaging to the nation as to the individual. Malnutrition is debilitating; those so affected cannot perform optimally. Current estimates of the numbers so affected are unreliable but the cost in human waste is great indeed and the effect in terms of future performance cannot be accurately measured.

EFFECT ON THE INDIVIDUAL The effects of malnutrition on the infant and young child can be devastating. In its severest forms, as with kwashiorkor or marasmus, it can lead to death. Overt malnutrition can produce physical impairment, marking the individual for life. The poorly nourished child, the hungry child will have a shortened attention span which interferes with learning even though there be no mental impairment. Malnutrition in early childhood has obvious implications for future manpower and economic progress. It adds a fearful urgency to the whole problem.

Human and animal studies have provided evidence that the nutritional state of the mother is an important factor in maternal illness, fetal deaths, premature deaths, neonatal deaths, and morbidity of infants. The high infant mortality rates in certain sections of the country and among certain ethnic groups in large measure may be related to poor nutritional status of mothers. The death rates of the young infants are vastly greater among the malnourished than among the well nourished.

Charles Lowe, MD, formerly Chairman of the American Academy of Pediatrics' Committee on Nutrition, has compiled information which begins to show a cycle of events which embraces the low-birth-weight infant. Poor nutritional status during pregnancy is one of several etiological factors related to low-birth-weight neonates. In progression, the infant is in danger of serious malnutrition which if uncorrected can lead to growth depression and possibly to mental retardation. An infant so endowed most likely will become a handicapped adult, if he survives. The female with this heritage when adult becomes a prime candidate to emulate her mother—completing the cycle.

EFFECT ON SOCIETY Hungry or chronically malnourished people are frequently resentful people.

Their resentment may be directed at fate, landlords, higher socioeconomic classes, or at society in general. But as long as they remain without hope of change, their resentment is seldom translated into action.

Hope is energy that fuels revolutions. As Crane Brinton points out in his famous study, *Anatomy of Revolution* (Random House, rev ed, 1957), a hungry, resentful people who begin to hope for better things, for change in their status, may suddenly acquire the furious energy of a forest fire. Change then cannot come fast enough to satisfy them.

The spark of hope has been dropped into the tinder-box of America's ghettos. Poor people, and especially black poor people, have heard from prophets both black and white that change will come.

Hunger and malnutrition is only one of the reasons for the fierce resentments of the US poor. But it is one that can be removed in very large degree. The cost of massive attack upon hunger and malnutrition will be great in money; the cost of doing nothing will be immeasurable in terms of lost human potential and social unrest.

The Role of the AMA

The specter of hunger and the misery of malnutrition are not really very contemporary problems. They have for years been visible—but have too often been overlooked. Now for perhaps the first time since the depression, public response demands programs of correction.

The private sector has been invited to become involved in the solution of problems of hunger and malnutrition. Hunger, per se, is a problem which society itself must solve. While it has a medical component, is is not a problem of direct responsibility to the medical profession. This is not to suggest that the medical problems associated with hunger are not the responsibility of the physician, but rather that the provision of food and the improvement of living conditions is in the public trust. The physician can provide a strong voice to arouse public concern, thus hastening corrective measures.

Malnutrition, on the other hand, is a medical problem that can be most appropriately resolved by intervention of the physician. Malnutrition and, to some extent, hunger are problems requiring a health orientation for solution. As governmental agencies begin to devise and revise programs to deal with the "newly discovered" problems, it is probable that both crash and long-range programs will be developed. It is important that the inherent nature of the problems be understood prior to the launching of any long-range programs. The information being obtained by the US Nutrition Program surveys will be meaningful to the development of programs to prevent malnutrition.

Most of the states had nutrition committees which were active during World War II to assist in nutrition education programs associated with food rationing. State medical societies may wish to encourage and provide leadership for the reestablishment of such committees to assist in general nutrition education programs. At the local level, it will become increasingly important for the physician to involve himself in the community affairs that pertain to the resolution of hunger and malnutrition.

The Council on Foods and Nutrition presented 13 recommendations to the Board of Trustees regarding the involvement of the American Medical Association in resolving problems related to hunger and malnutrition in this country. These recommendations can be categorized into three distinct groups: (1) those related generally to national policy; (2) those calling for AMA actions; and (3) those calling for messages to constituent and component societies.

The recommendations were approved, and through their implementation the AMA will exert its influence to help ensure that the federal government does not become concerned solely with emergency, short-range programs to relieve hunger and malnutrition. It will take an active part in determining practices and those causes of malnutrition that are likely to be amenable to preventive measures, as well as aid in the development of realistic long-range programs to improve the nutritional status of individuals and communities. Finally, the AMA will continue to emphasize the vital importance of the health sciences in determining national policy with regard to food.

Persuant to the recommendations, a letter was sent to President Nixon encouraging the development of a central coordinating agency for nutrition at a high level in the executive branch of the government. Since the major emphasis is now being placed on the problems of nutrition through activities such as child feeding programs, food distribution, and popular education, the need for a coordinating agency was evident.

A letter was also sent to Secretary Finch of the Department of Health, Education, and Welfare, encouraging the development of authoritative positions in nutrition within HEW. There is not, at the present time, a high executive position of responsibility within HEW which is concerned with nutrition. The Nutrition Program is a new office which is now devoted wholly to the US Nutrition Survey. It is essential that someone with extensive knowledge and experience in the field of nutrition provide guidance and leadership.

The Council on Foods and Nutrition, in cooperation with the Divisions of Nutrition and Continuing Medical Education of the University of Alabama School of Medicine, sponsored a symposium on "The Role of Malnutrition in the Pathogenesis of Slums" on Feb 11 and 12, 1970. In addition, three satellite conferences are tentatively planned in 1970 to explore further the etiology of malnutrition in various parts of the country.

The implementation of the recommendations may provide much of the information needed for the development of long-range programs to improve the nutritional status of all Americans.

F. Vitamin Supplements and Their Correct Use

Following is the text of a pamphlet issued by the Department of Foods and Nutrition, Division of Scientific Activities, American Medical Association, designed to communicate the AMA's viewpoint on the use of vitamin supplements to the interested layman. The text should be read in conjunction with the new U.S. Recommended Daily Allowances (U.S. RDA), prepared by the Food and Nutrition Board of the National Academy of Sciences and the National Research Council, which appear on page 174. Copyright © 1970 by the American Medical Association.

Vitamins are essential to maintain life. The usual and most reasonable source of vitamins is food. A diet selected from the variety of foods available can supply all the vitamins a person needs.

All metabolic processes in our bodies are dependent directly or indirectly upon vitamins. Nutritional studies during the past thirty years have given us information on the kinds and amounts of the vitamins required in these processes. The studies have enabled the Food and Nutrition Board of the National Research Council to establish the Recommended Dietary Allowances.

261

The allowances are daily nutrient intakes recommended to assure good nutritional status in healthy persons.

The homemaker does not find frozen packages, cans, or bags of vitamins in her supermarket; she finds foods. The four-food-group guide helps her select a variety of foods that will supply nutrients as listed in the Recommended Dietary Allowances. This United States Department of Agriculture guide classifies foods according to their contribution of several nutrients. Key foods that are important sources of certain nutrients are emphasized. The guide encourages wide choice in food selection.

4 Food Groups

This is the fundamental plan:

Milk Group: Some milk daily—

Children:

Under 9 years	2 to 3 cups
9-12 years	3 or more cups
Teen-agers	4 or more cups
Adults	2 or more cups
Pregnant women	3 or more cups
Nursing mothers	4 or more cups

Cheese and ice cream can replace
part of the milk.

Meat Group: Two or more servings, including—Beef, veal, pork, lamb, poultry, fish, eggs, with dry beans and peas and nuts as alternates.

Vegetable-Fruit Group: Four or more servings, including—A dark green or deep yellow vegetable important for vitamin A—at least every other day. A citrus fruit or other fruit or vegetable important for vitamin C—daily. Other fruits and vegetables including potatoes.

Bread-Cereals Group: Four or more servings—Whole grain, enriched, restored.

Other foods normally included in the daily diet, such as butter, margarine, sugars, and unenriched grain products, serve to fulfill the caloric and nutrient allowances.

Vitamins as Food Supplements

An adequate intake of vitamins is assured when one consumes a proper variety of foods in sufficient amounts. There might be times, however, when supplementation is necessary. Supplementation is useful when a person is unable or unwilling to consume an adequate diet, as during illness, allergy, or emotional upsets. Vitamin supplementation augments the diet but does not replace it. The physician is trained to determine the most beneficial supplement and also to help the patient remove disturbing factors causing poor eating habits.

Adults

A daily vitamin supplement should contain amounts of the vitamins no greater than the Recommended Dietary Allowances. Vitamin preparations should be administered only until the individual is able to resume his regular eating pattern. When for some reason a particular class of food is eliminated from the diet, the supplement used need contain only the essential vitamins associated with that food group.

During pregnancy and lactation a need for supplementation may occur. When the intake of vitamin D-fortified milk is low, 400 U.S.P. units of vitamin D daily may be prescribed. Supplementation with the minerals calcium and iron may also be recommended during pregnancy and lactation. Foods high in these nutrients should be incorporated into the meal patterns if possible during these times. An adequate supply of other mineral elements is provided by meals containing a variety of foods. There is no value in the combination of vitamins with minerals other than iron and/or calcium.

Infants and Children

Infants consuming commercial formulas or formulas based on whole cow's milk will receive adequate amounts of vitamins A and D. The physician may recommend supplements of vitamins A and D for infants who cannot consume sufficient amounts of formulas or who, due to allergies or disease, must be fed special diets.

While human milk contains some vitamin C, milk from cows has very little. Most commercial infant formulas contain added vitamin C. Infants fed formulas which do not contain a sufficient amount of vitamin C require an additional source. This may be in the form of fruit juice; or when this is not possible, a dietary vitamin supplement may be suggested.

The growing child should be introduced to a wide variety of nutritious foods, since food is the most convenient and economical source of vitamins and all other nutrients. If a child is not eating properly and vitamin inadequacies result, the doctor follows the same type of treatment he uses for an adult.

Vitamins as Therapeutic Agents

During any prolonged illness associated with decreased food intake or in other situations in which an individual is unable or unwilling to eat an adequate diet, the physician must decide whether dietary vitamin supplementation alone will adequately meet the individual's need for nutrients. When vitamins are needed in quantities larger than the Recommended Dietary Allowances they are prescribed in amounts usually designated as "therapeutic levels."

The mixtures designated as therapeutic vitamin preparations contain 3 to 5 times the Recommended Dietary Allowances. Therapeutic vitamin preparations are valuable in treating specific vitamin deficiencies and in maintaining good nutritional status in patients with chronic disease. Therapeutic vitamin mixtures should be so labeled, and they should not be used as daily dietary supplements. The decision to employ vitamin preparations in therapeutic amounts clearly rests with the physician. For example, the cause of an anemia is determined by the use of clinical and laboratory procedures; then the specific vitamin or therapeutic agent required is prescribed. There is no reason to use preparations which contain most or all of the antianemic factors, which include vitamin B_{12}, vitamin C,

folic acid, iron, and copper. Medical supervision
should be continued as long as a therapeutic preparation is used.

The use of vitamin mixtures in the self-treatment of
suspected disease is a dangerous procedure. An individual who "always feels tired" should contact his physician rather than employing remedies glowingly
advertised to the public.

In all cases, the reason for prescribing vitamins,
either as dietary supplements or therapeutic agents,
should be understood clearly; and the supplement employed should represent a logical approach to the individual problem.

Excessive Vitamin Intake

Many of the vitamin products sold directly to the
public contain large quantities of vitamins. A daily intake of amounts of vitamins A and D in excess of the
limits suggested in the Recommended Dietary Allowances is unwarranted and potentially dangerous. The
absence of excretory pathways for vitamins A and D
and for carotene makes it necessary to limit their intake in order to avoid the problems of excess.

Chronic vitamin A intoxication occurs more frequently in children than in adults. Depending upon
the severity of the intoxication, children may develop
loss of appetite, weight loss, irritability, fissuring at the
corners of the mouth, and cracking and bleeding of the
lips. Later signs include liver enlargement, loss of hair,
and severe bone and joint pains.

There is great variation in individual tolerance to
large amounts of vitamin D. Several factors influence
response to continued ingestion of excessive quantities
of this vitamin. These factors include age, exposure to
ultraviolet light, dietary calcium, and hormone excretion. With excessive intakes of vitamin D, nausea,
polyuria, and diarrhea are early symptoms of toxicity.
Later symptoms include weakness, the deposition of
calcium in soft tissues, and depression.

MINIMUM DAILY REQUIREMENTS

	Child	Adult
Vitamin A, I.U.	3000	4000
Thiamine, mg.	0.75	1
Riboflavin, mg.	0.9	1.2
Vitamin C, mg.	20	30
Vitamin D, I.U.	400	400

Vitamin preparations must bear labels that comply with the regulations of the Food and Drug Administration. In order to avoid the use of confusing units and weights on the label, the amounts of the vitamins are indicated as the proportion of Minimum Daily Requirements (M.D.R.) These requirements have been established for the most commonly needed vitamins. The Minimum Daily Requirements for vitamins are generally slightly lower than the Recommended Dietary Allowances.

G. Vitamin Preparations as Dietary Supplements and as Therapeutic Agents

The Council on Foods and Nutrition of the American Medical Association has expressed its views of vitamin preparations in a statement that covered their use to supplement the human diet as well as in medical therapy. The AMA Council approves the concept of the new U.S. Recommended Daily Allowances (U.S. RDA) mentioned in several sections of this book, both for nutrition labeling and for use on vitamin-mineral supplement labels. The main argument put forth by the AMA Council in this statement remains unchanged, even though suggested combinations have been superseded by the U.S. RDAs. This statement was originally published in the Journal of the American Medical Association *(January 3, 1959), and is reprinted by permission; copyright © 1959 by the American Medical Association.*

Vitamin preparations are used extensively and are valuable when used properly. For the most intelligent use and beneficial results in preventive or therapeutic medicine, the values and the limitations of vitamins should be realized. It is important that a clear differentiation be made between vitamins as dietary supplements and vitamins as therapeutic agents. The Council on Foods and Nutrition has reviewed the indications for administration of vitamins in supplemental and therapeutic amounts, the composition and dosage of vitamin preparations, and the possible dangers of excessive use of certain vitamins. The following is the Council's present position on this matter.

Recommended Dietary Allowances of Vitamins and Their Occurrence in Food

Vitamins are essential nutrients, and their usual source is food. All the nutrients essential to the maintenance of health in the normal individual are supplied by an adequate diet, one which fulfills the Recommended Dietary Allowances, revised 1958, developed by the Food and Nutrition Board, National Research Council (Publication 589). The levels of nutrients recommended are desirable goals in nutrition for all normal, healthy persons. They are believed to be adequate for maintaining good nutrition throughout life.

NORMAL DIETS.—A convenient guide to the composition of an adequate diet has been prepared by the United States Department of Agriculture (Leaflet 424). Foods are classified according to their contribution of several nutrients, although emphasis is placed on key foods as important sources of certain nutrients. This daily food plan gives a basis for an adequate diet but permits the individual wide choice in his food selections. This is the fundamental plan:

Milk Group: Some milk daily—
    Children ....3 to 4 cups
    Teen-agers ....4 or more cups
    Adults ....2 or more cups
    Pregnant women ....4 or more cups
    Nursing mothers ....6 or more cups
    Cheese and ice cream can replace part of the milk.
Meat Group: Two or more servings, including—Beef, veal, pork, lamb, poultry, fish, eggs, with dry beans and peas and nuts as alternates.
Vegetable-Fruit Group: Four or more servings, including—A dark green

or deep yellow vegetable important for vitamin A—at least every other day. A citrus fruit or other fruit or vegetable important for vitamin C—daily. Other fruits and vegetables including potatoes.

Bread-Cereals Group: Four or more servings—Whole grain, enriched, restored.

This fundamental plan will supply the adult with one-half to two-thirds of the caloric allowance, four-fifths of the iron, four-fifths of the thiamine, nine-tenths of the niacin, and all of the riboflavin allowances. These nutrients and others not mentioned will be raised to adequate amounts by the other foods normally included in the daily diet but not specifically mentioned in the basic plan. Foods such as butter, margarine, other fats and oils, sugars, desserts, jellies, and unenriched grain products serve to fulfill the caloric and nutrient allowances. Therefore, if the diet contains the key food groups in sufficient amounts, nutritional supplementation should be unnecessary. The proper selection and preparation of foods are important to the achievement of an adequate diet.

MINIMUM DAILY REQUIREMENTS.—The Recommended Dietary Allowances should not be confused with the Minimum Daily Requirements established for labeling purposes by the Food and Drug Administration. Nutrient contents can thus be expressed in terms of the proportion of daily requirements supplied. Minimum Daily Requirements are the amounts of nutrients needed to prevent symptoms of deficiency and to provide a

Table 1.—Minimum Daily Requirements Compared with Recommended Dietary Allowances

Vitamin[a]	M.D.R., Adults	R.D.A., Man, Aged 25	M.D.R., Children, 6-11 Yr.	R.D.A., Children, 7-12 Yr.
Vitamin A, U.S.P. units	4,000	5,000	3,000	3,500-4,500
Thiamine, mg.	1.0	1.6	0.75	1.1-1.3
Riboflavin, mg.	1.2	1.8	0.9	1.5-1.8
Vitamin C, mg.	30	75	20	60-75
Vitamin D, U.S.P. units	400	...	400	400

[a] Comparable figures for niacin are not given since the Recommended Dietary Allowances include preformed niacin and niacin made available from tryptophan, whereas the Minimum Daily Requirements consider only preformed niacin.

small factor of safety. Recommended Dietary Allowances are amounts of nutrients which will maintain good nutrition in essentially all healthy persons. Table 1 demonstrates the basic differences between the two concepts. Throughout this statement the Recommended Dietary Allowances will be used.

Vitamins as Dietary Supplements

Healthy persons whose diets are ordinarily considered adequate may benefit from supplementary vitamins at certain special periods of life, such as during pregnancy and lactation. Vitamin supplementation is useful during periods of illness or deranged mode of life, which may result in impairment of absorption of nutrients or deterioration of dietary quality. Supplementation may also be of value to the individual who, through ignorance, poor eating habits, or emotional or physical illness, does not eat an adequate diet. The physician's primary responsibility for these patients is to remove these disturbing factors rather than merely to alleviate their results. Nevertheless, until the disturbing factors have been discovered and, when possible, removed, supplementary vitamins are valuable in assuring adequate intake.

INFANTS AND CHILDREN.—The daily diet of the artificially fed infant should be supplemented with vitamins C and D if the diet does not supply 30 mg. of vitamin C and 400 U. S. P. units of vitamin D. The diet should be brought up to these amounts, with care exercised that the intake of vitamin D is not excessive. The requirement of the breast-fed baby for vitamin D is not accurately known, but it is accepted practice to advocate 400 U. S. P. units of vitamin D supplement daily. Administration of vitamin D and, in artificially fed babies, of vitamin C should be started with the introduction of artificial feeding. Too often administration of vitamin C is delayed even into the second month. When administration of the vitamins is started, the amount of vitamin D is often too great and the amount of vitamin C too small. Maximum calcium and phosphorus retentions are obtained with 300 to 400 U. S. P. units of vitamin D daily. Not only are retentions no greater with larger amounts, but the use of 1,800 U. S. P. units or more daily for several months decreases appetite and, as a consequence, reduces the total retentions of calcium and phosphorus and slows linear growth. Infants receiving unfortified skimmed milk formulas also require supplements of vitamin A (1,500 U. S. P. units daily).

Healthy children fed adequate amounts of wholesome foods need no supplemental vitamins except vitamin D, which should be supplied throughout the growth period. An adequate intake of vitamin D-fortified homogenized milk or reconsituted evaporated milk (1½ to 2 pt. daily) provides the vitamin D required. The physician should determine the approximate amount of vitamin D supplied by foods before supplementing the diets. In certain instances, physicians may wish to supplement the diets of infants and children with preparations containing vitamins A, C, D, and certain B vitamins. The Council believes that such preparations containing the B complex are not needed for routine use but would be of value for children with special problems. It is important that the growing child be introduced to a wide variety of wholesome foods, since food is the normal source of nutrients.

ADULTS.—Healthy adults receiving adequate diets have no need for supplementary vitamins except during pregnancy and lactation when 400 U. S. P. units of vitamin D daily are required if the intake of vitamin D-fortified milk is low. In these periods of physiological stress, if any doubt exists as to the adequacy of the previous or present diet, supplementary vitamins in addition to vitamin D should be administered.

Supplementary vitamins are useful during periods of emotional illness, which result in bizarre food habits or greatly diminished food intake. The choice of vitamin preparations to be used to insure a desirable nutrient intake in such instances should be based upon the physician's evaluation of the patient's dietary pattern.

When restricted or nutritionally inadequate diets are prescribed for pathological conditions, vitamin mixtures as supportive supplements are indicated. Examples of conditions in which such diets may be instituted include allergic states and chronic diseases of the gastrointestinal tract. Vitamin supplementation also is indicated when it is necessary to employ parenteral feeding. The character of the supplementation required will depend on the diet, the nutrients administered, and the period of time the regimen is maintained.

In any prolonged illness associated with decreased food intake or in other situations in which an individual is unable or unwilling to eat an adequate diet, the physician must decide whether supplementation is necessary. The extent of the illness or the nature of the dietary restriction should be evaluated to determine whether the level of vitamin supplementation should be equal to allowances under normal physiological conditions or in excess of them.

Nutrition surveys in several areas of the United States have indicated that a variable fraction of certain segments of the population is not receiving sufficient varieties of foods to supply vitamins in amounts necessary to meet the Recommended Dietary Allowances. Generalization of these findings as a basis for vitamin supplementation of healthy individuals is not rational. The methodology employed in these surveys and the standards used for interpretation have varied considerably. It is necessary for the physician to evaluate each person individually. Correction of inadequacies should then be instituted, preferably by a proper diet, although supplementation with vitamins may be necessary until dietary adjustments are made and the body stores repleted. Avoidance of excessive or unnecessary supplementation is, of course, desirable.

Multivitamin Combinations

Multiple vitamin preparations should contain only

those vitamins shown to be essential in human nutrition or metabolism. The Council recognizes that certain foods such as liver, yeast, and wheat germ are excellent sources of some of the vitamins but finds no evidence to justify special claims for such materials or their concentrates in multivitamin mixtures. The combination of vitamins in a supplementary mixture should have a rational basis. Several combinations meet these criteria.

1. A combination of all the vitamins that have been demonstrated to be essential in human metabolism may be desirable for supplementation of certain restricted diets. Such preparations would include vitamins A and D, ascorbic acid, thiamine, riboflavin, niacin, pyridoxine, pantothenic acid, folic acid, and vitamin B_{12}. Vitamin K is not included, because dietary deficiency rarely occurs and because this vitamin has special uses which are not adapted to inclusion in multiple vitamin preparations, for example, prophylactic use for pregnant women and newborn infants. Vitamin D would be included in preparations for children, adolescents, and pregnant or nursing women and would be optional in others.

2. A combination of vitamins having complementary metabolic functions should prove useful in supplementation of certain restricted diets. These preparations might include (a) a combination of the B vitamins, thiamine, riboflavin, and niacin, with or without pyridoxine, pantothenic acid, folic acid, or vitamin B_{12}; (b) the B vitamins listed under (a) in combination with ascorbic acid; or (c) a combination of a calcium salt and vitamin D in a stable form.

3. A combination of vitamins that might be expected to be lacking concomitantly because of their common distribution in foods also might be desirable for supplementation. Examples would include the fat-soluble vitamins A and D or vitamins of the B complex as previously noted.

QUANTITIES FOR DIETARY SUPPLEMENTATION.—The quantities of vitamins included in mix-

tures for dietary supplementation should furnish daily
an amount which approximately fulfills, but does not
greatly exceed, the Recommended Dietary Allowances
for vitamins as given in table 2. The physician should
exercise more caution that his recommendations are
not increased in amount and that his patients do not
follow the precept that greater concentrations of vitamins are justified, in light of the little additional cost.
There is a tendency for the patient to believe that, if a
little is good, more would be better. It has not been
demonstrated that larger amounts are beneficial under
ordinary physiological conditions; in fact, an overdosage of vitamins A or D can be harmful.

The multivitamin preparations available today fall
into three general categories, those that supply (1)
about one-half the Recommended Dietary Allowances,
(2) one to one and one-half times the Recommended
Dietary Allowances, and (3) three to five times the
Recommended Dietary Allowances. The Council considers the first class of preparations useful in dietary
supplementation in situations as noted in the section
entitled Vitamins as Dietary Supplements. The preparations containing one to one and one-half times the
Recommended Dietary Allowances (group 2) would
be useful when supplementing therapeutic diets or
when prolonged illness or other causes significantly
reduce food intake. After the normal diet is instituted,
these higher potency preparations are not needed. The
third general type of preparations containing three to
five times the Recommended Dietary Allowances should
be reserved for use in therapy as discussed in the section on Vitamins as Therapeutic Agents.

Recommended Dietary Allowances have not been
established for pyridoxine, pantothenic acid, folic acid,
or vitamin B_{12}, although all these substances are
essential in human metabolism. The amounts present
in diets considered adequate in other factors should
serve as a guide for quantities to be used in supplementation. The amount of folic acid in supplementary
vitamin mixtures should be no greater than that available from an abundant dietary. Common experience

indicates that this is a quantity which will seldom
support hematological function in pernicious anemia
and therefore will not mask the diagnosis of this disorder. Although this quantity is still to be determined,
0.3 mg. of folic acid is suggested tentatively as a proper
maximum amount for supplemental mixtures.

An abundant dietary provides 2 to 10 mcg. of vitamin B_{12}, 5 to 10 mg. of pantothenic acid, and 1 to 3
mg. of pyridoxine. Therefore, these levels are considered satisfactory in vitamin mixtures for dietary
supplementation. Supplementary vitamins administered in the amounts suggested are safe. If the amount
of one or more of the vitamins in these mixtures is
markedly less than the recommended allowance, the
supplemental value of the preparation may be limited
accordingly.

*COMBINATION OF VITAMINS AND MINER-
ALS.*—Minerals have been combined with vitamins in
mixtures for dietary supplementation. Although certain
supplemental vitamin mixtures with calcium, iron, or
with both minerals have proved useful, there is no good
evidence to support the inclusion of the 12 or more,
mineral elements essential for man. Few of these minerals are likely to be lacking, even in restricted diets.
When iron is needed as a dietary supplement, it should
be given as such in most instances. Iron and calcium
might be included as optional ingredients in certain
supplemental vitamin mixtures, for example, for administration during pregnancy. A combination of calcium and vitamin D in stabilized form may be useful.
Sodium, chlorine, and iodine are usually supplied by
iodized table salt. Supplementation with copper is rarely
needed since it is usually adequately supplied by the
diet. Evidence is lacking that addition of the trace
elements, such as manganese, zinc, cobalt, and molybdenum, to the human diet is needed.

Vitamins as Therapeutic Agents

Vitamins in therapeutic amounts have proved valuable
in both specific therapy and in supportive therapy in

numerous pathological states. Vitamins in therapeutic amounts are indicated only in the treatment of deficiency states or pathological conditions in which requirements are increased.

Therapeutic vitamin mixtures should be so labeled and should not be used as dietary supplements. The decision to employ vitamin preparations in therapeutic amounts clearly rests with the physician, and the importance of medical supervision when such amounts are administered is emphasized.

The quantities of vitamins included in mixtures intended for therapeutic use in the treatment of multiple vitamin deficiencies should approximate simple multiples of the amounts recommended in the National Research Council's Recommended Dietary Allowances, revised 1958. It is seldom necessary to administer vitamins in amounts greater than three to five times the Recommended Dietary Allowances. In the rare instances in which larger quantities seem indicated, the vitamin(s) in question should be given separately. Although there is little danger of harm from larger quantities of the water-soluble vitamins because the excess is excreted readily, there is real danger of toxicity from larger amounts of fat soluble vitamins because the excess accumulates in the body. In multivitamin preparations, the amount of vitamin D should not exceed three times the Recommended Dietary Allowances as previously stated.

The combination of vitamins in mixtures intended for therapy should have a rational basis. Suitable combinations include (1) vitamins that have complementary metabolic functions and (2) vitamins that might be expected to be lacking concomitantly according to their common distribution in foods, or to similar chemical properties which influence absorption and biological availability. Examples would include (1) a combination of the B vitamins, thiamine, riboflavin, and niacin, with or without pyridoxine and calcium pantothenate; (2) a combination of these B vitamins with ascorbic acid; and (3) a combination of fat-soluble vitamins A and D or A, D, and K. In addition, a combination of vitamins A, D, ascorbic acid, thiamine, riboflavin, and niacin, with or without pyridoxine or calcium pantothenate, may be desirable.

There is little evidence which warrants inclusion of folic acid and vitamin B_{12} in therapeutic amounts in vitamin mixtures. As noted previously, folic acid in therapeutic dosage may mask the diagnosis of pernicious anemia and permit neurological lesions to develop while maintaining hematological remission. When folic acid is indicated in therapeutic quantities, it should be administered separately. The need for inclusion of vitamin B_{12} in therapeutic vitamin mixtures in an amount in excess of that supplied by an abundant dietary has not been demonstrated to date.

Before vitamins or other therapeutic agents are prescribed in the treatment of anemia, the etiology of the anemia should be determined. This will permit administration of the proper hematinic agent, which will usually be a single factor, namely, vitamin B_{12}, folic acid, or iron. Preparations containing all or most of the known antianemic factors, vitamin B_{12}, intrinsic factor, folic acid, iron, ascorbic acid, and copper, are in the opinion of the Council, not justifiable.

Toxicity of Vitamins A and D

Inclusion of excessive amounts of fat-soluble vitamins in therapeutic mixtures is scientifically unwarranted and potentially dangerous. The absence of excretory pathways for vitamins A and D and for carotene makes it necessary to limit their intake in order to avoid the development of hypervitaminosis. Daily dosage of more than 25,000 U. S. P. units of vitamin A should be followed carefully for toxicity.

HYPERVITAMINOSIS A.—Apparently the body can tolerate quantities of vitamin A 100 times greater than the daily physiological requirement, but there is a definite possiblity of harm from the prolonged ingestion of vitamin A in excess of 50,000 U. S. P. units daily. Chronic vitamin A intoxication occurs more frequently in children than in adults. Depending upon the severity of the intoxication, children older than one year may develop anorexia, weight loss, irritability, fretfulness, pruritus, seborrhea-like cutaneous eruptions, fissuring at the corners of the mouth, and cracking and bleeding of the lips. Later signs include hepatomegaly, hydrocephaly, alopecia, painful swellings over the long bones with bone and joint pains and bone tenderness, hyperostosis, deep, hard, tender swellings in the extremities, and cortical thickening in tubular bones. Serum vitamin A levels are increased and are useful diagnostically. Vitamin A intoxication in adults causes symptoms which are similar to those of hypervitaminosis A in children but are usually milder. Structural bone changes are not likely to occur, and bone and joint pains are not so severe. Menstrual alterations, exophthalmos, and pigmentation of the skin have been reported. Transitory increased intracranial pressure has been noted in severe acute toxicity.

HYPERVITAMINOSIS D.—There is great variation in individual tolerance to large amounts of vitamin D. Several factors influence response to continued ingestion of large amounts of vitamin D, including exposure to ultraviolet light, dietary calcium, and the endocrine system. A daily intake of 1,800 U. S. P. units continued over long periods of time may be mildly toxic in children. However, in the uncommon syndrome, refractory rickets, as much as 50,000 to over 100,000 U. S. P. units daily may be tolerated or, indeed, required.

The early symptoms of vitamin D intoxication include anorexia, nausea, headache, polyuria and nocturia, and diarrhea. Pallor and lassitude are also common findings in children. Later symptoms and signs include weakness, fatigue, renal damage, metastatic calcification, and depression. Hypochromic, normocytic anemia with azotemia has been reported in adults with hypervitaminosis D. When large dosages of vitamin D are administered, frequent determinations of serum and urine calcium should be made. An increase in the serum calcium to a level above 11 mg. per 100 ml., occurring in association with a high intake of vitamin D, is an indication for interdiction of the vitamin D supplement.

Comment

Vitamin mixtures, other than those discussed herein, may be demonstrated to be useful in therapy by further research. Until adequate scientific evidence is presented as to their value, however, such mixtures should not be advocated for general use. Public health will be served best by insistence on a factual basis for vitamin supplementation and therapy. It is sound judgment to emphasize repeatedly that properly selected diets are the primary basis for good nutrition.

Index

280

ABOUT THE AUTHOR

MARTIN EBON is the author of *The Truth About Vitamin E* and *The Vitamins in Your Food*. Mr. Ebon, an expert researcher and writer, is on the staff of the Playboy Book Club and resides in New York City.